BASEBALL'S FIRST INDIAN

THE STORY OF PENOBSCOT LEGEND LOUIS SOCKALEXIS

Ed Rice

Camden, Maine

Down East Books

Published by Down East Books
An imprint of Globe Pequot
Trade division of the Rowman & Littlefield Publishing Group. Inc.
4501 Forbes Blvd., Suite 200
Lanham, MD 20706
www.rowman.com
www.downeastbooks.com

Distributed by NATIONAL BOOK NETWORK

ISBN 978-1-60893-673-1 (paperback)
ISBN 978-1-60893-674-8 (e-book)

™
The paper used in this publication meets the minimum requirements of American National Standard for Information Sciences—Permanence of Paper for Printed Library Materials, ANSI/NISO Z39.48-1992.

Printed in the United States of America

For

Dad, "Brother" Mike, and, especially,
to this dad's marvelous moptop of
a daughter, Meisha . . . Here's looking at you, Kid!

In Memoriam:
Mom, Ruthe Rice, and brother, Gary Rice;
and two inspirational heroes,
Ginny DelVecchio and Terry Fox.

CONTENTS

PREFACE TO THE PAPERBACK EDITION

As the author of this 2003 biography of Louis Sockalexis, I am honored to have Down East Books of Maine acquire the rights to my manuscript, re-issue it and, in so doing, significantly contribute to an on-going effort to properly celebrate this extraordinary athlete and largely unrecognized civil rights icon.

Deepest gratitude from me goes, first and foremost, to Michael Steere and then to all other staff members from Down East Books and its parent company, Rowman & Littlefield, who have played a role in bringing out a second edition of my work.

I am forever grateful to Scott Kaeser and all the members of his staff at Tide-mark Press in E. Windsor, Connecticut, for first publishing the book and for over fifteen years of wonderful support.

In this introduction to commemorate the new edition, I would like to offer a couple of new concepts I have developed about the man and his times since I first published.

I remember that when I set out to write a Sockalexis biography I was greatly concerned about not overwriting my manuscript. Writers in his own day—and the handful of writers who had weighed in over the many years that followed when he was largely forgotten and barely a footnote in baseball history—had fallen victim to several historical mine fields. These run the gamut from reliance upon the flagrantly subjective, sensationalized press accounts of the American press of the late 19th century, to informa-tion they had not verified on their own, to myths and inaccuracies not corrected through their own initiatives where vitally-needed research was required, and to their own outright hyperbole in dealing with an athlete who was legendary in his own time. I determined, as both a veteran jour-nalist and newspaper editor and college journalism instructor, to carefully monitor my own editorializing.

Yes, Louis Sockalexis was absolutely legendary in his own time, an almost mythical figure, doing seemingly mythical things on the playing fields of baseball at every level he ever played.

And, in these fifteen years, I have come to recognize something I did not reflect upon enough back then: Louis Sockalexis did not need Cleveland and his brief professional baseball career to be regarded as one of the great-est players of his era, the 19th century.

Pure and simple, since its invention, during the mid-19th century and for the first two decades of the 20th century, baseball was far more popular with people who played the game themselves or watched their more skilled amateur peers, playing on local town teams or their regional college entry.

Further, all variety of ills beset professional baseball, beginning with its inception in 1871 (the very year Sock was born). Cities with teams and leagues for them to participate in evolved suddenly and disappeared just as rapidly. The teams attracted largely uneducated ruffians since those who attended college had little interest in playing for so little money and needed to find far more respectable, better paying professions. With only one umpire on the field trying to watch all the action, professional players frequently cheated on offense (i.e. cutting across the field while running the bases) and cheated on defense (e.g. infielders tripped runners rounding bases and fielders hid baseballs in the tall grass of the outfield for emergency use when a blow to their territory threatened to turn into a big scoring inning). Because of a brawling style of play and continuing streams of vulgar language by the players, women who considered themselves respectable ladies were largely not interested in attending these contests. And men found it very challenging to attend even if they had an interest: Men generally worked six days a week with only Sunday off. Since there were no lights, there was no night play. Since Ministers Associations were very powerful influences in most states at the time, the teams were prohibited from playing on the only day most people were available to attend games: Sunday. Finally, since the professional game was generally considered a "low-brow" form of entertainment, the players found themselves regularly associating with some of the worst elements of society, especially gamblers.

For all these reasons and more, there is little to respect about professional baseball in the era Sockalexis briefly played, except for some of the exceptional players and exceptional performances that have become part of the legend and lore of the game and its celebrated history. These would certainly include things like Cy Young's historic pitching record of 511 wins (achieved over a career that was split between the 19th century and the 20th century) and Wee Willie Keeler's 44-game batting streak, set in 1897 (and only broken by Joe DiMaggio's 56-game streak in 1941).

No, Sockalexis did not need a compelling professional baseball history to merit greater appreciation than he gets. It is something organizations like the professional Cleveland franchise, Sports Illustrated magazine and even the Baseball Hall of Fame seemingly have never understood; each should recognize and correct painful slights to his reputation. And, it would be wonderful if the people of my home state of Maine would, finally, recognize that we do not need institutions like these to determine the level of respect Louis Sockalexis deserves.

The Cleveland pro baseball team has, of course, what is today largely regarded as an inappropriate nickname (yes, Sockalexis inspired it during spring training of 1897 although it was *not* meant to be disrespectful) and, arguably, the most racially-insensitive logo/mascot in use in America. Chief

Wahoo has nothing whatsoever to do with Sockalexis, having been created in 1946, when Sockalexis had long been forgotten. Cleveland regards Sockalexis as merely a footnote to team history, something to be appropriated and used to justify their callous disrespect. When one considers the extreme racial prejudice Sockalexis suffered as the first-known Native American to play professional baseball, it is a sorrowful charade that has existed in Cleveland, from the time the nickname was officially adopted in 1915 to this very day, more than 100 years later, as I write these words.

Then there is *Sports Illustrated* magazine. For its issue that spanned the end of December 1999 and beginning of a new century, January 2000, the magazine published a list of each state's "50 Greatest Athletes." The magazine absurdly and ignominiously omitted Sockalexis entirely, while including such entirely questionable luminaries as LL Bean, for inventing all-weather rubber boots, and a teenage kid, for making the luckiest of half-court shots to win a state high school basketball championship. The magazine had also published two articles on Sockalexis, one in 1973 and another in 1995, replete with historical inaccuracies and riddled with myths this author has proven as false. When informed that the "facts" in their two accounts were deeply flawed, *Sports Illustrated* spokesperson Scott Novak told this author that the magazine had "already done the Sockalexis story" and had no interest in correcting anything it had gotten wrong. In 2009, ESPN, the bombastically self-proclaimed "Worldwide Leader in Sports," proved it, too, had no interest in history and operated upon a puerile memory that barely stretched a quarter of a century. It created a "Mount Rushmore" to celebrate the four greatest athletes from each state and joined *Sports Illustrated* in anointing, quite appropriately, Joan Benoit Samuelson as an obvious choice (the winner of the first-ever women's marathon in the Olympic Games, in 1984, was also *SI's* pick as Maine's #1 greatest athlete); however, ESPN's other three selections were all contemporary figures (one, hockey great Paul Kariya, is really from British Columbia) with nowhere near the achievements or historic distinctions of Louis Sockalexis.

Finally, there is the National Baseball Hall of Fame and Museum. Yes, it has been an honor for the author of this book to be invited to speak at the hall, twice, in 2005 (to discuss Louis Sockalexis) and 2009 (to discuss Sockalexis and the Native American pioneer players as part of a panel). Appealing, in both instances, for the hall of fame to match appropriate celebrations for the pioneer Afro-American, Hispanic/Latino, and women players in its exhibition areas, I implored administrators to do right by the earliest American Indian players, who also suffered mightily for the right merely to play. The administrator in charge of determining such displays responded dismissively and without further comment: "We don't have space for such an exhibition."

For a number of years now, I have felt that there should be a Louis Sockalexis monument, and it should be located somewhere in Maine. Recently, I joined forces with Theodore Bear Mitchell, the last Penobscot Nation representative to the Maine Legislature, and John Bear Mitchell, Passamaquoddy storyteller, professional actor, and former director of the Native American Studies Program at the University of Maine at Orono where he is a faculty member. We have formed an independent, non-profit entity, with the sole goal of properly showing respect and paying honor to Louis Sockalexis.

It seems only fitting that Maine show the nation how this is done. In Bangor, there is the Paul Bunyan statue, a mythic figure who did mythic things. When we have built Sock's monument, we will have built a lasting memorial to a real man who did mythic things.

—Ed Rice
April, 2018

INTRODUCTION

The Abenaki Adonis . . . Deerfoot of the Diamond . . . The Red Romeo . . . Those images suggest an Indian hero as powerful and fleet as he is handsome and bigger than life. Adonis and Romeo may need no introduction, but "Deerfoot" is probably Lewis Bennett (1830–1897) of the Cattaraugus Reservation in New York, who is considered the premier distance runner of the nineteenth century.

Penobscot tribesman Louis Sockalexis began his baseball career as the sort of arresting figure whose daily achievements were described in terms of hyperbole, but who remains an enigmatic figure to this day. Of such stuff, legends are made.

It is clear to me that Sockalexis is entitled to yet another title, one wrongly stripped from him. This book's title is an attempt to reassert the place of Louis Sockalexis as the first Indian baseball player. More than eighteen years of research have reinforced my belief that this designation was unfairly taken from Louis Sockalexis and given instead to James Madison Toy, who has been the individual most frequently identified as "the first Native American to play major league baseball."

The claim that Toy was the first Native American to play major league baseball appears to have originated in 1962, when historian Lee Allen of the Baseball Hall of Fame bestowed this distinction on Toy. Unfortunately, no reference material of any type accompanied Allen's declaration, and close scrutiny of the claim reveals it to be based on word-of-mouth tales handed down from direct descendants. The historical Toy played baseball rather uneventfully during the two seasons of 1887 and 1890.

Even if documentation could be found to prove that James Madison Toy possessed Indian blood (see Chapter 4, where Toy is discussed at length), the title that would most accurately describe him would be "the first man with a Native American background to play major league baseball." Toy's impressive handlebar moustache and Caucasian features, make it very doubtful that contemporary baseball players, fans, and sportswriters knew that he possessed Indian blood — if indeed, he did. Louis Sockalexis, on the other hand, was clearly recognized as an Indian by all of his contemporaries, and was accordingly both heckled and acclaimed throughout his debut season with Cleveland in 1897. It is he who deserves recognition for being the first Native American to play major league baseball.

Louis Sockalexis also deserves to be remembered as one of the greatest collegiate baseball players of all time and as a charter member of the College of the Holy Cross's Sports Hall of Fame, created in 1956 in Worcester, Massachusetts. Furthermore, the very participation of Louis Sockalexis as a member of the Cleveland team in 1897 inspired the nickname that the baseball franchise holds today.

That Louis Sockalexis lies buried in relative obscurity on Indian Island, Maine, beneath a monument sculpted and scripted in a manner reminiscent of the plaques honoring the legendary greats at the Baseball Hall of Fame in Cooperstown, New York, is one irony in a story replete with them. His Greek-sounding name carries a kind of irony as well. Sockalexis's athletic accomplishments were heralded with the fanfare associated with epic heroes. Like many heroes, Sockalexis experienced dramatic triumphs, widespread adulation, and finally a wrenching fall from grace, prompted in his case by an addiction to alcohol. Ultimately he failed to achieve the greatness that his peers and sportswriters of the time attributed to him.

At his best, Sockalexis wore the mantle of hero so easily that it seems only natural that he would have served as the model for one of the most famous of fictional baseball heroes, slugger Frank Merriwell. Maine-born novelist Gilbert Patten of Corinth, writing under the pseudonym of Burt L. Standish, began producing his sporting yarns about Merriwell of Yale in 1896, paralleling perfectly Sockalexis's spectacular exploits at the College of the Holy Cross and his meteoric rise in professional baseball. Patten had been a manager on the opposing team when Sockalexis played in a Maine summer baseball league in 1895.

It is unfortunate that Louis Sockalexis, the nephew of a Penobscot chief, was not carved from timber nearly so durable as Frank Merriwell. Yet at the height of Sockalexis's career, comments such as the following, made by Hughie Jennings, were typical: "Louis Sockalexis had the most brilliant career of any man who ever played the game. At no time has a player crowded so many remarkable accomplishments into such a short period of time as Sockalexis. He should have been the greatest player of all times—greater than Cobb, Wagner, Lajoie, Hornsby or any of the other men who made history for the game." John McGraw, one of baseball's most respected managers, said, "If Sock had stayed up for five years he could well have been better than Cobb, Wagner or Ruth."

Considering Sockalexis's awe-inspiring collegiate exploits and his status as the man who inspired the name of a major league baseball team (Cleveland was the only professional baseball team ever nicknamed for an individual), Louis Sockalexis deserves lasting fame. Unfortunately, even in Maine the unique distinction that Sockalexis achieved has most often either gone unnoticed or been disputed.

I hope this book clarifies the record of Louis Sockalexis, explains something of his life, and helps him circle the bases and come home in a manner appropriate to a truly gifted athlete—one who might have been one of the greatest stars in the baseball firmament.

1
The Early Years

L OUIS FRANCIS SOCKALEXIS was born on Indian Island, Maine, on October 24, 1871, the same year as the inaugural season of organized baseball in America. The reservation of the Penobscot Indian nation that settled in central Maine, Indian Island is located just across the Penobscot River from the small community of Old Town, and some thirteen miles north of what was once the booming "lumbering capital of the world"—Bangor, Maine.

Born into the Bear clan, Louis was the great-nephew of chief Tomer (Thomas) Sockalexis, who was born in 1813 and died in 1870. In 1832 Tomer was the chief of the tribe, and the Penobscots attempted to name him "chief for life." The Maine legislature, however, told the tribe that such an action was illegal. The Penobscots switched to a tribal governorship in 1867. Joseph Attean, who was the last chief of the tribe, was elected its first tribal governor. Louis's great-uncle Tomer Sockalexis returned to leadership as the tribal governor in 1868 and served one year. Louis's father, Francis Peol Sockalexis, who was born in about 1841 and who served as tribal governor from 1895 to 1896, married Frances Sockabasin, also born in 1841. The couple's first child was Louis. Apparently, several later siblings died in infancy. Louis had one surviving sister, Alice, who was six years younger. She married Thomas Pennewaite, had two daughters, and died in 1928.[1]

The Penobscots, members of the Wabenaki Alliance (which included the Maliseet, Micmac, and Passamaquoddy nations), had been proud and victorious warriors in an earlier day, soundly defeating the Iroquois, much feared; in fact, they were in James Fenimore Cooper's fictional *Leatherstocking Tales*. Known as the "Fighters of the Six Nations," the Iroquois were reportedly the reigning power from the Gulf of St. Lawrence to the Mississippi River, but after suffering heavy losses in their encounters with the Penobscots, they kept a respectful distance from the region that is now Maine.

Growing up on the small island reservation, "Soci" (as he was called then) attended the local school, which was run by Jesuit priests, as well as the old village chapel on Sundays. As a young boy on the island, he topped all his mates, demonstrating an exceptional blend of power and speed in such childhood games as running, jumping, and swimming. In high school, he excelled in football, track, and baseball.[2] Some Penobscot sources claim that Louis was the first person from Indian Island to graduate from high school, but there are no official records.

1

Sockalexis was discovered by a priest, who showed inspired scouting judgment and encouraged the Indian youth to continue both his education and ball playing. This paralleled the discovery of baseball's greatest legend, Babe Ruth. Ruth left St. Mary's in Baltimore, Maryland, for a professional career. After attending the small school on the island and the high school in Old Town, Sockalexis left for St. Mary's School in Van Buren at the very northern tip of Maine to continue his education and, perhaps, polish his baseball skills. It was the first of several significant steps up a long ladder the Penobscot youth would climb before reaching the professional ranks.

One of the earliest summer town teams for which Louis Sockalexis played might have been the one on Squirrel Island, just off the coast of Boothbay Harbor. Rob White, editor of the Squirrel Island Squid newspaper, wrote in July of 1994 that baseball games were played on the island as early as 1876. And in 1888, the editor of that issue of the Squid announced, with great pride, that "one of the greatest attractions here this summer will be baseball. The Island will have a nine made up of…well known players." The island team faced rivals from Rockland, Bath, Richmond, Bowdoinham and Ocean Point.

Four days later the newspaper announced: "Louis Soclexis [sic], who has recently arrived at Squirrel from his home in Oldtown, is about 15 years of age [actually in the summer of 1888 Sock would have been 16], and is one of the most powerful pitchers the Island has seen for years. He has all the curves." Perhaps the mystery of when and where Louis Sockalexis hurled those alleged three no-hitters has a possible solution here.

According to player Walter Emerson, reporting in the Lewiston Journal, the island had "an almost unbeatable team" in the late 1880s for two years. Emerson, the team's first baseman, was a member of championship team at Colby College in the early 1880s, said the team consisted of "Catcher, Louis Soxalexis [sic], an Oldtown Indian who afterwards became famous as a Big League player in the outfield of the Cleveland team… [and] second base, Joe Soxalexis, another Oldtown Indian player…"

The Squid also talked about some notable female players, including one named Harriet Holden who was pitching "inshoots and drops" to "catcher Louis Sockalexis (who retired after the seventh inning, somewhat the worse for wear)." While several players were credited with "parking at least one ball on to the library steps" outside the field's dimensions, Rob White commented, in a letter to the author, that an island veteran showed him areas where Louis "had hit balls beyond the library" and on to the more distant tennis courts.

After two semesters at St. Mary's he inadvertently auditioned for the next rung while playing a game in Orono against a town team from Houlton. The

2

Houlton club was made up mostly of young men attending Ricker Classical Institute in that northern Maine town. The club was coached by a Prof. L. W. Felch, a physical education director at the school. So impressive was Sockalexis's performance that, following the game, Felch and many of the Houlton players gathered around him, urging the talented athlete to come to Ricker to play during summers for the Houlton team. An added inducement was that the Houlton players were paid. Sockalexis liked the arrangement, and in 1890 he entered the school and joined the team, making his home with a family in Houlton.

A puzzling aspect of the early Sockalexis story emerges here: that he was able to maintain his amateur status, allowing him to play college baseball, while accepting pay for playing in several prominent summer leagues over the next several years. A number of college players used fake names and played for pay in leagues both in Maine and around New England. Yet Sockalexis, who was notable both for his race and his stellar play, always played under his own name, and in any case, no form of deceit would have been likely to protect his identity.

The Houlton town team was a member of the Maine–New Hampshire League. Sockalexis joined as a pitcher, and in his first season the team won 26 of 28 games and captured the league title. Olen B. Rideout was Houlton's first baseman (his brother, Percy, was the catcher). He once recounted how a disenchanted teammate, pitcher Horace Newenham, had said that he "would go down state and pick up college players and bring them back to Houlton to beat us. He got the players all right, but they didn't beat us." Sockalexis, of course, was what made the difference, but he had to outwit the cagey Newenham. Rideout recalled how the hurler "knew just how to pitch to each of us, [but] would not throw a strike to Soc." Avoiding any possible damage Sockalexis might do on his own, Newenham walked him on his first three appearances at the plate and then successfully retired the other Houlton batters. As Sockalexis prepared for his fourth at bat, Rideout remembered the slugger determinedly telling his teammates: "Let him pass me again, and I will score." Sockalexis was as good as his word. Newenham, again, deliberately walked him. Sockalexis successively stole second base, third, and home to score. Rideout reminisced: "He would run like a deer and then slide the remaining distance. On his run from third to home, he knocked the catcher flying, and also the ball. We won the game, 1 – 0."[3]

As extraordinary as they were, Sockalexis's speed and batting prowess never quite reached the legendary descriptions prompted by displays of his throwing arm. Even when Sockalexis was a high school youth, the strength of that right arm brought many challenges and provided many exhibitions. Purportedly, Sockalexis could throw a baseball more than 600 feet, from

Indian Island across the Penobscot River to his father, waiting to make the catch on the Old Town side. At fair time in nearby Bangor, according to first cousin Henry Mitchell, Sockalexis would throw a baseball over the length of the grandstand and over the top of the towering flag pole at the fairgrounds, or he would amuse patrons by having an easy game of catch across the width of the racetrack oval with his father—all, of course, throws of prodigious length.[4]

Some of the stories, still occasionally printed, are clearly out of line with reality, such as the tales of Sockalexis batting or throwing a baseball the length or width of several-miles-long Indian Island. Author Salisbury, visiting Indian Island in 1982, related a throwing tale that even one of Sockalexis's kinsmen could not swallow. Salisbury interviewed the then eighty-eight-year-old host at the tribe's historical society office, a Miss Violet, who told him that Sockalexis "was reputed to have thrown a ball from Oak Hill on Indian Island that hit the smokestack of the Jordan Lumber Mill. Miss Violet thought 'Louie' might have ranked with Babe Ruth if he hadn't been a drinker, but doubted he threw a ball from Oak Hill to the lumber company, because it is a distance of 4,000 feet."[5]

Still, a great many stories, by self-professed eyewitnesses, about Superman-like throws, endure. At Maine's nationally famous Poland Spring resort, reportedly on a dollar bet, Sockalexis is said to have successfully thrown a ball over the tower of Hiram Ricker's Hotel. Olen Rideout, too, recalled that "Soc performed many feats with a baseball — such as standing on the home plate of the Ricker grounds [in Houlton] and throwing the ball out of the field, over two rows of houses across Heywood Street, where we lived, so my brother could catch the ball in our yard."[6]

Another summer town team for which Louis played was the Hutchins Sasparilla of Augusta. According to Robert E. Foye of Sidney, Maine, he and Joe Sockalexis were members of the 1893 club that also featured Foye's grandfather, Orville Brown, the club's first baseman. A photograph of the team, sent to the author by Foye, shows a youthful Sock sprawled on the ground in front of a couple of rows of teammates, holding what appears to be a catcher's mitt. On the back of the portrait Louis Sockalexis is, again, identified as the team's catcher and his relative, Joe Sockalexis, is seated right behind him in the first row and is listed as the club's second baseman.

After playing in Houlton for two summers, Sockalexis first played with a stellar town team representing the Poland Spring House, in 1894, and then played that same summer for the Warren team in Maine's Knox County League, a popular coastal league featuring town teams from Rockland, Camden, and Warren. Mike "Doc" Powers, a collegiate star with Holy Cross, had done the catching for both the Poland Spring and Warren clubs,

4

and what he saw of Sockalexis impressed him greatly.

In this league populated largely by talented college players, young Sockalexis's play first became the stuff of storybook legend. For it was in the Knox County League that he was observed by Gilbert Patten, the manager of the Camden team who went on to pen a series of very famous baseball stories for young boys. Indeed, Sockalexis is considered by several reputable sources as the real-life role model for one of the most famous of fictional baseball players, superhero Frank Merriwell. Patten was born in Corinna (just outside Bangor) in 1866 and wrote under the pseudonym of Burt L. Standish. He began writing his sporting yarns about the fictitious Merriwell of Yale in 1896, paralleling perfectly the zenith of Sockalexis's Holy Cross exploits and his meteoric rise in professional baseball. Patten wrote the adventures of Frank and brother, Dick Merriwell, for eighteen years. The stories were published in *Tip Top Weekly*, a magazine for boys that flourished before World War I. According to the *Maine History Gallery*, Patten's lifework sold more than 125 million copies. His much-beloved Merriwell adventures delighted readers for decades, telling of the last-minute heroics of a genial, well-meaning athlete with a knack for doing everything imaginable right. Baseball historian Harry Grayson, in his 1944 tome, *They Played the Game* (a book of thumbnail sketches describing more than fifty of baseball's greatest players to that date), specifically made the link, noting that Patten was managing one of the clubs in this Maine league at the same time Sockalexis was routinely winning games single-handedly in the summer circuit. Grayson wrote, "While playing with the college men in the Knox County League in Maine, Sockalexis inspired the manager of one of the clubs to create the immortal Frank Merriwell under the pen name of Burt L. Standish."[7] Powers was also a baseball captain at Holy Cross College and, following the summer league season in 1894, he persuaded Sockalexis to come with him to Worcester, Massachusetts, to play with his college team.

A legendary player inspires stories of legendary feats, some less plausible than others. Consider this one: Sockalexis's father — said to have enjoyed long-range games of catch with his son — was reportedly angered when Louis became so engrossed in the sport of the white man that he threatened to leave the tribe. So upset was the father that he embarked upon a Herculean canoe journey, down the Penobscot River to the sea and along the Atlantic coast until he came to Washington, D.C. There, he hoped to visit President Grover Cleveland and to procure the papers that would allow the Penobscots to forsake their tribal governorship and return to being governed by a chief. He would thus be able to make his waywardly heading son, Louis, chief of the Penobscot nation and circumvent any notions of his leaving the area to play baseball. According to writer Frederick John, "This was the last desperate move by the elder Sockalexis to bind his son to the tribe, to make the call of the woods stronger than the call of the diamond. When the father returned from his long canoe trip, he found that his son had already departed."[8]

Writer Dick O'Donnell also offered a version of the story, a tale that surfaced in several publications after the turn of the century, again at the time of Sockalexis's death in 1913 and still again at the time of a rededication at his gravesite in 1934. O'Donnell's detailed story went this way: On a chilly June morning, at sunrise, Francis Sockalexis departed, determined to end his son's "fascination" for "a child's game played with sticks and balls."[9] He built a tiny birch bark canoe, approximately six feet in length. It took four days to travel ninety miles down the Penobscot River to the Atlantic Ocean. His progress was slowed because of dangerous rapids, and often he was required to leave the water and carry the canoe over land. Then came the Atlantic Ocean. The tribal leader quickly discovered it was safer out on the lonely ocean away from the shore. On Sockalexis's first day on the ocean, tidal waters kept pulling his canoe toward the shore, where dangerous rocks waited. He paddled farther away from land. And every day, just before twilight, the Penobscot would head back to the shore. Once there, he checked the underside of his canoe and repaired any damage caused by saltwater eating away at the bottom of the little craft. Then he cooked the food he had available and spent the night on the beach. He was able to do some fishing while on the ocean.

Finally, the Penobscot tribal leader arrived at Buzzards Bay on Cape Cod, where President Cleveland had a summer home, during the middle of July. His hopes, O'Donnell noted, "were smashed" when he went to "Grey Gables," where the president spent his summers. Sockalexis was told that President Cleveland had returned to Washington, D.C. Three days later, after repairing his canoe and buying supplies, the undaunted elder Sockalexis was back on the open seas again, bound for Washington.

The tribal leader did not reach the nation's first city until the middle of August. His canoe trip had covered 700 miles and had taken almost two months. Alas, there was more unhappiness for him when he knocked on the front door of the White House. President Cleveland was in the South on political business. The canoe paddler was obviously sick of the Atlantic, but he was not the type of person who was easily defeated. He decided to rest for a few days and then head for Florida, where Cleveland was scheduled to be two weeks later. By then, Sockalexis's epic sea journey in a canoe had been given a great deal of space in the press. Members of the Maine congressional delegation arranged lodging for him and made certain that his name was at the top of Cleveland's appointment list, when the latter returned to Washington. They also chipped in and bought him a return train ticket back home, shipping his canoe to the reservation. Early in September, the great day arrived. "The chief [*sic*], dressed in his finest tribal outfit, and wearing a magnificent feathered headpiece, went to visit the President of the United States." Again, O'Donnell gives us the purported conversation.

"Mr. President, it is not right for my son to spend his time playing this child's game," said Sockalexis. "He will not listen to me, but if you speak, he will obey you." (O'Donnell then interjects a curious thought: "Even if down deep in his heart, Cleveland had been willing to help the father, his political wisdom would have overruled him. After all, baseball was the national pastime.")

The president reported, "I am sorry Chief [*sic*], but I am unable to help you. I do not have the authority to order your son not to play baseball. Even if I did, it would be wrong of me to issue such an order."

O'Donnell's account concludes: "The two leaders spent a friendly hour together discussing many subjects, including life on an Indian reservation. Perhaps others might have been cheered by such a happy visit with the leader of the nation. Not Chief [*sic*] Sockalexis. He was broken-hearted. The president had been unwilling to help him. His son Louis was free to play baseball."[10]

It is not possible to verify that such a trip or meeting with President Cleveland took place, yet the story should not be dismissed entirely as myth. To do so is to think purely with a white man's sensibilities. The Penobscots, then and now, celebrate a long tradition as runners and canoeists and make trips of marathon proportions. Today, these trips include teams of Penobscots traveling to the far reaches of North America for weeks' long canoeing trips in wilderness areas and the sacred 100-mile run, from the reservation on the Penobscot River outside Old Town, up to Mount Katahdin, undertaken annually in late August.

2
The Holy Cross Years

OCKALEXIS WAS an immediate sensation at Holy Cross, although he attended the school for only a little more than two years and never graduated. The athletic record he established in several sports was so notable, however, that Sockalexis topped the list of candidates as the earliest of the charter members named when Holy Cross initiated an athletic hall of fame in 1956. He joined such standouts as Bob Cousy, Bill Osmanski, Willie Turness, Jack Barry, and Andy Kelly as the greatest names in the school's athletic history to that time.

According to author Luke Salisbury, "College baseball was more important in the 1890s than in this century." He noted that colleges recruited baseball players back then the way they do football players now. Salisbury listed the best teams in the country as Brown University in Providence and Holy Cross in Worcester, Massachusetts.[1]

Sockalexis's obituary in the *Bangor Daily News* said of the period: "Worcester went mad about him and immense crowds flocked to the little school on Mount St. James to see him.... He played in a time when college teams were truly great...including 'Billy' Lander, Bustard and Fultz of Brown; Carter and Greenway of Yale; 'Doc' White and Buck of Georgetown; Powers, Curley, Sox, McTigue, and Pappalau of Holy Cross, and Highlands and Scannel of Harvard, and even then experts universally proclaimed him the greatest college ball player of all time."[2]

Writing many years after the fact, some journalists claimed that Sockalexis was a star pitcher for Holy Cross when he was not playing the outfield and credited him with pitching a number of shutouts, including three no-hitters. There are, however, no Holy Cross records or collegiate box scores to substantiate those claims.

Even these legendary pitching feats would be eclipsed by Sockalexis's performances in hitting, base running, and fielding. In an exhibition game on April 10, 1895, his first appearance in a Holy Cross uniform, the *Worcester Telegram* reported that he had two hits and stole three bases in a 5–2 victory over the neighboring Sacred Heart Lyceums of South Worcester.[3] In his first official game at Holy Cross, he reportedly hit three triples against the Springfield Eastern League entry and pitcher Jimmy Callahan, later a standout big-league player who eventually managed the Chicago White Sox.

Then, in games against what was considered to be Brown University's greatest team to that date, Sockalexis recorded two home runs, two doubles, and six stolen bases. One of the home runs was a titanic smash, where the ball

8

cleared the field and crashed through a window of the Brown University Baptist Chapel.

Topping even that blow, however, was the special story behind his extraordinary feat of stealing six bases in a nine-inning game in the first home contest of the season at Worcester on April 19. Early in the game, the Holy Cross second baseman, a standout player named Walter Curley, injured himself reaching first base. Following the rules of the game as played then, the Brown University captain was allowed to select a player from the Holy Cross contingent to run for Curley. According to one often-repeated account of the game, the Brown captain selected the "lazy looking Indian who was lying on the ground near the baselines"; Sockalexis subsequently stole four bases running for the impaired Curley, and two more running for himself.[4]

The *Worcester Telegram* account for April 20, 1895, read a little differently, suggesting that Holy Cross had selected the replacement runner and that Brown had merely agreed. The *Telegram* reported that a crowd of about 3,000 people turned out for Holy Cross's first home game of the season on its "hill grounds" and left "satisfied that Holy Cross has a team which is capable of sustaining the reputation of the college on the diamond." Sockalexis was declared an immediate success: "The Indian, Sockalexis, was the hero of the game. He plays from the time the pitcher handles the sphere until the last out ends the game. The Browns were easy, Curley was lame, and the visitors were asked if Sockalexis could run for him. They assented. Sockalexis stole four bases for Curley and two for himself."[5]

Curley, injured before the game had started, was the second batter to hit in the first inning and reached first base when he was hit by a pitch: "Curley allowed an out drop to hit him and went to first. Sockalexis ran for him. He went down [stole second base] on the first ball." Browns pitcher Robinson struck out W. J. Fox. On the third strike to Fox, Sockalexis "went down" to third and this second steal of the inning resulted in a run: Third baseman "Lowney was way off the base and [Browns catcher] Lang threw wild, Sockalexis scoring." Sockalexis had only one hit, a double, in the game.[6]

Holy Cross clobbered Brown 13 – 4. The Holy Cross team had Powers as its catcher, with Jack Pappalau and Bill Maroney as principal pitchers. The infield featured "Long" John McTigue at first base, Curley at second base, Big Bill Fox at third base, and Little Bill Fox at shortstop. Joining Sockalexis in the outfield were Bickford, Gaffney, and Kelly. Five of these Holy Cross players made it to the major leagues. Besides Sockalexis, they included Powers, Pappalau, Curley, and William H. Fox. Writing in a 1936 issue of the publication *The Holy Cross Purple*, John T. Parpal exalted:

In those far days, even as today, Holy Cross was second to none in baseball. Every year the cream of the country's clubs, semi-pro and collegiate, went down to defeat before the Crusaders. But it was with Sockalexis that real baseball glory came. . . . Crowds flocked to see his marvelous playing, and they never went away disappointed, for the Indian was forever doing the unexpected, whether it was driving the ball up the bank onto Linden Lane, or racing up the same bank, catching a fly, and then completing a double play. When, in 1895, with Sockalexis in center field, Holy Cross defeated Harvard for the first time, 1800 people saw the game, a record for that day.[7]

That embankment was in left field, the position Sockalexis primarily played during his first season at Holy Cross. In a "prospects" story written about the 1896 team, this description accompanied Sockalexis:

> First and foremost among the returnees and of himself no small drawing card is Louis Sockalexis, the Indian, who played left garden last year. As is well known, left field is probably the hardest position to play on the Holy Cross grounds, as it includes a high embankment, and it is next to impossible to get a ball when running up a side hill. Sockalexis is a sprinter of no mean ability, and an accurate thrower, and in order to give him an opportunity to cover more ground than he did last year, he will probably be placed in centre field, while whoever plays left field will probably be placed farther over towards the left, Sockalexis being depended upon to cover some of that ground which it usually falls upon the lot of the left fielder to look after.[8]

It was in another Harvard game played at the Crimson home field that he made his so-called "lightning throw." A ball was hit out of the playing field, which had no fence, beyond some trees and onto a tennis court, where Sockalexis was finally able to race it down. The Worcester newspaper account stated that he "was after the ball in a flash, and made a lightning throw, directly into the pitcher's box, reducing a home run to a triple." The throw was ensured legendary status when, after the game, two Harvard professors measured the distance at a whopping 414 feet and declared that Sockalexis had established a "world's throwing record of 138 yards."[9]

According to writer Francis W. Hatch, Sockalexis's opponents were no less awed by his feats. Hatch wrote that Lewis Perry, a longtime headmaster at Phillips Exeter Academy, had told him of a game that Perry had played in Worcester in 1896 as a member of the Williams College team. "Sockalexis hit a ball on the line over the center fielder's head and was across the plate before the fielder had caught up with the rolling ball." Hatch continued, "Perry said it was murder for a man to try to score from second on any outfield single that Soc could get his hands on. His throw to the plate was so swift and accurate that the runner found the catcher, ball in hand, daring him to slide in. Soc never made a bouncing throw to the catcher. His were always special deliveries on the line." [10]

Sockalexis made yet another celebrated throw. Edward A. Dineen, class of 1920, recalled that Sockalexis's career was "replete with wonderful bullet-like throws to the plate." One of "the most remarkable instances," he said, came against the champion Springfield club of the New England League. In the sixth inning, with one man out and a Springfield runner on third base, the batter hit what looked like a certain home run. Sockalexis, playing center field,

> took one look at the ball and turning around sprinted madly for the fence. Looking over his shoulder he saw the ball coming and thrusting his gloved hand in the air caught the spheroid just as it was about to go over the fence. It was a marvelous catch, but the throw was even more amazing. As the runner on third started for the plate "Sock" threw straight as an arrow to the Purple catcher. Powers, standing on home, received the ball not two inches from the ground, just as the Springfield man from third base was sliding into the plate. All "Doc" did was tag the runner with the ball. It was by far the prettiest play of the game. [11]

It turned out to be a very pivotal play as Holy Cross narrowly won 3 – 2.

Robert Smith wrote that the legend of Sockalexis's throwing developed not only from game situations but from more throwing exhibitions: "There has never been a stronger throwing arm in the professional leagues than Louis Sockalexis owned." According to Smith, while Sockalexis was touring with the Holy Cross team, he frequently gave throwing exhibitions before games. Sockalexis "would stand in deep center field and hurl the ball in to the catcher, straight and fast as if he had pitched it from the mound, and high enough to be called a strike." [12]

Even the staunchest Holy Cross supporters, however, found the stories of some of Sockalexis's feats a little too much to swallow. On the occasion of Sockalexis being named as one of the charter members of the Worcester college's athletic hall of fame, *Catholic Free Press* columnist Gus Cervini turned his thumb down on one of two claims about Sock's fielding prowess. In his "Sports Chatter" column for January 27, 1956, Cervini called purely fictional a catch Sockalexis made in the top of the ninth inning to save a victory against Boston College at Holy Cross's Fitton Field by diving into a river adjacent to the field and swimming to the opposite shore.

The setup for this story went as follows: With two runs already in, the bases still loaded, and only one run more needed to tie the game, the Boston College team had a tiring Holy Cross pitcher on the ropes. There were two outs, but the Boston College batter had a three-ball and two-strike count, and the Holy Cross pitcher had little choice but to be absolutely sure he put the ball across the plate, lest he walk in the run that would tie the game.[13]

Cervini related that the pitcher "summoned up all his waning strength, and put everything he had on the next pitch. The crack of the bat was solid enough to sink the hearts of all the Purple rooters. The white pellet sailed for deep left field, where Sockalexis was playing. The Indian raced to the edge of the Blackstone, looked up, then plunged into the creek, swam to the other bank, reached up and hauled in the ball to save the game."[14] *Worcester Telegram* writer Burt Whitman, writing in April 9, 1951, agreed "the yarn" was not to be taken seriously at all. Whitman simply noted that in the days Sockalexis played, the Holy Cross team played baseball not on Fitton Field, but on a field "high on the hill, on a terrace far from the river."[15]

Even the legendary moment that columnist Cervini wants to claim as factual does not square with the Holy Cross record book. Cervini, quoting a story told to him by a former Holy Cross baseball coach named Pat Carney, described a game between Harvard and Holy Cross at the Purple's home field. According to this legend, Harvard had arrived to play the game with the bare minimum of nine players. Around the sixth inning, the Harvard shortstop injured himself and had to come out of the contest. The center fielder came in to play shortstop, but that still left Harvard short an outfielder. Harvard asked for the loan of a player, and Carney supposedly responded by giving them Sockalexis to play center field. Then, in the ninth inning, with Harvard ahead by just one run, Holy Cross put runners on second and third, with two outs and "a big hitter" coming up to bat. Cervini wrote: "The game was in the bag as the Purple batter bashed the first pitch to deep center. It was a sure triple. But the speedy Holy Cross man playing for Harvard turned his back at the crack of the bat, raced for the football field and made one of the most spectacular catches ever recorded in the record books to win the game for Harvard."[16]

There are several problems with Carney's story. Again, it is claimed that Sockalexis played at Fitton Field. Carney may well have been the coach, although he is not listed in the Holy Cross records. Both Jesse Burkett and James "Chippy" McGarr presumably stopped coaching the team around mid March to join spring training and play professional ball in Cleveland. Both Burkett and McGarr were Worcester residents and members of the Spiders, suggesting an obvious link to Sockalexis and his signing a Cleveland contract. McGarr, a third baseman, was replaced in Cleveland by Bobby Wallace in 1897, the year Sockalexis broke into the major leagues. Therefore, Carney could have been the coach of the team. More revealing is the Holy Cross record against Harvard in 1895. Holy Cross beat Harvard 4–3 in the first meeting of the season, on April 30 at Cambridge. Then, in the second and last meeting of the two teams, on the home field at Holy Cross on May 15, the outcome was a Holy Cross 7–1 victory. In Sockalexis's second and last season at Holy Cross, in 1896, the two teams did not meet.

In his first season playing baseball at Holy Cross, Louis Sockalexis hit a hefty .436 with 3 home runs, 11 triples, and 9 doubles. In 1896 he hit .444 in 26 games, with 56 hits in 126 at bats, and made another memorable visit to Brown University, where he reportedly inflicted more property damage, this time slugging a grand slam home run that supposedly broke a fourth-story dormitory window beyond the outfield. From his position in center field, he threw out nine runners. An advertisement for a game in 1896 read: "Don't miss seeing Sockalexis…baseball's heaviest hitter and the fastest base runner in the country."[17] To this day, according to the Holy Cross Sports Information Department, Sockalexis has been a member of every Holy Cross All-Time Baseball Team, no matter who has done the choosing.

Following the Holy Cross 1895 baseball season, Sockalexis joined college teammates Powers and Curley for another season of summer baseball, playing with the Warren town team in Maine's Knox County League. Sockalexis was apparently much in demand for summer baseball. Before signing to play in Warren again, he was targeted by the New England League. According to an article about the 1895 league in the Rockland, Maine, *Courier-Gazette*, for June 18, 1970: "Sockalexis is a man much wanted by the New England league teams. He is an awful slugger, sure catch, is as fleet as a deer, and can throw as straight and as far as a new fashioned rifle. . . . A six-footer, Sock was a murderous left-handed batter, and could really fire the ball from the deepest point in any park."[18] Sockalexis played center field in the summer league, and when he returned to Holy Cross for his second baseball season, he played center field for the Purple. Although he played for only one game, the New England League got its man after the Warren season concluded. After sitting on the team's bench and watching the Lewiston club play a contest in Bangor, Maine, in early September, Sockalexis agreed to play in the final game of the year for Lewiston's coach, Garrity.

On Saturday, September 7, 1895, Sockalexis played center field and batted fifth in what the *Bangor Commercial* touted as the league's "best game of the year" at the city's Maplewood Park. Sockalexis and Lewiston probably felt very differently: For the Bangor club, entering the ninth inning losing 7–4, exploded for six runs to win the game before a crowd of better than 600 fans. The *Commercial* said, "Sockalexis's playing in the centre garden was worth going a long distance to see." In one instance, Sockalexis tracked down a long drive, caught it, and then "made a wonderful throw" to the plate that narrowly missed catching a man who had tagged at third and was attempting to score on the play. His presence certainly could not have pleased Tom O'Brien of the Bangor team: O'Brien's "hit was one of the longest ever seen on the grounds and it would have easily been good for a home run but Sockalexis made a wonderful catch." The official statistics for the New England League record that, in his one game for the 1895 season, Sockalexis had one hit, a double, in four at bats, scored a run, and made three put-outs. After the Saturday contest, Sockalexis played for the Bangor team in a benefit game on Monday, September 9. He performed in a throwing exhibition (the distance recorded, 129 yards, 9 inches, "failed to break his own record") before returning to Holy Cross for another season in 1896.[19]

Yet Sockalexis's legend at Holy Cross was built on far more than baseball. The first mention of his name in athletic competition at the school came on December 11, 1894, when he finished second in the 40-yard dash, during the first indoor track meet ever held at Holy Cross. As a freshman, he won five out of the six track events he entered at a meet held at the old Worcester Oval. The wins included the 50-yard and 100-yard dashes (the latter won in 10 and 2/5 seconds), the broad jump (for which he held the school record for many years, with a leap of 21 feet, 3 inches), the hop-skip-and-jump in almost 41 feet, and the baseball throw, with a toss of 126 yards. According to Holy Cross student Dineen, Sockalexis "astounded the students and enthusiasts of the national game by throwing a baseball a distance of 409 feet, a world's record which stood for years" — and just a little short of his unofficial "lightning throw" of 414 feet.[20] A number of accounts claim various distances as the greatest throw by Sockalexis. Supposedly, on a challenge at Poland Spring in 1894, he threw the ball 137 yards, or 408 feet, but since the throw was not made under certifiable conditions, it was not counted as a new world record. The accepted record, during that time, was a throw by John Hatfield of 133 yards, 1 foot, and 7½ inches recorded in Brooklyn on October 15, 1872. While at Holy Cross, Sockalexis had a documented, official throw of 393 feet, 8 inches, which established a new national amateur record and "official" boasting rights as "the best arm in college baseball."

Several sources claim he could run 100 yards in ten seconds flat, even in his baseball uniform. Sockalexis regularly competed in three events in track at Holy Cross: the 40-yard dash, the mile relay, and the hop, skip, and jump; he was a consistent point scorer. He arrived at the school at a time when both indoor and outdoor track were particularly popular in New England. Holy Cross fielded an especially strong mile relay team; Sockalexis ran the third leg on a championship relay team.

His obituary in the *Bangor Daily News* claimed:

> Sockalexis was likewise brilliant in all lines of sport, especially in track athletics, where he ran all distances with equal facility. "Tommy" Connoff, the

world's champion mile runner, was a student at Holy Cross in those days, and often was hard pressed for his honors by the swift footed Indian. In competition the young redskin ran the "hundred" in ten seconds flat, and "Bernie" Wefers, then in his prime, declared that Sockalexis would surpass him if he gave his time to the sport. But Sockalexis loved baseball too well to care much about other pastimes.[21]

Yet when Holy Cross fielded its first football eleven in 1896 to play Worcester Polytech, Sockalexis was a charter member of the team and subsequently a standout. Writer Dick Dooley recounted some of Sockalexis's feats on the gridiron, even though his career was limited to the one six-game season played by Holy Cross in its inaugural football year. Dooley cited a *Worcester Telegram* assessment of the team on December 8, 1896, that named Sockalexis "the speediest man on the team" and a "sure and hard tackler. His sprinting abilities when coupled with the good work he is capable of putting up in other branches of the game, makes him one of the most valuable players at the college."[22]

Since it was the inaugural season of the sport of football at the school, the *Worcester Telegram* reported that almost everyone who played was new, or "green," to the game — everyone except a man from Bangor, Maine, the home area of Sockalexis. Edward Hixon had been the team captain and played three years of football as a fullback at Bangor High School. Hixon, according to that December *Worcester Telegram* article, "came to Holy Cross with a wide football reputation acquired in Maine." He was "the only player on the team who could follow the lines of the opposing team." By the end of that first season, Hixon had distinguished himself so much that "his playing was far superior to any of the other players."[23] Hixon was elected captain of the team for the next season. In the team photo, Maine residents Hixon and Sockalexis stood side by side in the back row.

Holy Cross lost its first game, Dooley reported, by a score of 10–0, "but the game had its moments. Sockalexis, whose knowledge of football at the time was minimal, succeeded in getting thrown out of the contest early in the second half. Unfortunately, it was never explained just what the big Indian did to incur official displeasure." He was ruled off for "unfair playing," about which Dooley commented, "In those days, the infraction could have been just about anything from chewing someone's ear to tying a knot in someone else's leg." As for the contest itself, "The game was not wholly free from objectionable features, but the slugging and other unfair features were few." Dooley also mentioned that it required the "best efforts of mounted police to restrain excited fans from interfering with the players during the course of the game."[24]

The next two contests were 0–0 ties, with Boston University and the Newton (a Boston suburb) Athletic Association. Then came the inaugural match that evolved and remained, until very recent times, one of New England's most prized collegiate football confrontations: back-to-back games with Boston College. Holy Cross dropped the first encounter 6–2, and the return contest was played the following Saturday at Boston's South End Grounds. Noted Dooley, "To this day there can be found argument as to the actual final score. The *Boston Journal* gave the final score as Holy Cross 6, Boston College 4." Not so, said the *Boston Globe*, which reported the result was Boston College 8, Holy Cross 6. Accounts of the game differ widely. Holy Cross did manage to go ahead 6–4 well into the second half on the basis "of an unbelievable dropkick goal from an extremely muddy field by Linehan, the right end."[25] Holy Cross seemed to have won the game, but a brawl ensued. The Boston College players left the field because the referees would not count a touchdown that had been made during the height of the fisticuffs. The officials apparently awarded the game to Holy Cross, but, while the Crusaders were on their way to the locker room, Boston College players retook the field — alone — and scored the "winning" touchdown unmolested. This action, too, was approved by the officials.

Dooley noted, however, that it was during the muddy brawl that "Louis Sockalexis enjoyed his finest afternoon as a football player." Commented the *Boston Globe*: "Sockalexis, the Indian, played at halfback for Holy Cross and astonished the spectators by his ability…. On the massed tackle plays he was given the ball time after time. When tackled he squirmed along the ground like a snake, while in defensive work he broke up the interference well and brought down his man."[26] The *Boston Journal* also pointed out that Sockalexis did most of the Crusader ball carrying "through a sea of mud," and, on at least two occasions, he broke through to dump Boston College ball carriers for substantial losses.[27] The *Worcester Telegram* account cited him for "magnificent all-around work."[28]

Sockalexis was never a student at Holy Cross proper but was enrolled instead at its Mount St. James prep division, which, according to the tactful assessment of student Parpal, "was the refuge of those who excelled in brawn but were deficient in other respects."[29]

According to author Smith, Sockalexis received his original invitation to Holy Cross because baseball at the school "had sunk to a very low estate." This information conflicts with other reports from authors like Salisbury, who claim that Holy Cross had one of the best collegiate baseball teams in the country at the time. The account continues, "[Louis] and many of his teammates — all recent recruits from the professional ranks — were put in a 'special class' together." Smith reported that within a year, most of them were sufficiently educated to take up freshman subjects at the college, and of them (but not Sockalexis) stayed at Holy Cross for a number of years, "slowly gathering a very good education and helping make the ball team invincible. A few became successful lawyers and doctors after graduation."[30]

Sadly, though many descriptions of Sockalexis's athletic ability are available for scrutiny, extremely little is available that tells what kind of person he was. Author Smith wrote: "Sockalexis made a noble appearance. He had a fine gentle face and luxuriant hair."[31]

Parpal and Dineen, the students writing in the college publication *The Holy Cross Purple*, stated that he was extremely popular with his fellow students and was even "idolized" by some. During his major league career, when taunted by racial taunts and epithets, he was repeatedly praised for suffering them silently and just going about his business, in much the same way that Jackie Robinson would be praised when he broke the color line for major league baseball in 1947. From his collegiate performances it is clear that if racial antagonism was a daily or even an occasional challenge, Louis Sockalexis was more than equal to meeting it. Dineen recalled the climate around the campus and Sockalexis's first few days at the school, noting:

> The advent of a full-blooded Indian . . . was the cause of the greatest excitement. Blood-curdling rumors began to stalk through dormitory and corridor that scalping would soon be in order. When Sock arrived at the dorm the first night, towels were conspicuously adorning the noble brows of every occupant of the room. Whether an epidemic of headaches among the fellows was a coincidence it is difficult to ascertain. As the evening gradually waned without any Indian social activities, however, all took heart and agreed that headaches were out of order, and forthwith headaches and turbans disappeared. During his first week of college, an enterprising joke-ster, with the intention of making amends for the towel fiasco, placed a high silk hat — purloined for the purpose from one of the faculty — with a large rock inside it for ballast, at the doorway just outside the refectory. Sock, having finished his dinner, was leisurely essaying an exit, when he spied the high hat. Here was an excellent chance to show off his prowess to the pale-faces grouped about the entrance. Pushing a couple of them out of the way, he made a perfect placekick. Then and there he found to his sorrow that the stony heart of fate was beating against him or rather against his broken toe. After emitting a few war whoops and vowing vengeance on the perpetrator he made the acquaintance of the infirmary.[32]

Socially, it appears that Sockalexis found a way to fit in, and it may well have been at Holy Cross that his tragic acquaintance with alcohol began. Some sources claim outright that Sockalexis was reprimanded and written up for drinking by the strict Jesuit fathers at Holy Cross. A few others, like Robert Smith, state the reason that "the gentle Indian" left Holy Cross was that he was thrown out of school for drinking, which appears to be untrue.[33] Author Luke Salisbury quoted Miss Violet, of the tribe's historical society office, as saying she remembered "Louie" from her girlhood. Miss Violet corroborated what others have said about Sockalexis being a gentle person and pointed out that she "never saw him drunk or after sundown." Miss Violet also said he had "a reputation as a drinker at Holy Cross, and the Crusaders' coach used to post players at the corners of Sockalexis's bed to keep him from searching the night for liquor."[34] Citing the school's strict rules about alcohol use and the absence of his name in the "discipline diary" maintained by the Holy Cross administration, however, other writers claim that Sockalexis was alcohol-free during his days at the school. This assertion is supported by a letter held in the school's archives, penned in 1949 by teammate William J. Fox, who wrote that Sockalexis, so far as he and other team members knew, did not drink during his two years at the school and always behaved in an exemplary manner.[35] Yet one wonders how close the two were socially, since Fox went on to a career in the priesthood. Further, since Sockalexis was enrolled at Mount St. James rather than Holy Cross, his name might not have appeared in the college's discipline diary even if he had been reprimanded.

Because of the growing popularity of intercollegiate sports on campus, Holy Cross administrators and teachers came to believe that the school's lofty ideals and intellectual atmosphere were being compromised by a thirst for athletic glory. The presence of scholarship athletes and the popularity they inspired provoked disgust among academics. A drive to stem the athletic tide prompted some Holy Cross athletes to leave the school. One story suggests that star catcher and captain "Doc" Powers was offered the equivalent of a bribe to leave Holy Cross to play for a school in the Midwest known for both its academics and its athletics. Powers did leave in mid December 1896 to play at Indiana's famed University of Notre Dame, and the twenty-five-year-old Louis Sockalexis followed him once again.

3

Short Stay at Notre Dame

A FTER DISCOVERING Louis Sockalexis in a summer league in Maine and luring the Penobscot Indian star to join him at Holy Cross, Mike "Doc" Powers, a native of Pittsfield, Massachusetts, once again induced Sockalexis to follow him — this time to the University of Notre Dame.

During the summer of 1896, Sockalexis had joined Powers and former Holy Cross teammate John Pappalau on a summer town team representing Plattsburgh, New York. In a letter to the author, Gerry de Grand Pre reported his father, Dr. G.C. de Grand Pre, was given a photo of the Plattsburgh team by player Harry Guibord's son in the 1950s. de Grand Pre's grandfather was also on the team and he often talked about Sock, commenting about how he "could run like a deer" and what a great throwing arm he possessed. Pappalau, according to de Grand Pre's father, also was part Indian.

Powers later starred in the major leagues as a catcher with the Athletics of Connie Mack and died tragically. According to author Luke Salisbury, Powers was "a charismatic man, a year older than Sockalexis," and was studying to be a doctor. When he caught for the Athletics, he was regarded as an excellent defensive player who was not much of a hitter; he was, however, the favorite catcher of star left-handed pitcher Eddie Plank. Of Powers, Salisbury noted, "Like Sockalexis, his career was cut tragically short. Doc Powers caught the first game played at Shibe Park in 1909, and ran into a railing while chasing a foul ball. Two weeks later he died of gangrene of the intestine."[1] He was only thirty-nine years old.

Joining Powers and Sockalexis at Notre Dame was Holy Cross coach Jesse Burkett, an outstanding baseball player who won two batting titles in the major leagues and who was ultimately enshrined in the Baseball Hall of Fame. According to many sources, it was Burkett who urged Patsy Tebeau and the Cleveland club to sign Sockalexis. Explained author Salisbury:

> Sockalexis went to Cleveland because of Jesse Burkett, the .400-hitting Hall of Fame outfielder, who coached at Holy Cross during the winters of '94 and '95. In the 1890s it was common for a professional player to coach a college team during the winter. When the coach left for spring training, which in the '90s usually meant spring drying out, the college nine would be run by its captain and a manager, who was frequently a student. It wasn't until the second decade of the twentieth century that colleges got full-time baseball coaches.[2]

Just as Sockalexis had not enrolled for academically challenging courses at Holy Cross, he apparently was not a university student at Notre Dame either. According to Cappy Gagnon, a Society for American Baseball Research member and director of stadium personnel at Notre Dame, Sockalexis "took courses like geography and reading while the other students were taking Greek and Latin. But once he set foot on campus, he immediately became the best athlete in school. He was a Jim Thorpe figure."[3]

According to an article in the 1897 Notre Dame *Scholastic Magazine*, the reaction to the arrival of Sockalexis made "the hearts of the local fans glow with joy unbounded."[4] Sockalexis apparently intended to spend some time in the area because he had also signed a contract with a local South Bend team to play the 1897 season in the Tri-State League that summer. His stay at Notre Dame, however, was short-lived. An evening of wild partying led to trouble with the local authorities. According to the *South Bend Tribune* for March 18, 1897:

> The two disorderly drunks arrested yesterday afternoon were students from the University of Notre Dame, where the news was carried by telephone at an early hour last evening. On hearing of the conduct of the two young men the university authorities ordered their effects packed and sent to them with the information that their presence at Notre Dame was no longer desired. Both were released last night. One of them was Sockalexis, the noted young Indian baseball player, who was recently signed to play with the Cleveland National League club after the close of the season at Notre Dame, where he said he desired to finish his studies.[5]

Gagnon states that the newspaper shielded the identity of the other young man because he was "a popular student" who "stood high in social circles in this city."[6]

Writer H. G. Salsinger credits William E. Hindel of the Indiana State Fire Marshal Department "for a most illuminating chapter in the biography of the brilliant Sockalexis.... No living man is better qualified as an authority on the subject since Mr. Hindel played second base on the Notre Dame team of 1897, and Sockalexis was a teammate."[7]

Salsinger reported that "before he left Holy Cross," after playing two seasons in 1895 and 1896, Sockalexis signed with Cleveland. Other sources state he did not sign with Cleveland until he was at Notre Dame. *Sporting News* reported, in its issue for the week of March 13, that he signed with the Spiders while in South Bend. His contract contained a clause that he was to report to Cleveland after the college season of 1897. But he reported before the end of the season, and Hindel explained why:

It was during the college baseball season of 1897 that Sockalexis and another Notre Dame student, whose name I don't recall, decided to paint the town of South Bend. They loaded up on old Oscar McGroggins and wandered about in search of entertainment. They visited an establishment conducted by "Popcorn Jennie" and wrecked the place. While they were demolishing furniture and hurling the broken parts out of the windows the local gendarmes arrived. They tried to quiet Sockalexis but only annoyed him. He became so provoked that he flattened two of the coppers with perfectly delivered rights to the jaw but he was finally overpowered and dragged to the bastile [sic].[8]

Some sources claim the incident occurred after Jennie expressed a disinclination to provide her "services" to a man with red skin; furniture-throwing escalated into fisticuffs, it is alleged, when a member of the summoned police force made a racially insensitive remark.

The Salsinger account continues,

Sockalexis and his fun-loving pal might have gotten out of this mess if the *South Bend Tribune* had not heard the story and plastered it over its front page. This greatly displeased the Reverend Father Andrew Morrissey, then president of Notre Dame, and he expelled both Sockalexis and his companion from the university. Mike Powers wired the Tebeau brothers in Cleveland and advised them to hurry to South Bend and get their Indian out of hock.[†] The next morning Pat Tebeau arrived, squared Sockalexis with the law, and took him to Cleveland, where his major league career began a few days later.[9]

Besides straightening out Sockalexis's problems with the law, Tebeau purchased his contract from the Tri-State League Club, according to the story as reported by the *Cleveland Leader*.

Hindel told Salsinger he did not know where or when Sockalexis took his first drink, but "he does know that Sockalexis and bourbon whiskey were acquainted before Sockalexis ever came to Notre Dame." Hindel recalled that

he was just as great a ball player as they say he was. . . . How he could hit! And how he could run, and throw. I've seen the best of the major leaguers but I cannot recall seeing another player with the foot speed of Sockalexis. He could have been one of the great all-time track and field stars had he gone in for track events. He could throw a ball as fast as any man could hit one with a lacrosse bat and he was accurate. There was never another player

---

† Cleveland manager Patsy Tebeau's brother was a minor league manager for the team.

like him and, quite likely, there will never be another. Had he never tasted whisky he would have lasted a long time in the majors and left a record that generations could shoot at without ever matching.[10]

Another version, far-fetched but falling dangerously close to the time-line, of how Sockalexis came to leave Notre Dame and join the Cleveland club involved roughly the same set of circumstances but all supposedly arranged through the deviousness of Patsy Tebeau. According to author John Phillips, the legend went this way:

> The story of how Tebeau grabbed the Indian is one of the athletic legends at Notre Dame. Tebeau went to South Bend in the early spring and got in touch with the Indian and offered him a sum fabulous in those dark days of salary getting. But he would not sign. Not till the college season was over, he said. And then Tebeau tried a trick and got a ballplayer — the same trick with a reverse English that cost him a player a year later. He bought Sockalexis a drink and another and another till the primitive redskin's red-blooded soul boiled, and that night the Indian, a perfect athlete, a model for a Remington statue, committed some violation of social etiquette, measured by college standards. He had disgraced his college...and was told he would have to leave school.... The plan of Tebeau was well worked out. And then Sockalexis notified Patsy that he would join his team.[11]

Of this story even Phillips wryly noted, "Don't forget that even Tebeau exaggerated." He cited, as an example, Tebeau's famed assessment of Sockalexis's "broken foot" that could not have been broken: This was the injury Sockalexis suffered and then played with during the 1897 season, the injury blamed for the Penobscot star's increased drinking and rapid deterioration as a player.[12]

After Sockalexis received his first paychecks from the Cleveland major league team, he reportedly wired money back to Notre Dame to reimburse the school for the cost of his education.

4

No Longer "Spiders" but "Indians" Now

THERE ARE CONFLICTING reports about how and when Sockalexis officially signed with Cleveland. Recounting Notre Dame teammate Hindel's story, Salsinger claimed that Sockalexis had signed an agreement even before he left Holy Cross.[1] This particular assertion is easily rejected. The *South Bend Tribune* for March 18, 1897, reported his altercation with local authorities of the day before and noted that Sockalexis had "recently" reached terms with Cleveland while at Notre Dame, agreeing to join the Spiders when the college team's 1897 season ended.[2] Some reports claimed that star Spiders player Jesse Burkett, who was coaching at Notre Dame, had tried without success after Sockalexis left Holy Cross but before he was dismissed from Notre Dame to persuade him to join Cleveland.

Then what about the allegation that it was because Sockalexis was expelled from Notre Dame that Spiders manager Patsy Tebeau was finally able to sign him? Further, what about the legend involving a devious Tebeau plying Sockalexis with drinks to induce him to sign?

The timeline, between Sockalexis's signing the Cleveland contract and being arrested in South Bend on March 17 is a close one, but it appears that the signing came first. In its March 13, 1897, edition, *Sporting News* announced the signing with an article headlined "Tebeau Signs an Indian." The item read:

> Manager Tebeau of the Cleveland team went to South Bend on a little scouting expedition and the result was that he signed Sockalexis, the Indian player, whom several teams have been trying to land for some time. Tebeau first noticed this player last season when he was on the Holy Cross team at Worcester, Mass. An effort was made to secure him, but it failed at the time and a close watch has been kept on him ever since. Burkett was recently instructed to sign the player but failed to get him, and Tebeau finally located him. Sockalexis is said to be a fine outfielder and a wonderful batter. He is a full-blooded Indian.[3]

The most prevailing evidence and consistent reporting seems to indicate that Sockalexis, while still at South Bend and just before his arrest, was signed to a contract by Tebeau, allegedly calling for a salary of $1,500 for 1897. In reporting the ballplayer's arrest, the *South Bend Tribune* did state that Sockalexis had "recently" signed with Cleveland; presumably "recently" did not mean as a result of his previous day's difficulties or Tebeau's deviousness.[4]

Further, writer Salsinger, citing Notre Dame teammate Hindel's memories of the arrest and its aftermath, noted that Tebeau had to be summoned from Cleveland to bail Sockalexis out of jail. According to this account, Tebeau arrived the next day and, after settling things for Sockalexis with the law, the pair departed for Cleveland.[5] Still, the closeness of the timeline indicates the slim possibility that the arrest could have led to the signing or perhaps the even more remote possibility that Tebeau overcame the apparent difficulty Burkett had had in signing Sockalexis through a drinking ploy.

A number of sources report that Sockalexis signed his first contract for $1,500 for the 1897 season, a considerable sum for a first-year player in the 1890s. The veteran Cleveland club had one of the highest payrolls in the game at the time. Many of its star players, like Burkett, Tebeau, and Cy Young, earned the maximum salary of $2,400. According to Francis Hatch, because Sockalexis was so successful on the field during the first three months of the season and was such a stellar gate attraction, his salary was raised to that maximum figure of $2,400 by midseason.[6] Tebeau, quoted in a column by Hughie Jennings, commented: "We signed Soc for $1500 and raised him to $2,400 almost immediately."[7]

An interesting factor concerning Sockalexis's signing of a professional baseball contract—perhaps this very first one, considering the incident at Notre Dame—was that his off-field reputation followed him. Several sources maintain that the terms of one contract contained a stipulation that forbade him to drink. Baseball historian Lee Allen provides this recollection, "When an outfielder named Louis Sockalexis, a Penobscot Indian, signed a contract containing a clause that forbade drinking, [player James "Orator Jim"] O'Rourke read about it, then turned to a friend and said, 'I see that Sockalexis must forego frescoing his tonsils with the cardinal brush; it is so nominated in the contract of the aborigine.'"[8] Unfortunately, O'Rourke's quote is not accompanied by the year in which the stipulation applied.

From the moment he arrived in Cleveland, Sockalexis was an immediate sensation, on and off the field. Before the Cleveland season opened, local newspapers lionized Sockalexis, writing glowing preseason reports, hailing his skills even during practice. The "Cleveland Chatter," a column in *Sporting Life*,* wrote that Sockalexis

> throws from the outfield with the accuracy and sure-aim characteristics of his race in handling the bow and arrow. It is more than probable that John Montgomery Ward was not dreaming when he wrote [Cleveland owner] Mr. Robison, "I will back my reputation as a base ball player and prophet on

---

* This Philadelphia publication called itself "A Weekly Journal Devoted to Base Ball, Trap Shooting and General Sports" and sold for five cents a copy.

Sockalexis proving a wonder. Why he hasn't been snapped up by some League club before this time is beyond my ability to explain." In the six exhibition games thus far played the Indian has had no less than eight outfield assists, nailing four men at the plate, one each at second and third, and catching two men off first, a surprising record, when considered along with the fact that he also leads the whole team in hitting.[9]

Montgomery Ward was one of the great early players in baseball history and is enshrined in the Baseball Hall of Fame.

The *Cleveland Press* newspaper for March 19 offered this intriguing front-page headline, "War Whoop, Sockalexis Had None As He Came To Town, The New Cleveland Ball Player Forgot His Tomahawk and Took a Shave." It reported:

A full-blooded Indian walked into the Kennard House, Friday, and wrote his name in bold-faced letters on the register. The only war-whoop he uttered was a request to be shown to the barber shop and the only thing he carried that could possibly be mistaken for a tomahawk was a trim walking stick. As he came out of the tonsorial department, Captain Tebeau met him.

"Hello, Pat," said the Indian.

"Hellow [*sic*], Sox," answered Pat, for the new arrival was none other than Lou Sockalexis, the outfielder signed by the Cleveland base ball club. Sockalexis is a bright, intelligent-appearing Indian of massive frame and bulging muscles. To a "Press" man he said: "I have played ball two seasons with the Holy Cross team and am surprised and delighted to get into the league ranks so soon. I have had good success in finding the ball and in hitting it out hard. I think Captain Tebeau the greatest man in the business and I hope to get on all right under his guidance." Captain Tebeau says the Indian is a fast outfielder.[10]

A late March article in *Sporting Life* reported that "Sockalexis, The Indian, came to town [Cleveland] Friday, and in 24 hours was the most popular young man about the Kennard House, where he is stopping. He is a massive man, with gigantic bones and bulging muscles, and looks a ball player from the ground up to the top of his 5 feet, 11 inches of solid frame work."[11]

That article again repeated Ward's assertion that Sock would be "a wonder" and then under the subhead "They're Indians Now" noted that "there is no feature of the signing of Sockalexis more gratifying than the fact that his presence on the team will result in relegating to obscurity the title of 'Spiders,' by which the team has been handicapped for several seasons, to give place to the more significant name 'Indians.' 'Spiders' did well enough with men like Jay Faatz, 'Darby' O'Brien and the like on the team, but is peculiarly inappropriate to the present aggregation of stocky players."[12] That reference should help to settle the issue about the genesis of the nickname "Indians."

Although known as the Spiders when Sockalexis arrived for his brief tenure, the team was quickly dubbed the Indians, when not just referred to as the Clevelands. There were no official league nicknames. In his introduction to *Chief Sockalexis and the 1897 Cleveland Indians*, from a compilation of newspaper clippings following the team's progress that year, author John Phillips writes:

> This is the story of Chief Sockalexis's debut in major league baseball and how he temporarily transformed the Cleveland Spiders into the Cleveland Indians. As the nicknames of baseball teams were informal well into this century, this book uses those that were most popular in 1897. The Cleveland team, of course, had been called the "Spiders" for years. But in 1897, many newspapers began calling it the "Indians."[13]

The nickname Spiders originated in 1889 when the Cleveland team was admitted into the National League and the Detroit entry was dropped. Legend has it that a critic of the team's preponderance of skinny, spindly-looking players—who did not, apparently, impressively fill out their new uniforms—led to the disdainful crack: "They look awful....They're nothing more than spiders." The name caught on with writers. Speaking of nicknames, Phillips also notes that the two most common nicknames applied to Sockalexis were "Sock" and "Sox."

Sockalexis, of course, was not an Indian chief, nor was "Chief" a common nickname for him. Apparently, the only people who used the term chief in reference to Sockalexis were the fans who mocked him and the members of the media who disparaged him. Curiously, *The Official Encyclopedia of Baseball* includes the nickname "chief" in the entry for Sockalexis. A handful of authors also refer to him this way even though no game account ever used the nickname.

A study of box scores and roundups of baseball news from early in the 1897 season shows references to the Cleveland club as "Indians," though many are offered as derogatory slurs directed at Sockalexis. The nickname "Spiders" had almost entirely disappeared.

Racism was virulent. After all, this period is only twenty-one years after Gen. George Custer's ill-fated trip to Montana and just seven years after the massacre at Wounded Knee. Many of the players vocally objected to the presence of an Indian, and there were numerous remarks to the effect that baseball should be restricted to those with white skin.

Unlike the barriers facing the black man, however, no barrier existed for Indians. Author Luke Salisbury offered this explanation:

> Racists had every reason to fear Jackie Robinson, for the arena of baseball is the national imagination, and if the black man could play there, sooner or later he could play anywhere." It is not surprising that Robinson broke the twentieth-century color bar seven years before the Supreme Court ordered school integration.
>
> The first Indian was another matter. The Indian strikes a different psychic chord from that struck by the black man, and no one tried to exclude him from baseball. It's been many years since a forest full of Indians troubled the American mind. We slaughtered them and devastated their cultures so completely that we've even eradicated our guilt about it. Indians represent a past we want to remember: the struggle to settle the country, subdue nature and conquer the frontier. The black man is from a past that is not so easy to romanticize, and a present we can't ignore. The Indian hasn't been a sexual threat since the novels of James Fenimore Cooper. Sockalexis appeared four years after a distinct turning point in the American self-image. In 1893, an unknown history professor named Frederick Jackson Turner pointed out that since publication of the 1890 census, the United States no longer had a frontier.[14]

As Sockalexis proved to be a hot box-office attraction as well as a speedy and potent performer on the field, the same sportswriters began using the nickname "Indians" out of respect rather than as an ethnic slur.

Even in Maine, however, the source of the Cleveland nickname has been disputed. In his book, *Yours in Sports: A History*, former television sportscaster Don MacWilliams wrote a thumbnail sketch of Sockalexis in which he says, "The story that the Cleveland team changed its nickname from the 'Spiders' to the 'Indians' in honor of Sockalexis is not a true one, for the team had already taken on the latter appellation before the Maine Indian had been signed by the club."[15]

Sportswriters of that period employed their own nicknames to describe the doings of the team that had been informally known as the Cleveland "Spiders." It was the presence of the only Indian playing baseball in the major leagues at the time that obviously inspired the nickname "Indians," even before Sockalexis had played his first official game. MacWilliams misunderstood this point, as did others who wrote about Sockalexis, relying on MacWilliams.

This is a good place to address the controversial question, "Who was the first big-league Indian?" In *The Answer Is Baseball*, Salisbury writes, "In fact, the first was James Madison Toy, who played in the American Association in

1887 and 1890, but this is a discovery of research. The first man known and treated as Indian was Louis Sockalexis—a name that intrigued sportswriters in 1897, who thought it befitted a slugger. Sockalexis was a Penobscot born in Old Town, Maine, in 1871, the year of birth of Marcel Proust and the National Association. He was not full-blooded (the last full-blooded Penobscot died in 1853) and he was not, as the papers in 1897 liked to say, the son of the chief. The tribe did not have a chief in 1871."[16] The tribe was led by a tribal governor.

The phrase full-blooded frequently causes confusion. Though the Penobscot Nation frequently characterizes Louis Sockalexis as "full-blooded" because both his father and mother were American Indian, Salisbury is correct when he says that the Sockalexis lineage, like all the others on the Penobscot reservation by the time of Louis's birth, was not pure Penobscot. At the time Louis was attending Holy Cross, his father, then tribal governor, grew so upset with white influences on the island that he took the drastic, and very unpopular step, of banning all whites from living on the reservation. Further, Salisbury is correct when he credits Sockalexis as the "first man known and treated as Indian."

Salisbury may be wrong, however, to credit Toy as being the first Indian. There is no evidence that Toy ever claimed Indian heritage while he was playing, and, indeed, there is no documented evidence to prove he had any Indian blood whatsoever. Just looking at a photograph of the man creates uncertainty. A faded print shows Toy looking directly into the camera, displaying the physical characteristics that have brought doubt since the early 1960s about his status as the so-called first Indian to play major league baseball. Dressed in his uniform, with a baseball lying at his feet, Toy clearly has fair skin and a distinctive bushy moustache, features that show he would not immediately be recognized by fellow players or fans (or anyone he did not tell, for that matter) as an Indian. American Indians often do not have facial hair. Toy has been identified for his partial Indian lineage. His father was reportedly a Sioux, while his mother was a white woman named Caroline Caler.

Far more troubling than debates about full-blooded versus mixed-blood status is the true genesis of Toy's selection as the "first Indian player in the major leagues." It appears this title was stripped from Sockalexis as recently as the early 1960s by the late Lee Allen, an historian at the Baseball Hall of Fame in Cooperstown, New York.

Allen was on an ambitious mission at the time. He was trying to establish contact with the descendants of all major league players "so that in our library we might have a file of biographical information concerning the men who have made baseball the great game it is."[17] In 1963, Allen received a questionnaire back from a namesake nephew claiming that his ball-playing uncle, James Madison Toy, of the late 1880s, was part Sioux Indian. In a series of letters, now in the Toy file at the Baseball Hall of Fame, Allen and relatives of Toy pursued the legitimacy of bestowing the title of first Indian upon Toy. Toy's nephew, plus Mrs. Jean Wigel, a granddaughter, and the wife of an uncle, Mrs. Hannah Toy, all corresponded with Allen.

In fairness to Allen, he inquired about family records and photographs, clearly seeking authentication. Yet not one of the three relatives could offer a single shred of documented evidence that Toy was part Sioux. Each repeated the popular legend, as passed down generationally by word of mouth. The nephew forwarded Allen a copy of the photograph that shows Toy with a baseball at his feet, standing with crossed legs, leaning on a bat. Mrs. Wigel passed along another photograph of Toy, having noted in an earlier letter that "we have a tintype picture of a very stern looking man that looks very much like he could be an Indian."[18] Apparently these photographs and the claims by the distant family members meant "case closed" for Allen. He wrote an article for *Sporting News*, published in 1963, with a Cooperstown dateline, under the title, "Who Was Majors' First Indian Player?" It was accompanied by the portrait of the "stern," elderly Toy, as a white-haired gentleman with a prominent bushy, white moustache, dressed in jacket and tie. Allen stated that it "often has been printed that the first American Indian to appear in the majors" was Sockalexis and briefly summed up the Penobscot's career. Allen continued: "But now it develops that Sockalexis was not the first of the natives, that the honor should go to James Madison Toy." The only evidence that Allen had to offer: "A nephew of Toy who still lives in Beavers Falls writes that his uncle was Sioux, although it is not probable that he was full-blooded."[19]

Curiously, Allen did not seem interested enough to pursue the matter after receiving a letter, dated February 14, 1964, from a baseball researcher from St. Paul, Minnesota, J.F.A. Pietsch. Pietsch said that he had written to the newspapers of Beavers Falls "but got no response." Pietsch noted that he himself had been born in Mankato, Minnesota, "where they hanged 38 Sioux Indians during the Civil War when we had a Sioux outbreak, I never saw an Indian who had a mustache or whiskers, much less a handlebar mustache." Pietsch emphasized his incredulity at Allen's claim by stating, "As far as our history shows there were no educated Sioux in the 1850s when James Toy was supposed to have been born of Indians or part Indian Sioux, so I can never believe the story about Toy being a Redman or part Redman."[20]

Even accepting the idea that Toy had Indian blood, it is highly doubtful that anyone other than he knew about it. Consider this article from the January 26, 1887, edition of *Sporting Life*, under the title "Another Catcher for Cleveland." It noted, "The Cleveland Club yesterday engaged its thirteenth player in the person of James M. Toy, of Beaver Falls, Pa., as catcher.

He is a tall, athletic young fellow, a splendid back-stop and very fine thrower."[21] The article concluded in two more brief sentences, explaining that Toy had played 39 games in the previous year with Oswego and Utica, two New York clubs of the International League, with a combined .218 batting average and .903 fielding percentage. Toy's playing versatility was also proclaimed, with the notation that he could play first base and the outfield. The article ended with no mention of Indian heritage. Every article about Sockalexis, no matter how small, always identified him as an Indian. Since being Indian caused a sensation in every city in the league when Sockalexis appeared ten years after Toy, it is hard to believe that Toy's Indian heritage, were it known, would not have created the same stir.

Who was the real James Madison Toy? According to articles from the Carnegie Free Library's Resource and Research Center for Beaver County and Local History in Beaver Falls, Pennsylvania, Toy was born in Beaver Falls on February 20, 1858, allegedly the son of a Sioux father and white mother. The Allen profile is present in this collection, and almost all the other articles are dated after 1963 and feature Allen's background and claims. Toy was said to have come from an athletic family, his father having pitched for the town team of West Mayfield, Pennsylvania, located near Beaver Falls. Two brothers also distinguished themselves as athletes, one as a ballplayer, the other as a boxer. Toy was described in one article, clearly taken from the 1887 profile, as being "a fine athletic young fellow, a splendid backstop and a fine thrower." The *Baseball Encyclopedia* states that he stood 5 feet, 6 inches tall, and weighed 160 pounds. After playing for Oswego and Utica in 1886, Toy made it into what would have been the major leagues for baseball when he played for (ironically) the Cleveland franchise of the American Association in 1887. Appearing in 109 games for Cleveland, most frequently at first base, Toy apparently was gifted and versatile enough to catch and to play most of the infield and outfield positions as well. It is said that during his career he played every position but pitcher. Toy is listed as having 94 hits in 423 at bats, for a lowly .222 batting average. His Cleveland team had the worst record in the league that year, winning only 39 games and losing 92. In 1890 he resurfaced again in the American Association, this time as a catcher playing in 44 games with a Brooklyn franchise that moved to Baltimore during the same season. His batting average was only .181 that year. Toy apparently suffered a career-ending injury in 1890 while catching when a pitched ball bounced off a corner of home plate and struck him in the groin. This injury reportedly caused him pain until the day he died. Returning to his home area, Toy worked as a molder with a stove manufacturer in Beaver Falls. He was married to the former Ida May Shrum, and several families in the Beaver County area are identified as descendants of Toy. Toy died on March 12, 1919, and is buried in Beaver Cemetery. Significantly, even in Toy's home area, he is not identified as "the first Indian to play major league baseball," but as "the first major league baseball player with an American Indian background."

Even the great-great nephew named James Madison Toy, whose great uncle was the ballplayer in question, said by phone and in writing that he "can't substantiate" the Indian heritage of his relative. In a letter to writer Larry Rutenbeck and a phone call with this author, he said that "any reference that James Madison Toy was part Indian" was made by writers and by deceased relatives. According to the now elderly Toy, all court records had been destroyed in a Beaver County building fire, and to his knowledge, the family itself possessed no documentation for the claim. He remembered speaking, in the mid 1960s, to an elderly gentleman named George Parris. "When Mr. Parris was a youngster, he remembered Jim Toy. He mentioned that 'Uncle Jim' had taught him how to play baseball. In addition, Mr. Parris referred to 'Uncle Jim' as a Sioux Indian. At that time, I questioned the accuracy of his statement. I thought that he might have meant to say that Jim Toy was part Seneca Indian. The Seneca nation was and still is located in northern Pennsylvania and southern New York."[22] Other family members, too, occasionally talked about the relative who had been an Indian ballplayer, but no one, to this descendant's knowledge, had any proof or explanation for how a Sioux Indian came to be part of the Toy lineage.

Toy agrees that his great uncle does not appear to have American Indian features and doubts that he was American Indian. Further, he says he knows of no one in the family tree who looks the least bit American Indian.[23]

The concepts that Toy, age 60 at the time, died in Beaver Falls in 1919 and that his death certificate was lost to history, as a result of that fire which destroyed all earlier official Beaver County records, pretty much left the author resolved no further doors remained open to investigation at the time of this book's publication in 2003. Then an inquiry, in the summer of 2005, from a man who enjoyed both baseball and genealogy changed all that.

Michael Palmer, general manager of WVII-TV, Channel 7, in Bangor, Maine made a study of James Madison Toy that he said took very little time. Palmer quickly discovered there were no American Indians named "Toy" in the 19th century, according to census records, and there would not be any to be found until the 20th century when the name appeared with a western tribe far, far away from the Sioux nation. Clearly, both a father and a son named "James Toy," who registered with the Sioux tribe and claimed a Sioux identity did not exist. Palmer also discovered that James Madison Toy had not died in Beaver Falls but had died in Cresson, Pennsylvania. The author had a new door of investigation to open.

A request to the Pennsylvania Division of Vital Records revealed a roadblock the author, a former journalist, regarded as both unethical in practice and completely unfair as a restriction to honest research and historical discovery. Instead of seeing itself as merely the gatekeeper for open, public records – records any American should be entitled to see upon request – the Pennsylvania division closed access to anyone who was not a relative of the deceased. The author had been advised this would happen…and that all it would take to secure the document's release was the simplest of verbal acknowledgements that, yes, the one requesting the record was "a relative." No proof whatsoever necessary. Hardly credible "gatekeeping" by any responsible standard imaginable. And a completely arbitrary rule the author will always believe is unethical and, indeed, not a justifiable legal action.

The death certificate (see "A Gallery of Photographs") was received in January of 2006 and was a trove of information, all completely damning to the case that James Madison Toy should be regarded as having any Native American background. For category "4" under "Personal and Statistical Particulars," the individual's "color or race" box is filled in with the handwritten word "white." His father is identified as "James Toy" and that father's birthplace is listed as "Pennsylvania." Since the professional ball-playing son was born in 1858, also in Pennsylvania, it defies reason that any Sioux Indian was born in the early 1800s, sans a name like "Sitting Bull" or "Crazy Horse," this far to the east, in a largely, white, Irish, coal-mining community. And, indeed, there are several people named "Toy" found in the census for Pennsylvania for these decades, according to Palmer, and most of them list immigration from Ireland.

Yes, it is still possible that James Madison Toy had Native American blood but since he did not claim such a heritage and did not register with a tribe or actively associate with a Native American community he is certainly not deserving of any recognition or title. And he most certainly didn't suffer any excruciating racial prejudice and racial intolerance the way Sockalexis was, day after day. As the author stated, when releasing the death certificate to the media, in late January of 2006: "It's time for a sorrowful 43-year-old hoax to come to an end. Locally, regionally, nationally, it is time to restore the title of 'First American Indian to play Major League baseball' to the man who earned it—Louis Sockalexis."

Finally, the author of this book experienced an unexpected show of support, in April of 2017, when a Pennsylvania journalist, Tom Fontaine, staff writer for the Pittsburgh Tribune-Review, published an indepth feature story on Toy. This author was interviewed at length in preparation for the story and briefly contacted by phone following it when Fontaine chuckled and remarked: "I am NOT going to be too popular around here."

Wrote Fontaine: "Toy achieved baseball immortality—more than four decades after his death — because of a distant relative's baseless and apparently false claim about his heritage and a well-respected baseball historian's failure to investigate that claim."

Fontaine interviewed the same namesake, great-great-nephew who'd spoken to this author, who told him: "I'm not sure where it got started, but there were parts of the family that insisted he was part Sioux Indian," said Jim Toy, 57, of West Mayfield, Beaver County. "No one had any documentation to prove it. My dad always kind of questioned the claim."

"Others did not," Fontaine wrote condemningly before proclaiming in his introduction: "And so James Madison Toy, an average, white major league baseball player from Beaver County, became known, incorrectly, as the first Native American to play in the big leagues."

Fontaine followed up on this author's concern that the Baseball Hall of Fame should have but did not offer a correction for a former employee's obviously-objectionable pronouncement.

"Rice has urged Cooperstown to weigh in on the debate. But its library director, James L. Gates Jr.," told him: "The Hall of Fame is not a sanctioning body for ethnic backgrounds. (Lee Allen) was writing for himself when he made that claim. We don't stipulate anybody as being the first in terms of ethnic background."

Covering many of the same bases this author did, Fontaine crossed home plate with two potent, additional details this author did not possess: "Genealogical research and DNA analysis appears to show that Toy wasn't Native American."

Fontaine noted: "While numerous accounts suggest that the ballplayer's father was a Sioux Indian, records stored at the Beaver County Genealogy and History Center list the ballplayer's parents as James and Caroline (Caler) Toy. Toy's father was the son of Henry and Mary Toy, both of whom were born in Ireland."

"And results of a DNA test," Fontaine wrote, "added recently to Toy's file in Cooperstown show that the ancestral composition of another one of Toy's relatives, James Woods, who couldn't be reached, amounted to 0.0 percent Native American. Woods' great-great-grandfather John Wesley Toy was the ballplayer's brother."

Fontaine reported that Woods, writing in an email accompanying the DNA results, said that he took the test "not to discredit any family lore, but to accurately document my family history."

Some sources have attempted to make the case that Sockalexis was the first known player representing a "minority race." That case seems an impossible one to make. Many baseball authorities know, for instance, that Jewish outfielder Lipman ("Lip") Pike surfaced as early as 1876 to play with St. Louis and Cincinnati, part of the National League, for three seasons.

If the technical difficulties of full-bloodedness are rightfully set aside, however, Louis Sockalexis is entitled to be pronounced, as he was by the legendary Philadelphia manager Connie Mack in his memoirs, published in 1950, "the first full-blooded Indian to play in the major leagues."[24] Yet, even at the time of Louis Sockalexis's belated induction into the Maine Sports Hall of Fame (1985), Maine newspaper writers refused to credit him as the "first Indian to play major league baseball." They also declined to credit him as being the inspiration for the Cleveland baseball club's enduring nickname.

Not so at Holy Cross. Indeed, as the college alumni magazine would trumpet in the article "Sockalexis: The Greatest Crusader?" in 1950: "It was a red-letter day in the sports world when Sockalexis, the first Indian to play in the major leagues, decided to join the team coached by the famous Patsy Tebeau, the Cleveland Spiders." The article in the Holy Cross publication described the result of that choice this way: "In the fraction of one season . . . he attracted more fame, more adventure, and more publicity in his work than most moderns do in a lifetime. He changed the name of a big league ball team before he wore its uniform" in a regular season game.[25]

Another expression of the preseason excitement over Sockalexis came in *Sporting News* with this blurb, headlined: "New Spiders: Manager Pat Tebeau Thinks He Has Secured Several Stars." Reviewing new players, Tebeau says of the Penobscot, "Sockalexis the Indian is possessed of a wonderful physique. He has an immense chest and shoulders and his limbs are built for both strength and speed. He has a record of 100 yards in 10 seconds and wouldn't fall far behind in a trial at the present time."[26]

A notation in the March 27 issue of *Sporting Life*, in an article carrying the heading "They're Indians Now," said that "Sockalexis, the Indian, makes friends fast. He already knows half the sports in town, and has only been here three days."[27] Still, not everyone was happy about Sockalexis being in the league. Resentment at his mere presence was evident among players and fans who believed that only whites should be allowed to play in the major leagues. One of the five famous ball-playing Delahanty brothers reportedly said, "The League is all gone to hell now that they're letting them damned foreigners in."[28] Heckling, mock war whooping, and overt racial slurs in newspaper reports followed Sockalexis everywhere. Custer's Last Stand not long past, references to such events frequently appeared, even though Sockalexis's Penobscot and Down East Yankee heritage clearly distanced him from any connection with the warrior Sioux.

For example, a nationally syndicated newspaper column entitled "Crisp Base Ball Notes" reported, "That Tebeau's aborigine, Sockalexis, will not be forced to seek occupation as a stationary 'ad' for a cigar store is evidenced by his agile fielding and hard hitting in the practice of the Spiders. He sprints after outfield hits like a flock of Sioux giving General Miles' army a run. The Indian in athletics has demonstrated more than ordinary mechanical ability, as in the case of the Carlisle football players, but they seem to lack alertness of thought in a trying situation. The best test of Sockalexis's wit will come when he is on the bases."[29]

All this attention, and Sockalexis had still not played a regular season game. A *Boston Daily Globe* profile announced, "Indian In Right Field: Sockalexis, Penobscot From Oldtown, Will Play With The Cleveland Nine," complete with a line drawing of a gloveless Sock poised to hurl a mighty throw, with the caption "Sockalexis the Indian." This article, which was reprinted almost in its entirety in the May 1, 1897, issue of *Sporting Life* (this time with a handsome head-and-shoulders line drawing), commented:

> Sockalexis is not a well-greaved Greek, notwithstanding the Hellenic hint his name conveys. He is a well-educated Indian. Furthermore, says the New York World, he is a professional baseball player and during this season he will travel through the country playing right field with the Cleveland club. Of course the "rooters" will have no end of fun with his name, and it is possible, even now, to anticipate some of the gay changes that will be rung on "Sock" and "Aleck" as he merrily chases the ball over the field or legs it for bases. But Sockalexis is not to be sneezed at as a baseball player, and Capt. Tebeau of the Cleveland nine counts himself as a fortunate man in having him on his team.[30]

The article continues, detailing Sock's Maine heritage and describing him thus:

> His origin shows clearly enough in his dark complexion, straight black hair, and somewhat modified but still noticeably high cheekbones. He is over 6 feet tall, of powerful physique, and noted as a hard, reliable and safe batter. He is as nimble and fleet-footed in the field as he is safe at the bat, and he throws as straight as a rifle shot. Sockalexis never saw the wild west. To all intents and purposes he is a down east Yankee, and is, moreover, a very fluent, agreeable talker, the characteristic reticence of his race being entirely obliterated in his case. . . . Besides being a strong baseball player, Sockalexis is a good all-round athlete and one of the best handball players in the Cleveland club, even beating Capt. Tebeau, who is counted a remarkably alert player at this game.[31]

Author Salisbury addressed this curious "sensation" building steadily through the exhibition season:

Sockalexis was an immediate sensation. Fans got news through newspapers and by word of mouth. There were no newsreels and no action photos in newspapers. Expectations were built with adjectives on newsprint. Great feats were reported, and fans had to imagine the home run, the slide, or throw. Reading the Boston papers for April 1897, one gets a sense of something happening, something building, a phenomenon in the West — reports from St. Louis, Louisville, Cleveland, the *Sporting Life*, a weekly baseball bible and competitor of the *Sporting News*, reported that in six exhibition games in April, Sockalexis had ten outfield assists. [In fact, the article cited eight assists —*Author*.] That's enough to fire anyone's imagination.[32]

Salisbury also suggested that Sockalexis's physical makeup added to the allure: "Sockalexis was five feet eleven and weighed 190 pounds, which given the height of the average man in 1897, would be like being six-three or six-four and weighing 230 pounds today. He was as big as a football lineman of his day, and faster than the backs." Salisbury notes that several sources reported that Sockalexis could run a hundred yards in ten seconds flat, close to the world record at the time. An athlete who could hit the baseball, throw it prodigious distances, and run as fast as anyone in the world created anticipation for the "cranks" (the fans) of the day who expected that they would soon be seeing a superstar at their ballparks. Salisbury wrote: "Before fans saw Sockalexis, they heard about him, and created their own image of a man" who could do phenomenal things. "Anticipation is often sweeter than reality. It is its own excitement, but anticipation makes demands and extracts a price. Anticipation of Sockalexis must have been feverish."[33]

Maine writer Francis Hatch recalled the hoopla attending Sockalexis's first days as a professional player this way:

> Fans came to see him with the same curiosity that had attracted their parents to Barnum's Museum. . . . His bat was soon swishing customers through the turnstiles at a rate that warranted a mid-season raise to $2400. . . . Here was the first full-blooded Indian to come up and push an Irishman onto the bench. He was just under 6 feet tall, with a shock of hair bushing out from under his cap to shade high cheekbones and a good-natured smile. For Soc, baseball was fun — a case of doing what came naturally.[34]

Sporting News ran an article reviewing the teams and the race for the National League professional baseball title, "For the Flag: Best Race in History." Again, great expectations weighed on the shoulders of Louis Sockalexis. The account read:

> The Cleveland ball club needed but one accession last year to make them easy pennant winners and that is a heavy hitting outfielder. Such a fielder and

batter from every account seems to have been captured in the Indian. Sockalexis is a great batter, splendid fielder, and fast runner. He will be right at home with Cleveland while Harry Blake, who can play infield as well as out[field], will be what the Spiders needed, a capable substitute. . . . Team estimated as 12 percent stronger than in '96.[35]

On April 26, 1897, the *Cleveland Plain Dealer* carried a large portrait of the Cleveland team for the season, with Sockalexis standing prominently in the middle of the back row.

A few points are in order about the way baseball was played in Sockalexis's time. According to author Phillips, in the introduction to his book about the 1897 Indians:

Obviously turn-of-the-century baseball was somewhat different than baseball today. Some people say we would scarcely have recognized the game. My theory is that it would take us at least an inning to get used to it. Fair balls that bounced into grandstands or over fences were homers. The old teams sometimes batted first at home. The idea was to get first whacks at the ball when it was whitest and hardest, thereby quickly disheartening the visitors. "Wild pitches" weren't necessarily pitches that got past catchers; some were what we call "waste" pitches. "Wild-pitch hitters" such as Ed Delahanty were unpredictably troublesome; they'd reach out and clobber pitches they weren't intended to hit.[36]

When teams traveled, they used an omnibus or a bus that was horse-drawn.

Society for American Baseball Research member Richard "Dixie" Tourangeau disagrees slightly with Phillips over the notion that it would take as much as "an inning" for today's fans to recognize baseball 1897 style. He noted the distance from the pitching mound to the plate had already been established as 60 feet 6 inches and that most of the rules that fans today know were in place. He believes the most intriguing difference fans would notice was the practice of the fielders leaving their tiny gloves out on the field near their positions before coming in to bat, a practice that lasted well into the twentieth century.

One unnamed critic, writing in an early May 1897 issue of *Sporting Life*, did complain that the game was losing its civility:

Every year has its innovation in base ball. It used to be that when a pitcher hit a batter he would rush up to him, in apparent alarm, rub the contusion and accompany him down to the first bag, uttering solicitudes all the while. That was in the palmy days of old fashioned courtesy. Now your twirler kills a man, has a bored look while waiting an instant for the ambulance, rubs a little more dirt on the ball and asks for the next batter.[37]

Civility, or the utter lack of it with regard to opponents and umpires, might be the most shocking element for modern-day observers of baseball 1890s style. In addition to pitchers throwing at the heads of opposing batters, infielders tripped and interfered with base runners, and base runners slid into infielders with murderous intent. Flagrant cheating was commonplace. Spare baseballs were strategically placed in the long grass of the outfield, for use when potential extra base blows could be snuffed out — merely by seizing the substitute and whipping it into second for an easy out. Alert, devious runners would dash from first over to third by cutting across the infield. The rowdy play was matched with vile and obscene language on the field, barbs so despicable that sportswriters frequently complained about them. Further, umpires were shown little or no respect and frequently had to fight their way, literally, out of disputes arising from their calls. In the 1890s umpires resigned in staggering numbers. In 1895, for instance, the league went through fifty-nine umpires.

A major part of the problem seems to be that the rowdiest, most obscene, invective-spewing teams met with success on the field. One of the teams most celebrated for playing this style of baseball was the hated Baltimore Orioles, who captured pennants in 1894, 1895, and 1896. All the teams routinely complained about one another for fostering this despicable behavior. Baltimore, for example, railed that the Boston club was the worst proponent of such ungentlemanly play. For its part, Patsy Tebeau's Cleveland Spiders-turned-Indians hurled epithets and played rowdy baseball with the worst of them. One can only imagine what Louis Sockalexis — college student and first-known Native American to play major league baseball — thought of all this as he prepared to play his first game.

5

"Play Ball!" 1897

"**G**OOD DRAWING CARD: Sockalexis Is The Best Advertised Player In The Business." That headline ran above a *Sporting News* article by Charles W. Mears, reporting in a "special correspondence" from Cleveland during the week the 1897 baseball season opened. Mears wrote:

> Everyone in Cleveland, as well as other league cities for that matter, [is] talking Sockalexis and if the young Indian is not the best advertised new man that ever entered the big organization, then it will not be the fault of the baseball paragraphers of the press. They have discovered a novelty in it. The newspaper talk concerning the youngster has stirred up great local interest in the redman and of all the young players on the Cleveland's club list, he is the most talked of and it will be his appearance that will draw the greatest number of curious people at the opening of the season. His presence on the team may be the cause of drawing many patrons to the game. For if they go but once, just to see the Indian play, they may become interested in the game and go again and again until they may become regular patrons. Whether or not Sockalexis deserves all the good things that have been said of him and will make a place for himself on the team, it appears to me a good thing that Tebeau signed him for as forestated his connection with the Cleveland club has been noted everywhere throughout the country and the entire team has reaped the benefit given both the Indian and the organization. Down East one baseball scribe fell into hexameter over Sockalexis. There is little to be said about the Cleveland team at this time for nearly all the players are off on the exhibition trip and President Robison has not yet returned from the meeting in New York. However all the cranks [fans] are talking of the season's opening and I shall expect to see an immense crowd when the first game is played.[1]

Sockalexis had joined the team for spring training, which was held indoors at its outset at the Cleveland Athletic Club. A *Cleveland Plain Dealer* article marveled at Sockalexis's athleticism, noting that he went through conditioning exercises "that would tear the ordinary man in two."[2]

Further, Sockalexis's left-handed batting stance and swing were apparently unique. Another preseason *Cleveland Plain Dealer* article remarked: "Sockalexis, despite the peculiar way he goes at the ball, is hitting it pretty regular."[3]

The author never found another reference to the unique or so-called "peculiar way" Sockalexis swung the bat. Perhaps there is a tantalizing, possible answer to be found in the photograph of him holding a bat that graces this book's cover: He is holding it with a spread grip, his hands several inches apart at the bottom of the bat. A few players, from time to time, were known to do this for better bat control; indeed, Ty Cobb, arguably the greatest hitter who ever lived, would come along a few years later and make an art form of placing hits where he wanted with a spread grip.

The name Indians first appeared in the Cleveland newspapers when Tebeau split the team up for an intersquad game. Sockalexis played right field and batted fourth for a group dubbed the Indians, comprised mostly of Spider veterans, the regulars from the previous season. Opposing them, as the "Papooses," were the bench players and young hopefuls. On Burkett's recommendation, Tebeau had signed Sockalexis's Holy Cross teammate John Pappalau, but Pappalau made a miserable first impression, pitching very badly.

Sockalexis was making headlines and drawing tremendous attention even before the regular season began, and the moniker Indians was catching on as the new Cleveland nickname. The *Cleveland Press*, for instance, carried the following headline after an April 15 exhibition game that "Tebeau's Indians" won over Indianapolis: "Errorless Was The Game Played By The Indians. Tebeau's Team Wins An Easy Victory, Sockalexis's Work Was The Feature Of The Day." According to the account, "The Hoosier capital team, the second strongest club in the Western league, fell down before Oliver Tebeau's Indians, yesterday, in the easiest possible way. Sockalexis was the star of the game. He made a circus catch in the field, made a hit that brought in two runs and stole the only base pilfered by the Clevelanders."[4]

In an April 18 exhibition game in Grand Rapids, Michigan, however, the team was castigated in a headline that blared: "Shiftless Was The Playing of the Indians." The game account of Cleveland's 9–5 loss bluntly stated, "The game of ball put up by the Cleveland team, yesterday, wouldn't have beaten a club of 12-year-old boys. Neither Gear nor Pappalau could pitch a little bit, and not one of the visitors could bat.... Tebeau's warnings to his men about overdoing were greeted sarcastically by the crowd, as none of the Indians made any effort to win the game."[5] The box score showed that Sockalexis, batting in the fourth position, had one hit in two official at bats. He had one put-out in right field and also one assist.

On Thursday, April 22, 1897, baseball's twenty-sixth organized season opened. National League president Nick Young was quoted as saying, "Baseball is the best emblem of the American people I can think of. For our nation's game symbolizes the great traits in the disposition of Uncle Sam's children — energy, fair play and the wistful uncertainty that has marked the work of all Americans who have achieved name and fame in the passing of a day."[6]

Fans of the 1896 champion Baltimore Orioles were concerned about whether shortstop Hughie Jennings's arm had gone lame. The Orioles manager denied it. After threatening not to play yet another year because of a contract dispute [he sat out the entire 1896 season], one of the outstanding pitchers of the era, Amos Rusie, joined the New York Giants playing on the road in Philadelphia. On opening day Philadelphia unveiled rookie Napoleon Lajoie at first base. Future Hall of Famers Jennings, Rusie, and Lajoie are all significantly linked to the Sockalexis legend. Manager Connie Mack wrote in his memoirs, published more than fifty years later: "With fond memories I also recall Amos Rusie back in the 1890s. He was generally recognized by sport authorities as the great pitcher of his day."[7] The most prominent dignitary absent for Washington's home opener was President William McKinley. The team lost 5 – 4.

Twenty-five-year-old rookie Louis Sockalexis played in his first official game on April 22, 1897, in Louisville, Kentucky. He was hitless in three at bats, playing before 10,000 spectators, as Cleveland lost 3 – 1. Sockalexis replaced the 1896 starter, Harry Blake, in right field. The fans apparently derisively "whooped it up" for him at the outset but grew respectful thereafter. Cy Young, who appears destined to forever remain the winningest pitcher in baseball history, with an astounding career total of 511 wins, was the losing pitcher on this day for Cleveland. According to the account of the game in the *Louisville Courier-Journal*:

> Sockalexis, the Indian, was cheered at almost every move. As a matter of fact, he had little to do. He caught a long fly very prettily and the spectators remarked at his grace. He is certainly a ball player, but could not touch [Charles "Chick"] Fraser's delivery. As was predicted, the crowd tried to have some fun with Sockalexis' name and imitated the warwhoop of various Indian tribes, to all of which the handsome Indian smiled good naturedly. He is educated and cultivated.[8]

In his second game, again against Louisville on April 24, Sockalexis collected his first two major league hits while batting in the time-honored slugger's fourth position in the lineup, or "cleanup," slot. The safeties came against a left-handed pitcher named Still Bill Hill. Ironically, left-handed pitchers would generally prove frustrating for Sockalexis as the season progressed. In this game Cleveland was soundly defeated 9–3, and two Cleveland players, Jesse Burkett and Jack O'Connor, were ejected from the game for arguing with umpire Sandy McDermott. A few days later a "seething" captain Tebeau called umpire McDermott "a rank home team umpire" and supported players Burkett and O'Connor in their claims that

McDermott was "a robber," the allegation that was cited for the ejection of both players. Sockalexis had three hits in four at bats in his first game at Cincinnati, but the team again lost 6–3. A *Cleveland Plain Dealer* account of this contest noted:

Good pob

> The bright particular star of the game was Warrior Louis Sockalexis. He was naturally the center of attraction after the visitors reached the grounds. He was greeted with war whoops and Indian yells, but as the game progressed and Socks hit and fielded, he was given an ovation. The Indian is a star, at least that is the impression that the 4,420 fans drew from his work today. Every one of his fielding chances were of the most difficult order, and though it was the first time in his career that he played a sun field, he handled the ball perfectly. At the bat he easily led his side with two singles and a double.[9]

Under a bold headline of "Old 'Sox' Tried Hard To Win From The Reds, But Didn't Have Quite Enough Help," the *Cleveland Press* wrote of this game:

> Sockalexis and [shortstop Ed] McKean tried to play the whole game for Cleveland yesterday. With just a little help from the others they would have succeeded. The Indian made three of Cleveland's seven hits, and McKean accepted ten hard fielding chances with no sign of an error.... The contest, as a whole, was brilliant and dashing. The Indian was the center of attraction. His three put-outs were all difficult, each catch earning a round of applause.[10]

The team dropped its next two games to Cincinnati, leaving Cleveland winless at 0–5. Sockalexis went hitless in those two games, striking out three straight times against baseball's best-known left-handed pitcher of the era, Ted Breitenstein, in a 7–3 loss. This game alone easily puts to rest the apocryphal claim made by several sources, including a 1973 story in *Sports Illustrated*, that Sockalexis never struck out during the 1897 season.[11] According to Connie Mack, Breitenstein's performance as a player was remarkable for both its longevity and for the man's own personal strength in overcoming alcoholism, "Breitenstein...made a comeback and stayed on the mound and the water wagon as well until he was past fifty years of age."[12]

Sockalexis was hitless three more times in a 5–0 shut-out hurled by another left-handed pitcher, Willie Damman. Manager Tebeau had Sockalexis batting in the third position in the lineup against Damman. In an interview he gave in June, Sockalexis, a left-handed batter, confessed to a weakness in batting against left-handed pitching, a weakness he said he hoped to overcome with work.

Cleveland's luck changed in St. Louis. Sockalexis made a great catch to help preserve a 6–6 tie in the first contest at St. Louis. According to the

Sporting Life account of this game against the Browns, St. Louis "pulled an apparently lost game out of the fire in the ninth inning." Losing 6–4, St. Louis put together four straight hits to tie the score. Then, with the bases filled with runners and two out, "Sockalexis made a great catch of McFarland's long fly, which saved the game for his side," preserving the tie. The game was called because of darkness.[13]

In the next game Cleveland recorded its first win of the year, a 12–4 victory over St. Louis. Answering a taunt that he "get a tomahawk," Louis Sockalexis hit his first major league home run against a pitcher named Bill Hutchison. He had one other hit and reached base a third time when he was hit by a pitch. "Wild Bill" Hutchison was one of the premier right-handed pitchers of the early 1890s and formerly the star hurler for the Chicago team of the National League. The hard-throwing Hutchison won 42 games in 1890, had 44 more victories in 1891, and added 37 wins in 1892. The *Cleveland Press* celebrated this victory with a front-page cartoon that featured an American Indian under a headline that read, "One Scalp!"

Several accounts of the game, all citing unattributed remarks from the press and members of the smallish crowd of 900 fans, claimed that the Sockalexis blast was one of the longest home runs ever hit at the field. For instance, the *Boston Daily Globe* reported in its three-sentence account of this April 30 game: "The Clevelands won their first game this season by a score of 12–4. Costly errors by the Browns were responsible. Medicine man Sockalexis knocked the ball over the centerfield fence, one of the longest hits ever made on the home grounds."[14] *Sporting Life* carried this "Sporting Note": "Sockalexis made his first home run of the season at Sportsman's Park Friday. He also beat out a grounder to short by a phenomenal exhibition of speed."[15] The *Cleveland Plain Dealer* headlined its wrap-up of league games and standings with "Sox Old Boy, Hits The Ball For A Homer, First Victory." The account read:

> The game Pat Tebeau's Indians played here, yesterday, would have beaten any team in the league. Their fielding was clean and fast, the work of [shortstop Ed] McKean, [second baseman Cupid] Childs and [third baseman Bobby] Wallace bordering on the marvelous…. The big feature of the game, outside of Ed McKean's sensational fielding, was the home run hit of Sockalexis. The crowd was guying him and advising him to "get a tomahawk" when the red man let go at a straight one and smashed it against the fence.[16]

In that detail the *Boston Daily Globe* account is at odds with the *Cleveland Plain Dealer* story. At any rate, the hit was Sockalexis's first major league home run.

In the third game at St. Louis, Sockalexis "covered himself with glory. In five times at bat he made four hits, one a three-bagger when the bases were full," *Sporting Life* reported.[17] He also nabbed two stolen bases, leading the club to an 8–3 win. Before an estimated crowd of 2,300, little curve-balling pitcher Red Donahue of the Browns had a 2 – 0 lead until the top of the sixth inning, when a St. Louis error led to two Cleveland runs and a tie that held until the top of the ninth inning. Then, having collected three singles and the two stolen bases, Sockalexis hit a crucial bases-loaded triple that sparked a six-run rally and the victory.

Though hitless in four at bats in the fourth game at St. Louis, Sockalexis did steal a base, and his defensive play aided the team significantly as he recorded three put-outs and an outfield assist that resulted in a double play. The Indians took a 3–1 victory to complete the road trip with three straight wins against St. Louis. The *Cleveland Press* trumpeted the victories with this brash headline: "Great Work, Tebeau's Team Jumps Into Sixth Place By Taking A Trio Of Scalps At St. Louis. Now For 24 Straight Games At Home." The wrap-up story was no less enthusiastic if not politically correct by today's standards: "The whooping, howling red men from the Forest City left for home, last night, with three scalps swinging from their belts. They played the finest series of games in this city the people of St. Louis have seen in many a day. Their fielding was superb, their team work perfect, and their batting in three of the four games was savage."[18]

In the *Milwaukee Journal* of May 6, 1898, a nationally distributed roundup of notes concerning professional baseball called "Diamond Dust," Sockalexis discussed his attitude toward the fans' boisterous and often derisive behavior: "Sockalexis says that he doesn't mind in the least the war whoops, catcalls and yells that go up from the spectators every time he goes to bat. 'Had I cared they would have driven me out of the business long ago,' said Socks. 'I got it from the very first day I played. In fact, O'Connor got me used to it in practice. He used to get the other players to 'whoop it up' when we were training before the season opened.' "[19]

Still, like Jackie Robinson and Larry Doby more than fifty years later, Sockalexis faced daily pressures that went well beyond typical sports heckling. The newspapers casually discussed the "kidding" (taunting) and mock war whooping that attended his very presence at bat or in the field. *Sporting Life* politely but bluntly wrote: "In many cases, these demonstrations border on extreme rudeness."[20] Yet it is obvious from his many stellar moments on the baseball field that racial intolerance and indecent jeering failed to drive Sockalexis away.

6

Glorious Home Stand

THERE WAS GREAT anticipation as Sockalexis and his Cleveland teammates returned for a lengthy home stand. A "Sporting Note" in *Sporting Life* reported: "Sockalexis has not made an error in the nine games the Cleveland team has played away from home. His work in several of the games has been almost phenomenal. The eyes of the base ball world are certainly fixed upon the Indian."[1]

Cleveland's penchant for breaking bounds also extended to the team's owner, Frank Robison, who wanted his club to play a Sunday game in order to test the city's Blue Laws, which prohibited play on the Sabbath. Cleveland's mayor made it abundantly clear that he opposed Sunday games and threatened to have the players arrested if they attempted to play. Robison said the mayor could go right ahead and have the players arrested; he was prepared to bring the controversy to a head. Though it was rumored that Robison intended to sell the team, he denied the allegation, saying he was prepared to keep the club, even if that meant no Sunday games. In early May *Sporting Life* noted: "President Robison's lawyers, and there are probably none more able in the city, have advised him to go ahead with his arrangements to play Sunday games, and have assured him there will be little or no trouble so far as the law on the subject is concerned. Mr. Robison says he will follow their advice."[2]

Frank Robison was a trolley-car magnate struggling to increase his businesses despite tepid political support from Cleveland's mayor and outright opposition from the city's ministers. Robison had built the team's stadium, League Park, in East Cleveland, at Sixty-sixth and Lexington, adjacent to his trolley lines. Despite a franchise payroll ranking among the highest in the league at around $38,000, in 1897 the team suffered from consistently low attendance. Robison needed to increase attendance at Cleveland games. Not only was professional baseball played largely by undereducated white citizens with blue collar backgrounds, the games were watched (and frequently bet upon) by working class citizens of the same ilk, many of whom worked six days a week with Sunday as their only day off.

As Cleveland prepared for its first home stand of the season, the newspapers were full of high expectations for Sockalexis and the team, as well as Robison's determination to challenge the law that prevented Sunday play. In his first game before the hometown fans, Sockalexis encountered Ted Breitenstein, the pitcher who was fast becoming his nemesis. Sockalexis went hitless in three at bats. Breitenstein, who pitched a no-hitter in his first major

45

league start on October 4, 1891, is considered by some baseball historians to be the first left-handed pitcher "of distinction" in professional baseball. He had another no-hitter in 1898. Unlike Sockalexis, who later could not beat a drinking problem, Breitenstein reportedly did. In their first encounter, in a matchup in Cincinnati, Sockalexis struck out three straight times against him. In its account of the May 3 game, the *Cleveland Plain Dealer* said:

> Interest naturally centered in Sockalexis, and the big warrior was cheered and whooped every time he turned around. He made two clever catches and one clever throw in the field, but he was up against his Jonah at the bat. Breitenstein, who had such an easy time with the aborigine on the occasion of their first meeting, expected to toy with him again, but he was not so much of a plaything. In the first inning he struck out, mainly because he was forced to attempt a sacrifice, but in the second and sixth he hit the ball hard, but unluckily. In the fifth he got to base on balls, and was on third before anybody knew it. A faster man on bases is seldom seen.[3]

The second game of the three-game series was rained out. The Cleveland newspapers had no local baseball scores to report, but interest in owner Robison's plans was ripening. He was clearly determined to play baseball on a Sunday sometime during the home stand. He told reporters that if he or his players were arrested, he would "claim the Sunday laws are unconstitutional." He said he would "take the case to the highest court," noting that such a progression would prevent any resolution from taking place that year.[4]

In just his second game before the Cleveland fans, Sockalexis hit his second home run of the season off left-handed pitcher Willie Damman. He also claimed a second hit in the 3–2 loss. On defense he recorded another outfield double play, with a catch and throw to home plate that nabbed a Cincinnati runner trying to score. A headline in the *Boston Daily Globe*'s roundup of league games for the Wednesday, May 5, contest reads "Old Sox Was Very Deep In The Game" and carried this description of his exploits: "The Indian's playing was the feature of the game. The second time at bat he hit the ball over the fence in right field and through a store window on the south side of Lexington Ave. A minute later, with Irwin on third, Peits on first and no one out Ritchey hit a sharp fly to right. Old Sox made a pretty catch and then hurled the ball to Zimmer as straight as a rifle shot, Irwin being nailed six feet from the plate."[5]

A few days later, *Sporting News* claimed: "In throwing from outfield to home plate Sockalexis, the Indian who has a reservation in the Cleveland outer territory, recalls Joe Hornum, who often startled the fans of a decade ago with his long throws from deep left, nailing runners from third with more frequency than any outfielder of his day."[6]

Umpiring continued to draw the ire of the participants and the press. After a loss to Cincinnati on May 5, the *Boston Daily Globe* account complained that the Reds had their "usual luck" in the game Wednesday but "got away" with a victory that could just as easily have been Cleveland's "if fortune had been equally distributed." This competitive game, from start to finish, was "marred only by [Jim] McDonald's wretched attempts at umpiring. One of his decisions may have cost Cleveland the game." The situation related had Sockalexis on second base, Jack O'Connor at first, and Harry Blake at bat with one out. With three balls and one strike on Blake, "Jack and the Indian did some jumping around the base lines in an effort to coax a wild throw from a Cincinnati fielder." Subsequently, Damman pitched another wide one, but umpire McDonald yelled, "Ball three!" A chorus of "Four! Four!" was shouted in angry response around the ballpark. Then an appeal was made to the members in the press stand, and both the Cleveland and Cincinnati scorers told McDonald that, indeed, four balls had been called on Blake. McDonald would not be swayed. Damman's next pitch was a strike, and then, with two strikes on him, Blake had to swing at the hurler's next offering, flying out to center. The *Globe* account argued: "If [Blake] had been given his base, as he should have been, Zimmer's fly would have scored Sox from third, and more runs might have come in."[7]

About this same time, it was also noted in the *Cleveland Press* that both umpires McDonald and Tim Hurst had to be reminded by the participants that the hit-by-a-pitch rule had changed, amended to allow batters first base when hit on the forearm. Both of them had refused to grant passes to first base until the amendment was "shown them."[8] Chicago then came in for a three-game set, which included a truly memorable game for Sockalexis.

In the opening game, Sockalexis had one hit in four at bats as Cleveland topped Chicago 5–1. In the second outing, on Friday, May 7, Sockalexis put together one of his greatest games in one of Cleveland's most thrilling victories of the season. He led his team to a 6–5 victory with four hits in four tries, including a triple, and a great catch with two runners on base. He also had a walk, two stolen bases, scored two runs, and made a total of five put-outs in the field. The *Boston Daily Globe* account of this win noted: "Today's game was a slugging match, in which Denzer got a little of the worst of it. The Indians won by a close shave, a great catch by Burkett saving the game in the ninth. There was brilliant fielding by both sides, though the general work of the Colts [Chicago] was loose. Sockalexis made three singles and a triple in four times at bat, besides getting his base on balls once. His base running was a feature of the game, and one of his five put outs was a one-handed catch of a line drive with two on bases."[9] The *Cleveland Plain Dealer* exalted in its headline of the game: "A Really Wonderful Game Of Ball In Which Everybody Played To Win." The account raved:

The game played on the Dunham Avenue grounds between the Cleveland and Chicago clubs on Friday, May 7, 1897, will linger long in the memories of the 1750 shivering people present as one of the most sensational games they have ever looked upon. Other games have had two or three innings. This one had nine of them. Other games have been marked by one or two great plays. In this game there were at least a dozen. It is not an easy thing to distribute the credit marks for the victory of Tebeau's men, for all the players took part in one or more of the hair-lifting plays. Even the last play of the day was of the first order. The Colts had made two runs in the ninth and needed one run to tie and two to win. Thornton was on first when Ryan sent the ball screeching to left. It looked like a triple, but Burkett ran to the fence and dragged it down. Sockalexis' record for the day stands out particularly distinct, as the Indian made three singles and a triple in four times at bat; stole two bases and made five put-outs, one a sensational catch after he had first misjudged the ball.[10]

Sockalexis's outstanding performance the day before prompted a laudatory assessment from the *Cleveland Plain Dealer* on May 8 that also revealed Indian stereotypes typical of the time: "The man who said there are no good Indians except dead Indians, or words to that effect, surely never saw one Louis Sockalexis, late of the Penobscot tribe, but now of the tribe of Tebeau.... The baseball fans who witnessed Sock's performance yesterday will agree that he is the best Indian that ever wandered down the pike. Pocahontas was never a marker to him and all the other good Indians of history fade into insignificance before the new found hero."[11]

The team rose above the .500 mark for the first time that year, with an overall record of seven victories, six defeats. The Clevelands also moved from the rock-bottom rung of the twelve-team league listings, up to sixth position. In the final game of the Chicago series, again won by Cleveland by a score of 7–6, Sockalexis went hitless in four tries and committed his first error of the year.

Brooklyn then came to Cleveland for three games, starting Monday, May 10, and Sockalexis continued his hitting and running heroics. He collected a double and a triple in a 3–2 loss (a game in which he committed his second error), had two more hits and three stolen bases in a 7–0 victory, and doubled in a 5–3 loss.

Boston was next, and the Indian sensation doubled and tripled in the first contest, both hits coming against Kid Nichols, one of the league's top hurlers. The following day's game was rained out, so Cleveland played its first double-header of the year on Saturday, May 15. Sockalexis collected two more safeties in Cleveland's only win of the series and had one more base hit in the second game. The *Cleveland Plain Dealer* quoted Boston's star outfielder Hugh Duffy about Sockalexis: "The moment I saw that man in practice I realized that the stories about him were not exaggerated. He is a wonderful player, and the greatest find in many a day. He is not only wonderful now, but he will keep on improving, and I expect to see him the fastest fielder and one of the greatest batters the game has ever known." [12]

In his first twenty games, Sockalexis counted 29 hits in 79 at bats, batting at a solid .367 clip. Though he was not dominating every game as he had previously, he was proving that he could star as a professional.

We can only wonder and marvel at how successfully he was playing despite extraordinary scrutiny and heckling that was constant and often vile. Teammate Harry Blake had little reason to have sympathy for Louis Sockalexis: The outfielder had lost his starting position to him and then was sent off to play in the Western League in mid June. Yet, in June he told the *Cleveland Plain Dealer*, "there has been so much talk about Socks that the pitchers are all after him and pitch harder for him than for any man on the team. Then, the rooting he has to stand is something awful." [13]

On Sunday, May 16, everyone who stepped on the playing field in Cleveland, including the umpire, was arrested. The *Cleveland Press* newspaper headline blared "Men In Blue Send 15,000 People Home Sadly Disappointed, Police Stop The Sunday Ball Game, The Money Refunded and Nobody Hurt." [14]

No official league game had been scheduled for Sunday, but the Washington club arrived in Cleveland on Saturday evening from Pittsburgh for its three-game series with the Indians, to begin on Monday. Frank Robison met with owner Earl Wagner and manager Gus Schmelz of the Senators and assured them that the fans of the city were behind his plans for Sunday games and would turn out in force the next day at League Park. Earlier on Saturday the forces opposing Robison had discussed their strategy. Cleveland mayor McKisson, city prosecutor Kennedy, many city officials, and the Ministers' Association met at the police station. Robison's lawyers apparently advised him, wrongly, that the police were likely to allow the teams to play four innings.

According to author John Phillips, in accounts culled from Cleveland newspapers: "Cleveland is agog at the prospects of its first Sunday game. The Ministers' Association will try to stop it, and, no matter which side they take, most every Clevelander has an opinion. Frank Robison has placarded the city, promising to return ticket money if police prevent 4 innings from being played. He's ordered $400 in silver halves and quarters to expedite change making if refunds are necessary." [15] By noon on Sunday, however, Robison reportedly got the word that the police intended to intercede after the first inning. The *Boston Daily Globe* reported:

The police made good on their promise to prevent Sunday ball in Cleveland if an attempt was made to play today. At the end of the first inning between the Cleveland and Washington teams all the players on both sides and umpire Tim Hurst were arrested and taken to the central police station, four miles distant, where Robison gave bail for the prisoners and they were released. The game had been extensively advertised, and in consequence, there was a big attendance. All the railroads ran excursions, and a large number of enthusiasts from surrounding towns arrived in the city during the forenoon. Long before the hour for the game the grounds were crowded. The turnstile showed that 10,000 people had passed the gates. It was impossible to admit any more without letting them on the field and the gates were closed. Still, at least 5000 persons clamored for admission.[16]

According to Phillips, a massive crowd gathered at League Park and, after 9,500 passed through the turnstiles, Robison ordered the gates closed. Phillips reported that "estimates of the cranks" left outside ranged from five thousand to twenty thousand and that specially assigned police controlled throngs of fans still lining the streets for a block around the park. The police "obviously" feared "rioting" if the game was prevented, it was reported, and inside the park, the overflow spilled onto the field and behind the ropes.[17] The *Globe* article noted that at a conference held Sunday morning, Robison had discussed the scenario to occur with the police and that, after one inning had been played, both Robison and the police captain were to walk onto the field and play would be halted.[18]

From the Cleveland newspapers, Phillips recounted that Washington took the field first at 3 P.M. Burkett smacked one of Washington hurler Les German's pitches to center, where Senator captain Tom Brown caught it in front of the rope. McKean walked. Sockalexis flew out to Charlie Abbey, and Bobby Wallace lined out to Chewing Gum O'Brien. In the bottom half of the first, Brown decided not to bat in his usual leadoff spot, sending up catcher Jimmy McGuire. Brown reportedly "remained near the bench, instructing the Senators what to do if arrested." McGuire popped out to second baseman Patsy Tebeau. Kip Selbach singled to left field. Gene DeMontreville grounded to pitcher Zeke Wilson, who got the force out at second base. Duke Farrell lined out to Tebeau, ending the first inning.

At that point Cleveland police captain English, joined by Robison and a reporter from the *Cleveland Leader*, walked to home plate, accompanied by "a chorus of hisses." Some fans yelled: "Put them out!" Phillips' account noted that Robison raised his arms and, "smiling sarcastically," begged the crowd for silence to make the following announcement: "Ladies and gentlemen, we are ordered by the police to refrain from fracturing a state law. The law must be respected. I will take this case into the state courts and

I believe yet that we will be victorious." Phillips' account tells us that "thousands of cranks swarmed the field to shake Robison's hand." Police captain English then announced that the players and umpire were under arrest. Managers Tebeau and Schmelz were then asked by the police captain whether they preferred to be taken to the central police station in "hoodlum wagons" or in the team omnibuses. Both managers, "not surprisingly," chose their own conveyances. The Cleveland team members were granted time to change their clothes, but the Washington players had to report to the station wearing their uniforms. The arrested umpire, Tim Hurst, accompanied the Washington players.

Some members of the crowd reportedly jeered the police at the ballpark, although one paper reported that "most of the spectators didn't know what was happening." Many remained in their seats, apparently expecting the game to resume. Eventually those fans realized that the game had been called off; about half of them, it was reported, chose to get their money back, while others held on to their coupons, good for either one of the next two Cleveland games.[19]

Meanwhile, Sockalexis and his eight teammates were to assemble, along with the Washington players and umpire Hurst, at the jail. The *Globe* newspaper account noted: "The players took their arrest good-naturedly. The buses were driven rapidly to the central station, where the players and umpire were booked. Pres Robison promptly gave bail in the sum of $100 for each player. They were then released and went to their hotels."[20] Phillips' account wryly noted of the uniformed Washington team: "The usual motley characters at the station had considerable fun at the Senators' expense."[21]

The nine Cleveland players arrested were center fielder Harry Blake, left fielder Burkett, shortstop McKean, right fielder Sockalexis, second baseman Tebeau, third baseman Wallace, pitcher Zeke Wilson, catcher "Chief" Zimmer, and, in place of regular first baseman Jack O'Connor, Jack Powell. Phillips notes that Jack Powell, a pitcher, was not even on the Cleveland roster and had yet to play his first official League game before the incident. In the days that followed, it became clear why Powell had been added to the roster from Robison's Fort Wayne minor league team. He became "the guinea pig," the named party to be judged "guilty" or not of playing ball on Sunday, as owner Robison attempted to battle the issue in court. The Washington nine arrested included: Abbey, Brown, Jumbo Cartwright, DeMontreville, Farrell, German, O'Brien, Charlie Reilly, and Selbach.

Robison left the police station for a local restaurant and what one Cleveland newspaper termed "an indignation meeting." John Phillips quoted Robison's remarks from this session as follows:

The ministers who are making this fight on Sunday ball are a lot of unheard-of devines [*sic*] anxious to secure free advertising in the newspapers.... Sunday baseball is endorsed by the masses in this city, as was shown by the enormous crowd that wanted to see today's game. The inconsistency of the whole business is proven by the scores of Sunday amateur games that are being played in Cleveland and throughout Ohio today, to say nothing of Sunday professional ball at Cincinnati, Toledo, Columbus and Dayton. I will admit that there is a state law, now practically obsolete, that prohibits Sunday ball, but the prohibition is under a vague statute that forbids amusements in general on Sunday. It is an unpopular law, and antagonistic to the desires of the public. I will fight this case to the finish in the courts."[22]

At the time, Robison was not sure what the next step should be. If he demanded a jury trial in what was called police court, he was aware that even if he were to win, the ministers could make local officials enforce the state law. Furthermore, since the Ohio legislature was not scheduled to convene again until 1898, he was fully aware that the law would remain in place until then. Worst of all, however, was Robison's belief that he had been betrayed. Cleveland newspapers reported that the anger of the Indians' owner was "deep" and directed at the mayor. Robison commented that he supported McKisson's campaign and claimed that McKisson had assured him the previous fall that the team could play on Sundays.[23]

Monday morning, before the scheduled afternoon game with the Senators, members of the Cleveland and Washington teams gathered in the detectives' office at the central police station. The players and umpire Hurst were represented by a former judge named Solders (acknowledged to be a friend of Robison's) and a lawyer named Harry C. Mason. Just after 11 A.M., after the officials had completed drawing up the documents, Robison, the attorneys, and the accused were called to appear in police court. They were charged with "participating in" an unlawful Sunday baseball game with "admission being charged," and, secondly, presenting "an unlawful exhibition," again with "admission being charged." Solders and Mason conferred with the presiding judge, a man named Fiedler, and it was announced that no plea would be filed until Wednesday. Fiedler continued the case until Wednesday. Solders told the newspapers he was going to seek to have the case dropped. Failing that, he would demand a jury trial. He said he wanted to settle the matter by the following Sunday because Robison hoped to play a game with Baltimore on the forbidden day. Robison told reporters that Wednesday's outcome would determine whether he would try another Sunday game. He said, however, that he really expected the case to go to the circuit court.

Solders was not successful in getting the case dropped, and no Sunday game was attempted on May 23 (and rain most of that day would have canceled it anyway). It was several more weeks before the case was resolved. The trial was not held until the week of June 7–12, with the case going to a jury for deliberation at 7 P.M., Wednesday, June 9.

On Thursday, June 10, the front page of the last edition of the *Cleveland Press* carried a line drawing of John Powell with the headline: "Pitcher Powell Found Guilty, Sunday Ball In Cleveland Does Not Go." At noon, a jury returned the verdict, declaring Powell guilty on two counts of violating the law against ball playing on Sunday. He was convicted of "participating in" and "the exhibiting of base ball on Sunday." Powell's defense attorney had tried to derail the case on a technicality, arguing that because a full nine innings, or an entire game, had not been played, a case could not be made that a baseball game had been played. The judge in the case was not buying any of it; he "especially instructed" the jury members that the playing of any part of one inning was sufficient to constitute illegal ball playing.[24]

Powell was fined only $5, but the court charges of $153 were the part of the punishment that, reportedly, "hurt."[25] The attorney representing Robison's player told the *Cleveland Press* that the case would be appealed to higher courts and, presumably, outside the city limits of Cleveland. The real issue—the legality of preventing ball playing on Sunday—would be tested. Robison publicly threatened another Sunday game that season. The *Cleveland Press* noted that the police were "prepared for more arrests."

Captain manager Oliver "Patsy" Tebeau wired his views from Baltimore, where the team was on its eastern road swing. He wrote:

> I think that the conviction of Powell was a mistake. I am no lawyer, but it seems to me that the men who built the game are competent to judge what constitutes a game of ball. The rules say that nine innings constitute a game. How can a man participate in a game when none was played? I hope that President Robison will carry the case up to the highest court. I think he will win in the end. I favor Sunday ball playing. Without it, I am afraid, Cleveland will not have a league team. Sunday ball keeps men out of mischief.[26]

An explanation from one of the jurors concluded the *Cleveland Press* account of the guilty ruling. After leaving the courtroom, juror Seth Hull said, "All of the jurors were personally in favor of Sunday base ball, but they were compelled to render a verdict of guilty." He added, "If we did not find Powell guilty, we would have perjured ourselves.… Judge Fiedler took a great portion of the testimony for the defense away from us and then told us that we should base our verdict on the evidence. We came into court for instructions and he told us that as a matter of law one inning or any part of nine innings constituted a game of base ball. There was only one thing to do after that."[27]

The long home stand, which began on May 3 and lasted for the entire month, became a showcase for Sockalexis and the Spiders-turned-Indians. After the arrests on Sunday, May 16, the Cleveland club continued its outstanding home showing. Cleveland swept three straight games from Washington, split a doubleheader with New York, swept three more games from Philadelphia, and closed out with a two-game split with Baltimore. Against Washington, Sockalexis literally and figuratively ran wild. He stole two bases in each of the first two games and one more in the third contest. In two of the games he had three hits in four at bats.

Following the first game of the series, Washington owner Wagner condemned Tim Hurst's umpiring. He told National League president Nick Young that Hurst "let the Indians win" because he hated three of the Washington players (naming Brown, O'Brien, and Cartwright). In his telegraph wire to Young, Wagner allegedly wrote: "Hurst will never umpire a game of ball in Washington again if it costs me every dollar I'm worth. He harbors ill feeling toward three of my players and he made the threat publicly that he will get even with these three every chance he can get."[28]

For the second straight game against Cleveland, Doc McJames pitched for Washington, and although Sockalexis did not hit him nearly as well as he had the day before, he collected an infield single and stole two bases. The newspaper account noted that Sockalexis beat out an infield roller after swinging at "a wild pitch." A newspaper account a few days earlier stated that Sockalexis "loves wild pitches. In a recent game against the Browns, he got two hits on pitches that were a foot from the plate. And like Larry Lajoie, the only pitch he has trouble with is a slow curveball."[29]

In the third game of the series, batting against Winnie Mercer, Sockalexis collected a double and two singles, again legging out an infield hit. Umpire Hurst came under fire again after the contest won by Cleveland 8 – 5. The *Cleveland Press*'s game account bluntly reported: "Tim Hurst's futile attempts at umpiring was the feature.… Someone had intimated to the scrappy referee that his reputation for being an away-from-home umpire was slipping away from him and Tim hastily proceeded to make it good." The newspaper charged that captain Tebeau wound up being charged for two errors when Hurst missed seeing two men tagged out by the Cleveland manager. Further, Hurst was charged with failing to call Cy Young's pitches strikes unless they were "directly across and waist-high."[30]

Hurst would prove no more popular several weeks later in Pittsburgh. Under the headline "Tim Hurst Mobbed," the May 28 issue of the *Cleveland Press* reported:

The Pittsburgh directors will have a nice time of it explaining to the league why Umpire Tim Hurst was allowed to be mobbed in that city, Wednesday. Hurst is notoriously an away-from-home umpire, and is in fact the only member of Mr. [National League president Nick] Young's staff who can be said on every occasion to give the visiting club an equal show with the home team to win. For this reason Hurst has been kept away from Cincinnati, where it has been feared an even break on close decisions would not be tolerated. Pittsburgh was regarded as not quite so partisan a town.... After the game, Wednesday, in which Pittsburgh had been outplayed at every point, 500 men, drunk with rage at the home team's defeat, followed Hurst to the dressing room. Vile terms were used and a stone hurled at him. Hurst resented the attack, plunged into the crowd and scattered his assailants right and left. While thus engaged he was struck in the face and head by the mob. After a long wait the Pittsburgh players came to the rescue. Hurst was hurried away by fifteen special police and left for Chicago after supper.[31]

An account of the third game with Washington said: "The batting of Sockalexis was, as usual, a notable feature."[32] A "Between Innings" note, published in the *Cleveland Press*, raved: "Sockalexis keeps on hitting any kind of pitching he is compelled to face. For a new man in fast company, he is certainly a marvel."[33] Later, according to an unidentified newspaper account cited by John Phillips, Washington pitcher Mercer told a reporter: "I have been watching the Indian Sockalexis closely and I believe I have discovered his weakness. Feed him a high one over the outside corner and he will masticate it as though he were going for a plate of Indian corncakes. But get it knee high about opposite the low water mark of his knickerbockers and you have him guessing. Like Jesse Burkett, he is not stuck on a low curve."[34]

The New York Giants were the next team to visit Cleveland, but rain and wet grounds prevented games on Thursday and Friday, May 20 and May 21. Cleveland had a record of 12 wins, 10 losses, and stood in fifth position in the league. Sockalexis told an unnamed writer on one of these off days: "I have seen all the good outfielders of the League, and I am just as good as any of them." The writer editorialized: "Who's to dispute that?" Commenting on "Sox's wondrous throwing," captain Tebeau reportedly told the same writer that the skill comes "naturally for Indians, who frequently throw primitive boomerangs."[35]

When famed pitcher Amos Rusie and his New York club mates played the opener of a doubleheader on Saturday, May 22, with the Indians, the contest went into extra innings and set the stage for another sterling Sockalexis moment. It was the Indians' real Indian who knocked in the winning run off the future Hall of Fame pitcher, getting a base hit in the tenth inning to give Cleveland a 4–3 verdict. He had had another hit, earlier in the game, off

Rusie, and the theatrics of that game would serve to stir the cauldron for an even more dramatic moment when the two men faced each other again less than a month later at the Polo Grounds in New York.

The doubleheader attracted 8,000 fans, and captain Tebeau tried out a new batting order, putting Sockalexis in the leadoff spot. The return of infielder Cupid Childs from injury to his post at second base allowed Tebeau to return to his usual first base position. Childs batted second, followed by shortstop McKean and left fielder Burkett in the cleanup slot. Batting fifth was third baseman Bobby Wallace, followed by center fielder Harry Blake, Tebeau at first, catcher Chief Zimmer,* and the pitcher.

In a memorable first game, Cleveland pitcher George Joseph "Nig" (the nickname is a racial slur, frequently saddled on players with dark complexions, for many decades in the professional game) Cuppy's slow balls matched Amos Rusie's "thunderbolts," and the game remained tied at 3–3 from the fifth inning until the bottom of the tenth inning. A Sockalexis line shot, "cracked" into the outfield, scored Tebeau from third base with two outs, and "put the 7,900 spectators on their feet," according to the game account in the *Cleveland Press*.[36]

In the "Cleveland Chatter" column for June 12, *Sporting Life* columnist Elmer E. Bates recounted how the dramatic moment helped overcome one New York writer's skepticism.

> I have remarked before that queer things happen in baseball. In a ten inning game with the Giants, I sat beside Eddie Roth of the *New York World*. In the tenth with a man on third Sock came at bat. Two out and a hit needed to win the game. Mr. Roth murmured, "I've heard so much about this Indian, but I don't see where he comes in." Just then the redman smashed a hot one to center and as the winning run came in Mr. Roth added, "But he seems alright in a tight place."[37]

In the second game with New York, Cleveland collapsed, losing 11–2. Sockalexis went hitless in three at bats but did throw another runner out from the right field. One Cleveland columnist said: "Outfielders might gain a few valuable hints by watching Sockalexis throw. He sends the ball on a line no higher than six feet from the ground, and it invariably comes to the infielder or backstop on the first bound. This is much safer than the long high throw to the infield."[38] Sockalexis then hit in all three wins over Philadelphia and the split of two contests with Baltimore, collecting three more two-hit games, to complete a stellar home stand.

---

*The veteran catcher came by his Indian nickname because he had formerly played for a New York minor league team with an American Indian nickname.

In the first two games with Philadelphia, the Indians overcame three-run deficits in their last at bat to win 9 – 8 and 10 – 9. Cleveland pitching, which had delivered second-place finishes in the two previous years, was inconsistent. Cy Young, who had averaged nearly thirty wins a season during the previous four, "was not himself this year," one scribe noted. In a Philadelphia contest, even the opposing pitcher, Taylor, reached Young for a home run. The Indians were losing badly until they pounded Taylor for four runs in the bottom of the ninth inning to win the game, without making a single out. Sockalexis had two hits, scored two runs, and committed one error in the game.

Cleveland's second star, veteran hurler Nig Cuppy, was not faring much better. One of the league's "notorious" slow-ball pitchers, Cuppy had averaged more than twenty wins a season, but he too was throwing inconsistently. Handed a 5 – 0 lead in the second Philadelphia contest, Cuppy gave up two runs in the seventh inning and then, after errors by McKean and Childs, got belted around for seven runs in the eighth. Aided by a string of walks served up by Philadelphia pitcher Kid Carsey, Cleveland overcame a three-run deficit in its final at bat for the second straight day to win the game. Sockalexis smacked Carsey for a triple.

A tremendous catch preserved the third straight victory over Philadelphia as former circus acrobat Harry Blake made "a circus catch" to give Cleveland a 4 – 2 win. Philadelphia slugging stars Ed Delahanty and Larry Lajoie led the way as both teams collected twelve hits. Sockalexis had two hits but committed another error.

The script was not much different when Baltimore arrived in town to complete the month-long home stand. Cy Young was again hammered, this time for seven hits and three runs in two innings, and left the pitching to Mike McDermott. The Indians mounted a late charge, scoring six runs in the last two innings, to nip Baltimore 8 –7. Sockalexis had one hit, but Tebeau, with four safeties, and Burkett, with three, led the way.

Rain washed out the scheduled second game of the series on Friday, May 28. The home stand concluded with an unhappy twist to the usual fall-behind-early-but-rally-to-win script. Again, Cuppy was badly battered. He and mound successor Zeke Wilson gave up eighteen hits. This time, though, Cleveland was unable to mount an offensive counterpunch. Sockalexis, however, delivered two of Cleveland's five hits, a double and a single.

Cleveland finished its twenty-one-game home stand with a 17–12 record and held fifth position in the National League standings. Still, after two successive years finishing in the league's runner-up spot, the poor start was disappointing. Since stars like Cy Young, Nig Cuppy, and Jesse Burkett were not playing at stellar levels, the spotlight honed squarely on Louis Sockalexis.

As Cleveland completed its long home stand, Sockalexis was hailed as the toast of the town. His popularity reportedly stirred some jealousy among some of Cleveland's established stars, like Burkett, a two-time batting champion (hitting .423 in 1895 and .410 in 1896) and future Hall of Famer. *Cincinnati Enquirer* columnist Eddie Burke, who reported on the games in Cleveland, was quoted by a *Cleveland Press* writer as saying:

> I believe that Jesse Burkett, the champion batter of the world, is a little jealous of Sockalexis. Yesterday, when the crowd was cheering and whooping for the Indian, I said to Burkett, "They think pretty well of old Socks up here, don't they, Jess?" "O, I don't know," said he. "He's pretty warm just now. All new ones are. He'll cool a bit after a while; 'new broom sweeps clean,' you know." Just then Socks hit up a fly and Jess yelled, "Hold on there, Socks, you will never make money hitting 'em up in the air; soak 'em on the floor." [39]

Sockalexis's fellow rookie sensation in major league baseball, "Frenchman" Napoleon "Larry" Lajoie, was hitting extraordinarily well at the outset of the season. By early May the writers were suggesting Lajoie "looks as if he might take Irishman Ed Delahanty's batting title."

Some of the league's usual top hitters were struggling, notably the Orioles' Hughie Jennings and Sockalexis's own teammate, Burkett, whose frustration over his own hitting may have prompted some of the reports of jealousy.

In his account, *Chief Sockalexis and the 1897 Cleveland Indians*, John Phillips offers these remarks from a Washington player, Princeton Charlie Reilly, the Senators' third baseman:

> Jesse Burkett and Sockalexis are about as popular with each other as a pair of rival tenors in the same opera company. The redskin has been connecting with the ball every day and leads the Spiders in batting, while Burkett, the champion stick wielder of the League, has not yet struck his batting eye. In our last game at Cleveland last week, the Spiders had men on first and second, and Burkett was on the coach line opposite third. I knew that Jesse and the child of the forest were frosts with each other, and I tossed Jesse a quiet josh. The Indian was at the bat, and I asked Jesse if Tebeau had ordered his Hibernian aboriginal to sacrifice. "Can Sock sacrifice, Jess? I hear he can dump 'em down as often as yourself and beat 'em out." That started Burkett's wheels and he yelled, "Don't ask me about that bead peddler. He's a Jonah. I haven't hit over .100 since he joined the team. Tebeau has just signaled for the redskin to cut a hit through the infield. If I were at that bat, Pat would make me sacrifice!" And just as Jesse had finished, the Indian drove a single through the right side of the infield. "Great hitter, that redskin, eh, Jess?" I yelled. "Hit nothing," said Jess. "That was one of those

chance blows. Wait till I strike my gait and I will make him go back to the woods and look for a few scalps."[40]

Near the end of May, Cleveland owner Frank Robison, his brother, Stanley, and his wife and daughter traveled to St. Louis. Robison held a meeting with St. Louis Browns owner Chris Von der Ahe and Washington Senators owner Earl Wagner. Robison remained upset over the issue of Sunday baseball and continued to use the local newspapers to wage war and make threats. He claimed that at the beginning of May, he had decided to move his franchise "if the preachers" continued to thwart his efforts. He further claimed his team would be "making three times as much money" if baseball were allowed on Sunday.

Playing on fears that Cleveland might lose the team, Robison claimed that a theatrical firm, Dickson and Talbot, had been making proposals to buy the team since the day after the players were arrested. Robison told the papers that Dickson and Talbot would move the team to Buffalo, where Sunday ball was legal. Another variation on the same theme featured Robison's threat to keep the team but move it to St. Louis — since, the press dutifully noted, he "loves" the game.

After Robison's visit to St. Louis, Phillips quotes the following remarks of Washington owner Wagner:

> Buffalo is a splendid ball town, five to one better than Cleveland, especially with Sunday ball.... I believe, though, that Mr. Robison wants to remain in baseball and would prefer to transfer his franchise to St. Louis and would become one of the heavy stockholders in the St. Louis club. What would become of Cleveland is problematical. But I would say that Mr. Robison has the consent of the other 11 clubs to do whatsoever he thinks will benefit him the most.[41]

Also, what would happen to the existing St. Louis team if the move occurred? These variables helped to contribute to one of the most unusual franchise exchanges in the history of professional sports. Before the 1899 season, the Robison brothers, who by then had majority ownership of both the Cleveland and St. Louis baseball franchises, took the best players from their Cleveland franchise and created a powerful St. Louis team. The not-so-select St. Louis players were then shuffled off to Cleveland to play on what was to become absolutely the worst team in the history of professional baseball. The 1899 Cleveland club won only twenty games and lost an astounding 134 games.

Not all the interest in Cleveland baseball was prompted by a purist's love of the game. According to a newspaper account in Cleveland: "There's more gambling on baseball in Cleveland and Pittsburgh than anywhere else. Clevelanders like the old combination system of picking winners. There are thirty-two combinations of the six games that usually are scheduled each day. There's a secret gambling house on Superior Street a few blocks from the Hollenden House." [42]

Sunday ball playing continued to stir unrest and resulted in more arrests in the Midwest. On Sunday, May 23, for example, police in Paducah, Kentucky, arrested the players on the local team and those from the Terre Haute team on warrants charging them with playing baseball on Sunday.

7
A Home Run of Legendary Proportions

O N MAY 31, 1897, Cleveland began a long eastern road trip, visiting Brooklyn, Boston, Washington, Baltimore, Philadelphia, and New York. In each city attendance was reported to be unusually high, and attention was unabashedly focused on Sockalexis.

The Brooklyn opener on May 31, a 5–2 loss for Cleveland, was reported in the *Boston Daily Globe* as follows:

> The Cleveland team, including Sockalexis, the Indian, were [*sic*] made to bite the dust at Eastern Park yesterday afternoon by the Brooklyn team. There was no morning game, owing to the rain, but the management were [*sic*] not out of pocket as a result. An hour before the afternoon game was scheduled there was not a vacant seat in the stands. Fully 5,000 persons circled the outfield. The crowd, which was officially announced as 18,000, broke all attendance records at Eastern Park. It can be safely said that Sockalexis, the full-blooded Indian, was what brought many of the people. He didn't make any home runs; neither did his club mates, because [Harley "Lady"] Payne, the Brooklyn left-hander, was on his mettle.[1]

Sockalexis went hitless in four at bats and made only one play in the field, prompting one reporter chronicling the game to remark caustically: "As for Sox, he's merely a cigar store Indian except for catching one fly."[2] The "cigar store Indian" denigration would often appear in accounts on those rare occasions when Sockalexis failed to play a prominent role.

Even though Sockalexis had already stolen a batch of bases and scored a bunch of runs, one columnist repeated concerns that the Penobscot lacked the innate inability to do the job: "Poor Lo Sockalexis, who is doing a medicine dance at the expense of the twirlers in the western teams, has yet to demonstrate that he is not a cigar sign on the bases, as the critics still insist that the child of the forest is slower to think than the white man, and the football playing of the Carlisle Indians is advanced as an illustration."[3]

Outstanding base runner Tom Brown, captain of the Washington Senators, had a very different view. Brown, who stole 106 bases and scored 177 runs in the 1891 season, offered these impressions to the *Cleveland Press*:

> Sockalexis has the flatfooted glide that betrays his origin. Watch him closely when he's on the bases and you will discover that he plants the pedals firm on the ground at every step. He probably inherits this flatfooted tread from his forefathers, whose moccasined feet fell firm on the snow. You would think

Sock's emphatic habit of clouting the ground with the soles of his feet would handicap his speed. But he's one of the nimblist sprinters the League has ever seen. When he began professional ball playing, he found the spiked shoes clumsy, so he told me, and it took him one whole season to accustom himself to spikes. The heels of his shoes are about half an inch thick, almost as flat as moccasins, and are built on a special last for him.[4]

Another columnist chided Sockalexis in doggerel about an unsubstantiated lack of sophistication: "Lo the poor Indian, whose untutored mind / Sees hits in everything, / Sees 'em in his mind. / Sockalexis, Sockalexis, / Your necktie's up behind."[5]

Many of the scribes, however, as unequivocally racist as their banter ran, were firmly in his corner and extremely impressed with his playing exploits as well as the way he conducted himself in the face of derision from the stands. Wrote one, Joe Campbell:

Poor Lo Sockalexis, who has staked a claim in Tibeau's [sic] Hibernian reservation, has come to stay in major league company. This copper-hued child of the forest and stream throws as swift and sure as an arrow from the string of an archer, and he has an easy position at the bat, hitting from the left side. The philosophy of the stoic, which he inherits from his fathers, and curdles cold in his blood, is a big advantage in baseball. He is deaf and unconscious to the whoops of the fans, and his temper has never displayed the least symptom of a ruffle when the comedians blare a mock warwhoop.[6]

Throughout the eastern road swing Sockalexis hit consistently, going hitless in only two of the twelve games before he made his New York City debut. The team, by that time, had fallen back to the .500 plateau (with 20 wins, 20 losses).

In the second Brooklyn contest on June 1, Sockalexis collected one hit but Cleveland lost its third straight game 7–2. The team moved on to Boston. The opening game with the Beaneaters was a rout, with Boston clobbering the Indians 21–3. Even worse than the drubbing was the loss of Jesse Burkett, who appeared to be very seriously hurt when struck in the head with a pitch from Boston left-hand hurler Fred Klobedanz. Making his first appearance for the team, Jimmy McAleer took over for Burkett in left field. Sockalexis collected two hits in the game, scored a run, and had two put-outs but committed one of Cleveland's five errors.

The *Boston Daily Globe* heralded Sockalexis's first appearance in town with a line drawing of the young Penobscot formally dressed in bow tie and jacket, under which was written: "Right Fielder Sockalexis, Who Is Putting Up A Great Game For Cleveland." The many decks of the headline, celebrating the easy Boston victory, included one last comment that read: "Sockalexis Played Finely, Both At Bat And In The Field."[7]

The *Daily Globe* account of the game, from start to finish, was riddled with warring metaphors concerning hostile American Indians and rave observations about Sockalexis. The star Boston players and their mammoth hitting demonstration — 14 runs in the first two innings and 20 hits, good for 35 bases, overall — were mentioned in passing. It read:

> Yip, yip, how the feathers did fly yesterday at the South end ball grounds. The Tebeau Indians from the Cleveland reservation tried to steal a march on Capt. Hugh Duffy and his men. The red men were minus their bows and arrows, but they carried big clubs and looked like fighting machines as they marched into the open to prepare for action. There was a big crowd present, for it was known that it was to be no sham battle. The observed of all observers was the young chief from the Maine reservation, who has smoked the pipe with the Tebeaus and is now fighting like a Maceo for the men of the west. Sockalexis, the handsome young Indian, fought against great odds, but proved himself equal to any of his white brothers. His all-around exhibition was very fine, and the men under Capt. Duffy sent him to the fence until his legs grew weary and his speech fell to a whisper.... The features of the game were the batting of Sockalexis and the fielding of Tebeau and Blake for the visitors. For the home team Collins made the star play of the day, taking a well placed bunt from Sockalexis and cutting it over to Tenney like a flash, and none too soon to get the fleet-footed red man.[8]

The second Boston game, on Thursday, June 3, featured a matchup of two of the game's best pitchers, Kid Nichols versus Cleveland's struggling star, Cy Young. Nichols won the duel easily 6 – 1. Batting in the second position in the Cleveland lineup for this game, Sockalexis had one hit, a double, in four times at bat. Cleveland suffered its fifth straight loss, dropping the club's overall record to 17–16 and falling to sixth place in the league. The great Cy Young's record dropped to a dismal five wins, six losses. The third game with Boston on Friday was washed out after two innings because of heavy fog and rain.

The Indians moved on to Washington, where the losing streak came to an abrupt halt as the Clevelands feasted on Senator pitching. Winnie Mercer, who claimed to know the Sockalexis batting weakness, could not get him or anyone else out. The Indians delivered fourteen hits and collected a 10 – 5 verdict. Sockalexis had two hits and scored a run. In his first at bat against Mercer, as the game's leadoff hitter, Sockalexis slammed a single to center but was thrown out attempting to steal. In the third inning Sockalexis beat out a bunt and came around to score on Mercer's bad throw, Childs' single to short left field, and a McKean sacrifice fly ball. Sockalexis recorded two put-outs and threw out another runner from his post in right field. In his Washington debut, Sockalexis was described by *The Washington Post* as "stalwart, erect as a branch of briar, deep-chested and built on the architectural lines of an Apollo. He is as swift as the wind on the bases and covers a wide area of ground in the outfield." Regretfully, the *Post* then attempted to joke that Sockalexis "denies he is to receive a flask of Kentucky dew and a string of beads for this season's salary." [9]

On Sunday, Cleveland played an exhibition game in an attempt to help former pitcher and umpire Harry Mace introduce Sunday baseball in the Washington, D.C., area. After building a ballpark just outside Alexandria, Virginia, Mace rounded up a group of independent players, some of them former league players, and enlisted the support of several National League teams. The teams from Boston and Baltimore were said to have also agreed to play Mace's club in exhibition games. Though it was generally acknowledged that "Leaguers" hated exhibition games, Cleveland reportedly put on "an interesting and adept game." Sockalexis had three hits, and "the feature of the afternoon" was said to be his "long throw," though no further details were given. Cleveland built up a big early lead, en route to a 12–1 rout, and then had some fun — even catcher Chief Zimmer took a turn pitching an inning. Before Monday afternoon's game with the Senators, Sockalexis was reported to have visited Holy Cross rival, Georgetown University, to meet baseball players, students, and teachers.

According to an account in a Cleveland newspaper, Chicago star first baseman (and future Hall of Famer) Cap Anson regarded Cleveland captain Patsy Tebeau as "the Dr. Jekyll and Mr. Hyde of baseball." Anson commented that off the field, Tebeau was a "mild little gentleman" but that on the field, "he's a terror. His blue language has unraveled many an opposing pitcher." New league rules regarding "coaching" and remaining "speechless" were credited with restricting Tebeau's outbursts. Yet some critics of the change complained the game now lacked "life" and that the players were "performing mechanically." [10]

To bring some civility to major league games and to protect umpires, the league instituted two new rules for 1897. Only the team captain was allowed to confer with the umpire during a dispute, and other players were required to stand at least ten feet away. The league also banned the virulent bench jockeying from the coaching lines in an attempt to halt criticism about the ugly chatter directed at opposing players.

In a lengthy interview, Tebeau, who frequently proved to be an unreliable source, especially when describing injuries, was quoted commenting on the extent of Burkett's injury and about the presence of Sockalexis as "a curio" in the club. According to author John Phillips, Tebeau said:

> I am worried now about Jesse Burkett, who was hit in the head by the Boston lefthander, Klobedanz. The blow has, so the physician says, produced a slight disorder of the brain, which accounts for the spells of vertigo that have attacked Jesse repeatedly. We sent him home from Boston and he will not be able to play for at least a month. There is a danger that the blow may result in making Jesse timid against left-handed pitchers [Burkett was a left-handed hitter], as many a good batsman has been ruined from a blow by a pitched ball. But Burkett's heart is in the right place. He is one of the nerviest players in the League, and his resource of sand will stand by him and bluff off the close in-shoots of the twirlers.[11]

Burkett was injured on June 2, and Tebeau's comments were apparently reported on about the weekend of June 5–6. Tebeau's frightening description of brain injury and its repercussions was, however, belied by Burkett's almost immediate return to the team. He played in the Wednesday, June 9, contest at Baltimore, collecting two hits, and then resumed his regular play.

Tebeau also noted that, for the next season, he planned to "enlarge the curio department of the Spiders." He stated that at the present time the team offered two items: "Sockalexis is the feature of our museum now," he said, and joked that a "sabbath-breaking tie" owned by catcher and first baseman Jack O'Connor might also prove noteworthy. The next year, Tebeau boasted:

> I will place a five-foot-three Jap. This Jap is built like little Cub Stricker and is a relative of Sorakishi, the Japanese wrestler who died a few years ago. He was brought to my attention by Pete Gallagher, the old catcher who is now a politician in Chicago. Jap has played on amateur teams in Chicago. He is swift as a bullet and can hit in the .300 class, so Pete believes. He handles himself as a seasoned veteran. I will spring him on the public next season. These museum attractions on a ball team are box-office successes, and with Sockalexis next season the Hibernian blood in the game will begin to boil.[12]

On Monday, June 7, Sockalexis turned in a stellar effort, knocking out two hits, scoring two runs, stealing a base, and making three put-outs in the field. Cleveland collected fourteen hits and beat Washington 7–0 behind the pitching of Zeke Wilson. Cleveland's record improved to 19–16. In the ninth inning Sockalexis was credited with "a smart catch" of Jimmy McGuire's drive to right field. In a notes column accompanying the game account, the *Cleveland Press* noted that the catch "shows he's improving rapidly in chasing down flies and liners."[13]

After Tuesday's finale with Washington rained out, the team traveled to Baltimore, but without its two ace pitchers, Cy Young and Nig Cuppy. Both returned to Cleveland to "nurse sore arms." Still, Burkett rejoined the team, stating he was ready to play. The Cleveland newspapers, cited by John Phillips, praised Sockalexis for his stoicism in the face of the fans' daily derisive "war-whooping" and also for his level-headedness in dealing with umpire calls: "When the bleachers spring the calliope whoop on Sockalexis, the scout of the outer reservation, he broadens his copper-hued visage good naturedly and gives a heave of the chest and a funny little nod. He never executes the war dance when the man with the indicator mistakes a ball for a strike, nor does he spring the medicine man gag if the umpire calls him out on a safe slide. He is a paragon of grace and symbol of action from moccasin to feather."[14] Patsy Tebeau was quoted as stating: "The only weakness I have been able to discover about Sockalexis is his awkwardness in retrieving a fly ball or line ball that he has to catch on a forward run. But this is a fault he can remedy by constant practice. He is a sensible fellow and sees his weakness, which is a good trait in a young player."[15]

A quote about Sockalexis, his hitting prowess, and weakness, from Kid Nichols, the star Boston pitcher, was also making the rounds. Nichols remarked: "Sock is not stuck on a low curve, but if you keep them up around his neck and get it over fast for him he will go after it in a hurry and eat it up."[16]

Baltimore, the top team in the league, feasted on Cleveland's weakened pitching staff and took three straight games from the Indians. The feisty instigator John McGraw, the Orioles' star third baseman, wore a full headdress, with feathers stretching down to his derriere, on the field before game one, inciting the fans to taunt Sockalexis during the entire series with mock war whoops. The first game featured the pitching debut of John Pappalau, Sockalexis's teammate at Holy Cross, but Baltimore smacked fourteen hits en route to an 11–6 victory. Cleveland was losing 11–1 until the Indians scored five runs in the top of the ninth. The *Cleveland Press* account noted that "Sox was given a cheer and warwhoop when he first went to bat."[17] Sockalexis had two hits, scored a run, and had four put-outs in the field. That evening in Cleveland the jury began deliberating at 7 P.M. in the Sunday baseball trial or, more properly, in owner Robison's trial attempt to end the Sunday baseball prohibition.

Although still "ailing," Cy Young returned to the team and pitched the game on Thursday, June 10. Led by future Hall of Famers Wee Willie "Hit 'Em Where They Ain't" Keeler, Hughie Jennings, and John McGraw, Baltimore reached Young for a 3–0 lead by the third inning and prevailed by a final score of 4–2. Sockalexis went hitless in four times at bat. After the game the Indians learned that the team had lost the Powell case and that there would be no Sunday ball playing in Cleveland that year — or so it was thought at the time.

Nig Cuppy took the train to Baltimore for the series finale and pitched on Friday, June 10, as captain Tebeau attempted to salvage one game of the series. Tebeau also changed the lineup, dropping Sockalexis from the leadoff spot to seventh position. In the fourth inning Sockalexis belted a triple, driving in two runs. He also threw out another enemy runner, but the Orioles came from behind to take a 5 – 4 verdict. The loss dropped Cleveland to a record of 19–19, sixth position in the league. After the game Cuppy reportedly asked Tebeau for two weeks off to rest his arm. Whether he made the request or not, he wound up pitching the series finale in Philadelphia on the following Tuesday.

According to a note in the *Cleveland Press*, Cleveland hurlers Zeke Wilson and Mike McDermott "have been working with Sockalexis, throwing him nothing but low, slow curves in batting practice." The report added, "He is hitting them better now." The account offered a quote attributed to Sockalexis in which he is said to have confidently stated: "The foxy boys, such as Kid Nichols and Clark Griffith, are tipping off the other pitchers to my strong and weak points. Let them push their low, slow ones."[18]

Cleveland moved on to Philadelphia and lost its fourth straight game on Saturday, June 12. Sockalexis went hitless and Cleveland lost 5 – 0. Finally, on Monday, in game two of the series, Cleveland captured a 10 – 4 win behind the pitching of Cy Young. The Indians banged out fourteen hits, led by Burkett (showing no effects after being hit by a pitch on June 2), who had three safeties. Sockalexis had a double in five at bats and scored two runs, but he made two errors in the field. In the third game of the Philadelphia series, on Tuesday, June 15, Cleveland won 4 – 3 in a rain-shortened contest pitched by sore-armed Nig Cuppy. Sockalexis had one hit and scored a run.

The team then traveled to the famed Polo Grounds on Wednesday, June 16, for what was already being billed by the New York newspapers as a "revenge" game for Amos Rusie, the game where he would "strike the damned Indian out." Described in even the briefest of career accounts concerning Sockalexis, this game and the Penobscot's much-celebrated home run are often portrayed in near epic proportions — yet it has never been made definitively clear why Rusie entered the game vowing vengeance. The most obvious explanation is that he wanted to even the score after Sockalexis reached him for the game-winning hit in extra innings on May 22 in Cleveland.

A part of it, as well, could have been the extraordinary press hoopla and leaguewide attention Sockalexis was attracting and an interest Rusie might have had in maintaining his own reputation as the most feared pitcher in the league. A third, more remote possibility (remote only because no documentation has ever been offered and because Rusie himself may not have been available for such a confrontation) is that Rusie sought revenge because of an alleged home run Sockalexis collected against him in a preseason exhibition game. Several Notre Dame alumni have made this claim, as well as writers Hotaling, Robinson, and Salzberg.

According to all these sources, Sockalexis, as part of the Notre Dame team, embarrassed Rusie and his professional New York Giants teammates by clubbing a long home run against him in an early 1897 exhibition game. There certainly is no problem with the idea of a college-professional matchup; indeed, the Giants had played several of them with area New York City college teams that very spring. The problem, however, is that Rusie was still maintaining a year-long holdout against the Giants in a dispute over an alleged curfew violation and original $200 fine, which had grown into a $400 penalty. It was not resolved and Rusie did not pitch for his team until the regular season started. An intriguing possibility, allowing for the slim chance that the alleged encounter is true, relies on a coincidence. Rusie, the so-called "Hoosier Thunderbolt," was a resident of Indiana and had attended Notre Dame himself. Perhaps the encounter occurred with Rusie pitching for some professional barnstormers or other notable players living in the region. Although this alleged home run suffers severely for lack of proof, the home run by Sockalexis in New York City was accorded unusually substantial description and fanfare.

Salisbury wrote that this moment "was to be the high point of his career— his first trip to New York in June." According to Salisbury:

> Sockalexis had been in Brooklyn, but Brooklyn wasn't New York. Brooklyn was a separate city until 1898, when Chicago threatened to grow bigger, and Brooklyn was annexed to keep Gotham the biggest city in America. New York, then as now, was the media and cultural capital. The appearance of a new star did not go unheeded. The Giants' best pitcher was Amos Rusie, the Hoosier Thunderbolt, who had come roaring back after holding out the entire '96 season. The New York papers made much of the confrontation between the hardest thrower of the decade and the Indian from Maine.[19]

Maine writer Francis Hatch described the atmosphere at the game as "explosive.... For weeks there had been a build-up in the press. Photographers clicked close-ups of his throwing arm, his legs and his heap big Indian profile. New York writers had scoffed at the spectacle to come when the poor red man would face the fabulous Amos Rusie, owner of the most savage and elusive curve ball in league."[20]

Indeed, Rusie, who was elected to the Baseball Hall of Fame in 1977, is regarded by most baseball historians as the fastest and most intimidating of the nineteenth-century hurlers. Some baseball writers contend that because Rusie (with no other pitcher ever cited by name) so dominated hitters during the 1892 season, the pitching mound was moved back 10 feet to its present 60 feet 6 inches before the start of the 1893 season. The burly right-hander won 245 games during a ten-year career, achieving the thirty-victory mark four years in a row and winning twenty or more games eight successive times. He led the league in strikeouts and shut-outs on five occasions. Another important factor supporting Rusie's stature as the premier hurler to be feared was his wildness. He set records for walks allowed and figured in several frightening, life-threatening, hit-by-a-pitch beanings, including one involving Orioles star Hughie Jennings. Hitting a home run, a rarity in the "dead ball" era to begin with, was extremely rare against Rusie; he surrendered only six homers in more than 300 innings. So, apparently still fuming at Sockalexis for whatever earlier successes the Indian had already enjoyed against him, or recognizing the potential for a good newspaper story, Rusie pledged that he would "strike the damned Indian out."[21]

Commotion in the packed stands reached a near fever pitch as Sockalexis approached the plate as the third batter to hit in the top of the first inning. There was much war whooping. Not all of it was derisive, since about fifty fellow Penobscot tribesmen had made the long trip to New York to see him play. Many of the New Yorkers in the stands are said to have stood and sarcastically beat their cheeks or shouted war whoops. Amid the din, Sockalexis is said to have smiled and waved to his friends in the stands. Rusie, too, reportedly smiled at the hollering. Whether this is true is not to be gleaned from the *Boston Daily Globe*'s crisp summary, which makes no mention of any of it, nor from the equally terse account published in the *Cleveland Press*.

History makes clear who won this classic duel. Sockalexis slapped Rusie's first pitch, the much-celebrated, fastest breaking curve ball of the day on a sharp line, far over right fielder Mike Tiernan's head, for a home run. As frequently occurred during this era, to accommodate an overflow crowd (some sources claim as many as 5,200 fans), a rope barrier had been set up before the game in the deepest reaches of the outfield, and fans were allowed to stand around the field behind the barrier. The ground rules of the day held that the ball was still in play even if it went beyond the barrier. Outfielders had to retrieve the ball as best they could, despite the fans on the field. While Tiernan was chasing down the ball, Sockalexis sped around the bases for an easy home run.

Salisbury says: "What little literature there is on Sockalexis never fails to mention the confrontation with Rusie. Some accounts claim that the muscular Indian hit a 600-foot home run off Rusie, which would be a neat trick with the dead ball." As a yardstick to assess this highly doubtful Herculean feat, Salisbury noted that the longest measured home run ever remains Mickey Mantle's 565-foot blast off Chuck Stobbs in Washington's Griffith Stadium in 1955. Salisbury sarcastically added, "Unmeasured home runs have a way of getting longer." Ruth supposedly hit a 600-foot homer in Tampa and, judging by the accounts of that one, "You might think it was still going."[22]

The *Cleveland Press* account, under the headline: "Big Rusie Outpitched In A Game By Zeke Wilson, Indians Hammer The Ball At New York," simply related the big hit this way: "Sockalexis electrified the 4500 people present in the first inning when he made a home run. The great and only Rusie did the pitching for the New Yorks but Tebeau's men found no difficulty in solving his delivery." After praising the fielding of several infielders, the account continues, "Burkett made a great throw home, stopping a run. Sockalexis did likewise, later in the game."[23]

An article published in the July 20, 1912, edition of the *Bangor Daily Commercial* told the story under the headline: "Once Deerfoot of the Diamond, Now Charon of Penobscot":

> No fan who witnessed his debut in New York in 1897 will ever forget it. Sockalexis came heralded as great, but the big city, as usual was skeptical until it had seen. Tall, broad-shouldered, lithe limbed, dark, clear eyed and handsome, he strode to the home plate of the Polo Ground for the first time, a perfect specimen of his stock, the Algonquin, the truest type of the American Indian. He struck the plate with his bat and crouched. Amos Rusie, then in his prime, opposed him. Rusie wound up and uncoiled. The mingled roar of "Injun — Big Chief" and other similar cries of intended derision was silenced like magic by a resounding report. The ball, like a bullet, soared high and far to the wall in the outfield. Then up from the crowd in the grandstand across a curiously garbed group and a cry never before heard on a ball field, the war cry of the [Wabenaki], clear and vibrant, rang to the rafters, rolled over the field where the pride of the tribe was fleeing over the white paths, and rebounded from Coogan's Bluffs in the distance. The Old Town Indians, even their chief, had long before become proud of Sockalexis's fame on the diamond and had come there to greet him. That memorable home run was the forerunner of many.[24]

Unfortunately, that last remark is untrue, though no one would have suspected it at the time. The often-celebrated home run slugged against Amos Rusie would be the last major league home run Louis Sockalexis ever hit.

The story of the legendary matchup and the showing by Sockalexis in the game grew more spectacular in the retelling than the game's box score reveals. First of all, this was obviously not Sockalexis's first at bat in the major leagues. A number of writers apparently misinterpreted the meaning of the word debut. This was Sockalexis's first appearance in New York, his New York debut, and not—though the romantic notion of it clearly drove several writers to flowery descriptions—his first time facing major league pitching. Furthermore, he did not hit another home run, nor did he throw three men out at home plate in the game. The box score for the game reveals that he had one other hit, a single, and recorded one outfield assist.

Lost in the more glorified accounts of the game are moments that did not go particularly well for Sockalexis. After putting up a "1" on the scoreboard in the top of the first, he returned the favor for New York in the bottom of that same inning. Sockalexis, who had already committed seven outfield errors in the forty-two games previously played, mishandled a line drive by Tiernan with one out, allowing the outfielder to get all the way to third, where he scored on a sacrifice fly. In the second inning Cleveland hammered Rusie, en route to a 7–2 win, but the hurler did keep his pledge—for he struck out Sockalexis the very next inning. In its account of the game the *Boston Daily Globe* records:

> It is quite evident that Sockalexis, the Indian, whose phenomenal stick work has been one of the surprises of the season, has been giving the other Cleveland players some of his ideas as to how base hits should be made, for every player on the Cleveland team made at least one hit yesterday, and some of them made two. Rusie, the strongest pitcher the New Yorks have, was an easy mark to the visiting team, and they rapped out singles, doubles, triples, and, to cap the climax, a home run. Sockalexis started the hitting with a beautiful line drive over the right field ropes in the first inning for a home run. Rusie evened things up in the next inning by striking him out on four pitched balls.[25]

According to Salisbury, *The New York Times* ran a subhead with the game account that read, "Sockalexis' Usual Home Run," which "is revealing about the man's impact and reputation, considering he hit only three big-league home runs."[26] Of course, during this so-called dead ball era, a handful of home runs was considered a great many. The league leader that year, for instance, finished with just eleven. The *Cleveland Press* account noted, "Sockalexis' home run in the first inning was made after two men were out," with no further description.[27]

Salisbury wrote: "The newspapers of the day give the impression that fans liked Sockalexis. He never seems to have responded to 'ki-yi's' and war whoops, and fans may have liked that. Perhaps, as with all stereotypes, when people actually saw a flesh-and-blood Indian who wasn't in a circus,* their attitudes changed. Maybe, as later with Jackie Robinson, they came to respect the ballplayer, and learned to judge the man as a man. The papers, of course, may have whitewashed the way Sockalexis was treated."[28] Summing up the dramatics at the Polo Grounds, Harry Grayson wrote in his book, *They Played the Game,* "Sockalexis' home run off the fireball king Amos Rusie took its place in New York history along with the purchase of Manhattan Island from the Indians."[29]

In the interview, "A Talk with Sockalexis: What the Noted Indian Player Has To Say about the National Game," published in the June 19 issue of *Sporting Life,* Sockalexis addresses the alleged "jealousy" of players, particularly Jesse Burkett, on his own team.

> No ball player has been talked of more this season than Sockalexis, the right fielder of the Clevelands. The Indian has been a lucky find for the club in more ways than one. Not only has the team been strengthened, but many dollars will be added to the coffers of the club. In the different cities of the National League where the "Indians" have played, large crowds have been the rule. The Indian is having a troublesome time with the small boys who can be seen hovering near the grounds.

> While the Clevelands were in Brooklyn, Sockalexis was interviewed by Joe Vila, who reports his experience as follows: "At first the Indian opened his eyes with wonder, and edged away, but finally consented to talk. The red man is a well-built fellow. He is probably six feet tall and an athlete from head to foot."

> SOCKALEXIS: "If the small and big boys of Brooklyn and other cities find it a pleasure to shout at me I have no objections. No matter where we play I go through the same ordeal, and at the present time I am so used to it that at times I forget to smile at my tormentors, believing it to be a part of the game. But I do love to play ball. Ever since I was so high (lowering his hand to within three feet of the ground) I have played the game. Out at Old Tom [*sic*]. Me. Where I was born, I used to join other Indians and some white boys, and it has been my ambition to become a great player.

> "Will I succeed? Why, of course, I will. You have no idea how anxious I am to learn every point and trick of the game. There are many little things that come up in nearly every game which are new to me, but the white players are good to me, and are always ready to advise me."

---

*Buffalo Bill's traveling show, featuring Sitting Bull and other famous Indians, was immensely popular. It certainly could not have helped either that Libbie Custer was still touring the country heralding her husband's bravery and cause in dealing with the issue of "the red man."

VILA: "Are the Brooklyns a good team?"

SOCKALEXIS: "They are very strong. At least, they played well against the Clevelands."

VILA: "Who is the best pitcher?"

SOCKALEXIS: "All left-handed pitchers bother me, but I will in time overcome that weakness. [Brooklyn's Harley] Payne has been very effective against me, but I will find him by and by.

"I have seen printed in several papers that the Cleveland players are liable to freeze me out of the club because I am an Indian. That is all bosh, for the white players can't do enough for me, especially Burkett, who is said to be jealous because I lead him in batting. Jesse is proud of me because I have made such a good showing, he having recommended me to Manager Tebeau. It was while I was playing with the Holy Cross College team at Williamstown, two years, that John M. Ward told a League manager to sign me. Burkett, who coached the Holy Cross team, finally got Tebeau to let me have a trial.

"College base ball is much different from that played in the National League. The result of a college game generally depends on the pitcher, who is expected to strike out every man, and is apt to become wild. In the League the pitcher puts the ball over the plate, and you have a better chance to hit it, but their tricks are so many that you must keep your eyes open every moment. Maybe some day I will be a great player, but not yet. I have a good deal to learn and watch every player, some of whom may do something that may be of benefit to me at another time."

VILA: "How old are you?"

SOCKALEXIS: "I think I was born in 1871, and will be 24 years old next October 24. No! No! No! That's a mistake! I was born in 1873. I have so much to think of that I get things mixed."**

VILA: "Are your parents living?"

SOCKALEXIS: "Yes, they are at Old Town, and are very anxious to see me succeed. My parents are of the Penobscot tribe. Father's name is Francis P. Sockalexis and mother's Frances P. Sockalexis. While my parents are not rich, they are comfortable and are not depending on my salary.

"I first played with the St. Mary's College team, of Van Buren, Maine, and then with Ricker's College, after which I went to Holy Cross. I was a great favorite at Holy Cross, with which team I played centre field."[30]

**Sockalexis was born in 1871 and would turn twenty-six that fall. Perhaps he wanted to appear to be younger than he was to the public and members of the press.

In the issue of *Sporting Life* a week earlier (dated June 12) a blurb in the "News and Comment" section stated: "The father of Sockalexis is the chief of the Penobscot tribe and a well known Maine guide.*** Before going to Holy Cross college young Sockalexis played in Maine in a way to attract general attention."[31]

After the great win against Rusie, the Indians fared dismally in the balance of the New York series, Thursday through Saturday, June 17–20, which brought to a close the sixteen-game road trip that had begun in Brooklyn on May 31. The Indians lost two successive shut-outs by the same 5–0 count and then lost the series finale 8–4. Sockalexis had one hit and threw out a runner from right field in the first shut-out but went hitless in the second. He had two hits in the final loss at New York. On the road trip the club won only five games and lost eleven.

That Saturday, June 19, 1897, the Orioles Willie Keeler failed to get a hit off Pirates left-hander Frank Killen. It was the first game in forty-five games where Keeler did not collect at least one hit. Streaks, however, were no big deal in this era and little mention of it was made. Still, Keeler's record stood for forty-four years, broken only when Joe DiMaggio collected hits in fifty-six successive games in 1941. DiMaggio's string is regarded today as one of the greatest all-time achievements in baseball.

*** This is incorrect. He was the tribal governor.

8

Fall of a Meteor

SOCKALEXIS, BASEBALL'S MAN of the hour, the batter who hit with the so-called "velvet swish," rode a wave of extraordinary feats during the first three months of the season. By July 3, 1897, Sockalexis "was hitting .328 (81 hits in 247 at bats), with 40 runs scored, 39 runs batted in and 16 stolen bases."[1] Only future Hall of Famers Honus Wagner and Big Ed Delahanty boasted higher averages.

After Independence Day, however, the wave that carried Sockalexis to heights of recognition and acclaim crested, broke, and almost as quickly swept him toward obscurity. As Cleveland traveled from one major Eastern city to the next, the Penobscot Indian star faced the toughest scrutiny and the most skeptical analysis of his skills from sports writers in New York, Boston, Baltimore, Philadelphia, Pittsburgh, and Washington. A *Sporting Life* "News and Comment" column said:

> Sockalexis has turned out to be such an unqualified success that every Indian who can make a salary bluff on the ball field can obtain an engagement without difficulty. Sockalexis is receiving much attention in the East. Personally he is a most attractive young man. He has the racial features of the redskin but in his civilian clothes passes as a handsome fellow. He is well educated and has pleasant manners. Tall, lithe, straight as an arrow. Admirably proportioned. He is the most striking figure on the ball field.[2]

One New York writer commented about Sockalexis, "His fielding was spectacular, his base running supreme, and an ease and grace marked his playing, which rarely, if ever, has been equaled."[3] In one game summary from the series in Brooklyn an unnamed *New York Journal* writer recounted:

> But that was not all that he did. In the first inning Shindle drove a line drive deep to right center. It looked good for three bases at least. Sockalexis was away with the crack of the bat. By a splendid effort, running with the speed of a Brooklyn handicap winner, he reached the ball and pulled it down just as it seemed about to settle in safely on the ground. "Socks," yelled the crowd. "You're a peach!" And Socks, grinning contentedly, took off his cap and bowed his respects to the vast assemblage before which he had made his Eastern debut.[4]

The response in Boston was glowing, too. One Boston reporter claimed, "His batting was wonderful, his fielding marvelous, and his great speed enabled him to steal bases at will."[5] The *Boston Herald* introduced him as follows:

> The new player is the celebrated Indian player Sockalexis in right field. Doubtless many attended the game to gaze at the man who has done so finely since his entrance into professional baseball. Many present had seen him play before, as for several seasons he played in the East. He is finely built and handles himself with remarkable ease and grace. As a fielder he covers a great deal of ground and is a sure catch. He is today one of the finest throwers in the country and more than once yesterday gave proof of his excellence in that direction. He is a left handed hitter and bats very freely and strongly besides being a splendid hand at bunting. As soon as he hits the ball he is off in a jiffy and takes some sharp fielding to head him off on a hit to the infield. The young man found himself busy before and after the game in acknowledging the salutations of his friends.[6]

The *Boston Daily Globe*'s "Baseball Notes" poetically declared: "Sockalexis, straight as a fir balsam, strong as a hornbeam, graceful as a white birch sapling, riveted the attention of the spectators…. Sockalexis, whose fleetness of foot is like the visitations of lightning from cloud to cloud, aroused the bleachers to a scalp dance in the eighth with a double won by sprinting."[7] The *Boston Traveler* tribute said:

> In recent years there has been no ballplayer who has attracted so much attention in Boston as Sockalexis, and judging from his work of yesterday, he deserves all the good things which have been said of him. As a swatter of the ball there are few men who will make a finer record than the Indian. He goes up to the plate with the air of a man who is going to punch the ball out of sight or of grip of any fielder. He respects the pitchers personally, but has the air of a man who is very well satisfied that curves of high and low degree were simply intended for him to slaughter. It is really worth the price of admission to see Sockalexis on his way to first base. I never saw a deer run, but if a deer can run as fast as Sockalexis, then I can understand what a tough time my hunting friends have annually in the Maine woods. Each season the league generally produces something in the way of a sensation. This year the sensation is Sockalexis, and the chances are that he will grow greater as he becomes more seasoned, and I cannot help but think that it is a shame that Sockalexis doesn't wear a Boston uniform. He would be a tremendous favorite in this city and there was a time when the Boston management could have easily enough secured him but we must not expect too much from our management. Now that the nine is playing pennant ball they simply look wise and take in our dough as a great thing. And we must have it to live, but the Boston management could quite easily afford to give up some of the strawberry shortcake it gets on holidays for a man like Sockalexis. He is a

good Indian, a mighty big chief among the great medicine men, and our bonnets are off to him.[8]

A Cleveland writer gushed: "Sockalexis is mighty— the mightiest of them all!"[9] Only three months into his rookie season of professional baseball, Sockalexis was winning a place in the firmament of America's favorite pastime. The season opened in late April and by May 6, the *Bangor Daily Commercial* reprinted a poem by R. K. Munkittrick originally published in the *New York Journal.* "The Great Sockalexis" reads:

> This is bounding Sockalexis,
> Fielder for the mighty Clevelands.
> Like the catapult in action,
> For the plate he throws the baseball,
> Till the rooters, blithely rooting,
> Shout until they shake the bleachers.
> "Sockalexis, Sockalexis,
> Sock it to them, Sockalexis!"
>
> Like the Bison on the prairies,
> Plunging from the flames up-leaping,
> Snorting at the crimson billows
> That his hinder members frizzle,
> Till the condor notes the odor,
> And his wings flap in the prescience
> Of a rich and luscious banquet —
> So spry Sockalexis capers,
> Leaving far behind the whirlwind,
> When he starts upon a home run.
>
> All the crowd cries: "Sockalexis,
> Sockalexis, Sockalexis!"
> When he circles like the eagle
> Round the bases, or serenely
> Slides upon his solferino
> Pie and doughnut padded stomach,
> Wiping all the glaring war paint
> Off his nasal in a jiffy.
>
> Such is merry Sockalexis,
> Who can bat and knock the home run,

Who can scalp the blooming umpire
Till the rooters in their glory,
Knowing no fit terms of praise, all
Lift their voices: "Sockalexis,
Sockalexis, Sockalexis!"
Till the weikins madly splitting,
And the purple cave of echo
Sends back all the surging chorus;
"Sockalexis, Sockalexis,
Sock it to them, Sockalexis." [10]

Perhaps the situation was put into its clearest context in the May 15 edition of *Sporting Life*, when an unnamed columnist noted Sockalexis's first error of the season, made against Chicago. Yet the columnist offered a very different tribute to the Penobscot:

> Sockalexis made his first error of the season Saturday afternoon. All eyes are on the Indian in every game. He is expected not only to play right field like a veteran but to do a little more batting than anyone else. Columns of silly poetry are written about him. Hideous looking cartoons adorn the sporting pages of nearly every paper. He is hooted and howled at by every thimble-brained brigade on the bleachers. Despite all this handicap the redman has played good steady ball and has been a factor in nearly every victory thus far by Tebeau's team. Of course Sockalexis has much to learn about the game as it is played in the big leagues, but he is not only an apt but willing pupil. Captain Tebeau predicts that after one full season in the National League, he will be one of the greatest players ever joining the organization. [11]

The Indians returned to Cleveland on the weekend of June 19–20, 1897, with an overall record of 22–23, mired in seventh place in the National League standings. Tebeau blamed bad luck and poor hitting. Clearly pitching was a problem, as the team's top two hurlers, Cy Young and Nig Cuppy, continued to be plagued by sore arms. Young's record was a very uncharacteristic six wins and eight losses.

Washington owner Earl Wagner was quoted wondering whether the problem with Cleveland that year, after the Spiders had finished in second place in both 1895 and 1896, was not simply that the team's veterans had "gotten old together." [12] Captain Tom Brown, who was now serving as the manager of Washington after Gus Schmelz had been fired, had a very different thought:

I cannot possibly account for the miserable showing of the Spiders unless the new coaching rule is handicapping Tebeau and his Indians. Under the old rule, Tebeau was always after the young pitchers, joshing and abusing from the coach line and roasting any player of the opposition who could possibly be rattled. But all is changed under the new rule, and Patsy and his Indians are obliged to grin and bear it. It is no exaggeration for me to say that many a game won by the Spiders was due in no small measure to the coach line efforts of Tebeau, O'Connor and Burkett, who took their sting out of the pitchers every day and even rattled some of the old heads with their ribald comments.[13]

Brown said that, based on the personnel Cleveland had, it should have been "even stronger than last year as a team." Concerning Brown's theory, almost two weeks earlier Tebeau had been quoted in the *Cleveland Press* as being in favor of the new "speechless" rule for coaching and regarded it as no factor whatsoever in the team's poor performance.

My esteemed friend Chadwick, the papa of the game, used to indulge in considerable flower tossing at my expense in previous years, charging that I abused the young pitchers by word-of-mouth inelegancies, as Dad Clarke or Chris Von der Ahe would put it. He even predicted that in the event the coaching law was amended and restrictions placed on it the Cleveland club would miss my monologue and the team would take a downshoot in consequence. Now, these critics who have accused me of being the Hungry Joe and the Spike Hennessy of the coach line would be amazed if I were to tell them that I was one of the heartiest advocates of the change in coaching that was made at the League meeting by the rules committee last February. I figured that the restriction would save me a heap of unnecessary conversation. I had always made a point of coaching in a lively, scrappy style, and wherever we went the crowd expected me to orate. Now that the public has the speechless article, there are cries for the return of the old rule. If the Cleveland team is handicapped by the coaching law, I have yet to discover it. We are stronger this season than ever before since the team has been under my management. We were handicapped at the outset of the season by a lack of training, but we are sure to come and finish among the first three clubs.[14]

Concerning Tebeau's behavior and that of his team, critics of Cleveland still believed otherwise. Writing in the *New York Herald* on June 17, Hank O'Day railed, "It is a fine ball team but not one to engender local pride. The conduct of the nine tells plainly why Cleveland people refuse to support it. Spectators want more than good ball playing. They want sportsmanlike conduct and clean conduct on the diamond. The bulldozing and indifferent action which Tebeau and his men yesterday mixed up was disgusting in the extreme."[15]

On Monday, June 21, Cleveland opened a three-game series at home with Louisville. In the opener, "The Indians play even more miserably than the Colonels, thoroughly boring 600 [fans]," according to one game account of Cleveland's 6–5 loss. "Slumping" Cy Young surrendered eleven hits in losing his ninth game of the year. Shortstop Ed McKean had three hits but also made three errors. Sockalexis, however, had one hit and threw out yet another runner from the outfield. In game two, the Colonels pounded Cleveland and Sockalexis's Holy Cross mate, Pappalau. One Cleveland newspaper account caustically reported, "Ginger Pappalau pitches his first full game for the Indians and it could be his last."[16] He surrendered eighteen hits, walked six, and struck out three. Sockalexis had one hit in three at bats, scoring a run. In the third game with Louisville, Cleveland broke a five-game losing streak, winning 18 – 1 behind a surprising starter — Jack (or "Jake," as he was sometimes called) Powell. To that date, Powell's only "major league experience" had come in court, serving as "the guinea pig Cleveland had left behind to face the judge and jury" in Robison's testing of the law concerning Sunday baseball playing.[17] Powell almost matched the Colonels in hits himself. He gave up just three hits, two of them "scratches," and had two base hits of his own. Sockalexis had two of Cleveland's nineteen hits and scored two runs. The forecast of doom for Pappalau proved accurate. He was released to Detroit of the Western League in late June.

The team then left town for a one-city stop and a three-game series with Chicago. Behind Cy Young, Cleveland took the opener 5–2. Sockalexis had one hit in five tries and five put-outs. The Colts won the second contest 9–2, beating another rookie pitcher being given a trial by Cleveland, Henry Clarke, the University of Chicago's star pitcher. Sockalexis collected two hits in five at bats. In the Cleveland newspapers, Cy Young was quoted as saying he could not explain why he was having his worst season ever. He speculated that perhaps it had something to do with the Indians' "lack of an adequate spring training." He suggested that factor might be behind "the whole team's poor play."[18] In the final contest at Chicago, on Sunday, June 27, the Indians received another stellar performance from Jack Powell. This time he gave up only six hits and was the winner of a shut-out, 5–0. Sockalexis was hitless in five at bats, but made seven put-outs in the field. Cleveland's record improved to 25 wins, 26 losses, and the team was in seventh position in the league standings.

Returning home, Cleveland evened its record at 26–26 and passed Pittsburgh in the standings for sixth place, with a 12–2 win on Monday, June 28. Cy Young got the easy victory, surrendering only a total of seven hits, while the Indians collected eighteen safeties. Sockalexis continued his consistent, fine play, with two hits and a run scored. In this contest, using its prerogative as home team, Cleveland chose to bat first.

In game two Pittsburgh battered Tebeau's new collegian, right-hander Henry Clarke, en route to a 9–3 win. Sockalexis had one hit, stole a base and scored a run, and made an error in the field. The writer of the account of this game for the *Cleveland Press* made umpiring a major culprit in the loss:

> Umpire "Sandy" McDermott succeeded, Tuesday, in dispelling any doubts that may possibly have existed about his claim to the title "worst that ever happened." In every city in the league, except Cleveland, a cry has gone up, "Save us from Sandy." McDermott objected to any exception and proceeded to make the protest universal. It is not claimed that he gave Tuesday's game to Pittsburg [*sic*], but that he is utterly, completely and entirely incompetent.[19]

The writer continued in this vitriolic vein, claiming that pitcher Clarke and Sockalexis were two major victims. Clarke, the young collegian, "had curves and twists which McDermott never set eyes on before," and the writer believed the young pitcher "got a rough deal on balls and strikes." The bases were continuously "cluttered with Pirates," and the game, the writer dejectedly stated, was "lost in the fourth." The writer concluded:

> McDermott reserved his master stroke for a climax. With the bases full and one run already forced in and the Pirates six miles up in the air in the ninth, Sox hit hard to [Pittsburgh shortstop] Ely, who fumbled it, but did well to stop the ball. Sox was away beyond first when [first baseman] Davis got the ball and two runs were in, but McDermott shouted "out" and ran off to get supper. In the eighth he had called the Indian out on a similar play, and earlier called Wallace out for alleged interference, on the word of the Pittsburg [*sic*] players. The crowd followed McDermott off the field — at a respectable distance — and told him he was everything almost, except an umpire.[20]

On Wednesday, June 30, all the Indians hit safely in a 14–3 rout of Pittsburgh. Pitcher Jack Powell had his third straight outstanding outing. Sockalexis was outstanding, too. He delivered two hits, scored two runs, stole a base, and made three put-outs. He recorded another outfield assist when, after making one of those catches, he started one of the Indians' three double plays.

Sockalexis had a perfect five singles in five at bats, stole a base, and scored a run to pace the Indians as Cleveland defeated Kid Carsey and St. Louis at home 6–2 on Thursday, July 1. Cleveland pitcher Zeke Wilson gave up only four hits to get the victory. Because Sandy McDermott was ill, an amateur umpire named McGinty served as substitute. The team finally nosed above the .500 mark, at 28–27, and had moved into fifth place in the standings.

Meanwhile, Boston's Beaneaters had overtaken "a crippled" Baltimore team for first place in the standings. The account in the *Cleveland Press* of the game noted: "The batting of Sockalexis was the feature, the red man making five 'bingles' — as they are termed in the cultured east — in five times at bat."[21]

The recent play of the team had captain Tebeau very confident. He remarked to the *Cleveland Press*: "We are out for the Temple Cup now. We have eight good pitchers, four great catchers, and the best team of batters Cleveland has ever had. From now on we expect to play winning ball."[22]

For the second game of the series the members of the St. Louis Browns said they would not play if McGinty was umpiring again. As a compromise measure, which proved acceptable, Tebeau let Browns pitcher Red Donahue serve as umpire for the bases. In a game where the Indians rapped out eighteen hits and routed the Browns by a 13–1 score, McGinty was not a factor. But apparently Donahue, clearly trying to be as impartial as possible, gave every close call to the Indians as well as some that were not even close. Cy Young got the win, finally evening his overall record at 9–9. Sockalexis had three hits, including a double and two singles, in six at bats and scored three runs. He also threw out a runner but committed an error in the game. Burkett continued his recent hot hitting, collecting four safeties.

On Saturday, July 3, the Indians completed their three-game sweep of hapless St. Louis. Newcomer Jack Powell continued his outstanding pitching for Cleveland, securing his fourth straight win without a defeat, in an 8–4 victory that required ten innings to decide. Tied with the Browns at 3–3 after nine innings, Cleveland, which chose to bat first in the contest, erupted for five runs ultimately to provide the decisive margin. Sockalexis had one hit in five at bats and scored two runs. For the second straight game he made an outfield error.

At the end of play on Saturday, July 3, when the Cleveland players departed their home field, their record stood at 30–27, and the team was in fifth position in the league standings. Members of the Cleveland team, their fans, and baseball followers around the country could not have suspected that Louis Sockalexis's meteoric run as a sensation and his professional baseball career were nearly at an end. Sockalexis would never again appear as a game-in, game-out regular in the Cleveland lineup. Indeed, after such a wonderful start he was destined to play only eight more games during the 1897 baseball season.

No signs of self-destruction were apparent to the public. Certainly on the playing field, the hitting and running, fielding and throwing of Louis Sockalexis had been exemplary, with only the occasional lapse easily attributable to a newcomer playing at the highest level of competition. Off the field more sinister forces were apparently at work.

The first tangible evidence of Sockalexis's difficulties off the field came to light after a Saturday night on the town. Sockalexis, whom *Sporting News* had called the most popular player in the league in its issue for the week of June 19, had apparently spent the eve of July fourth on a binge and returned to baseball undone as a professional.[23]

In a widely repeated story, Patsy Tebeau is supposed to have recounted the evening when Louis Sockalexis suffered his literal and figurative fall from baseball grace. Hughie Jennings's "Rounding Third" column is the source of the account. Jennings was a great Baltimore shortstop who went on to an equally distinguished and lengthy managing career and wrote a nationally syndicated column about baseball. In a 1926 column he focused on the rise and fall of Louis Sockalexis, a player he saw perform in five games against his Oriole club. According to Jennings, Tebeau related the fall of Sockalexis this way:

> No other player, to my knowledge, ever sacrificed so much on the altar of his appetite than did this red man. We signed Soc for $1,500 and raised him to $2,400 almost immediately. When he began to drink and stay out all night I promised him $6,000 for the next season and $10,000 for 1899 if he would stay sober and play ball. He promised, all right, but he could not let the strong stuff alone. He celebrated the Fourth of July by an all-night carousal in a red light joint, during which he jumped out of a second-story window. His right foot was badly broken in the fall, but he bandaged it up and went with the other players to Pittsburgh that night. I went over next day and there in the bus was Soc, his broken foot swollen four or five times its natural size. I sent him back to his hotel in Cleveland, where a doctor put his foot in a plaster cast and ordered him not even to turn over in bed. But do you know, he would get up during the night and walk a block on his plaster foot to get a drink of whiskey? Poor Soc — he could have made $10,000 or $12,000. He was worth that for his playing alone, but also as an attraction. Nobody ever heard of Cy Young, Bobby Wallace or any of the others when Soc was with us.[24]

Clearly no doctor, Tebeau overdramatized Sockalexis's injury, as he had in describing Burkett's head injury. The foot, while badly hurt, could not have been "broken." When the team played in Pittsburgh the Indian star was, indeed, absent from the lineup for all three games, but he returned on July 8 and claimed two hits against Washington.

Author Luke Salisbury writes: "Another misconception is that the Indian was hitting .400 and then succumbed to drink. This, like the single-drink theory, is also not true."[25] Salisbury cited the research done by Cappy Gagnon, a Society for American Baseball Research member who, like fellow member Richard Tourangeau, undertook a game-by-game study of

Sockalexis's 1897 season. Gagnon, according to Salisbury, found that the origin of the ".400-to-.338 fall, the riches-to-rags archetype that dominates all discussion of Sockalexis," began with a list of the league's leading hitters published in the August 7, 1897, issue of *Sporting Life*.[26] Heading the list is a very young Honus (then called "Hans") Wagner of Louisville, batting .475. Slugger Ed Delahanty was at .424, and then, listed as third in the league, was Sockalexis, at .413. Gagnon, however, saw that the Indian's average was computed by dividing 151 hits into 365 at bats. Gagnon also noticed that not only was Sockalexis's hit total identical with Delahanty's, but so were his runs, doubles, triples, and home runs. Deciding this was too much of a coincidence, Gagnon reconstructed the Indian's season from box scores and discovered that Sockalexis was really hitting .335 on August 7, which is consistent with the .338 all-sources list as his final average.

Salisbury concludes: "Whatever happened to Sockalexis over the Fourth of July was so severe that he simply couldn't play anymore. His season wasn't a matter of hitting .400, beginning to drink, slipping, and then being benched. He steadily hit between .330 and .350, and then was benched. Whatever happened over the Fourth, in hotel rooms or saloons, was irreversible. Gagnon speculates that the team may have locked Sockalexis in a hotel room to keep him from drink, and the Indian may have injured himself jumping off a roof."[27]

Perhaps, since Burkett was Sockalexis's coach at Holy Cross, he may have suggested this strategy to Tebeau, if, as Miss Violet of the Indian Island Historical Society reported, at Holy Cross the manager posted players around Sockalexis's bed to keep him from going after whiskey. Certainly the Sockalexis obituary in the *Bangor Daily News* subscribed to this second theory:

> Just when the experts were predicting that he would become the greatest of all players, he broke; broke dismally. They say that the downfall of Sockalexis dated from his first payday. The lights of the big cities dazzled him. He was coaxed, threatened, cajoled, all to no effect. He simply would not listen to managerial advice or recognize any discipline. He was given every chance, but there was the aboriginal Indian thirst for fire-water which was unquenchable. One night in getting out of a second story window to avoid a guard on the floor below, he broke his ankle. That was the beginning of the end. He was never the same or even a remote resemblance to his top form. His leg became fairly strong, but his old speed was gone never to return.[28]

9

A Season's Sad End

WHEN THE TEAM played in Pittsburgh, the injured Sockalexis was replaced in right field by Lew McAllister. Cleveland won the first game of a morning and afternoon doubleheader on Monday, July 5, by a score of 4 – 3 but lost the second game 6 – 1. A crowd of 5,500 for the first game was reportedly disappointed by Sockalexis's absence, a game ultimately won on a clutch hit by Burkett.

The second game's loss resulted from Burkett's alleged "sulkiness" in failing to chase down a ball that went through his legs.[1] Finally retrieved by shortstop Ed McKean, the hit became a bases-clearing home run that paved the way to a loss. The next day Pittsburgh nipped pitching sensation Jack Powell 3 –2, scoring the winning run in the top of the ninth after exercising its home-field prerogative to bat first.

The *Cleveland Press* for Wednesday, July 7, reported: "The smash that brought in the winning run at Pittsburgh, Tuesday, was a triple over McAllister's head.... Sockalexis was badly needed, Tuesday. The Indian has a badly sprained foot and is almost unable to walk."[2]

A gossipy feature story appeared in a Cleveland newspaper that July describing the love letters and other fan mail Sockalexis received. According to author John Phillips, the story reported that "the matinee favorite or leading juvenile man of the Indians is the sporty scion of the Penobscots, Louis Sockalexis. His mail at the Kennard House in Cleveland is flooded with Cupid missives from palpitating maidens who pine for a photo of the shifty copper-tinted tender of Tebeau's outer reservation. Barrymore, Kelcey, or any of the thespian heart-players never aroused such an inflammable, consuming equatorial toridity in the feminine bosom as Sockalexis, child of stream and forest."[3]

The team traveled from Pittsburgh on Wednesday, July 7, to play a three-game series with Washington at home, where they learned that owner Robison had scheduled the games for Thursday, Saturday... and Sunday. With Washington owner Earl Wagner, Robison met with members of the press to say that he was expecting a decision at any moment from the court of common pleas regarding his Sunday ball-playing case. He said he had every reason to believe the court would declare unconstitutional the state law that prohibited Sunday ball. Cleveland's prosecuting attorney said he had a contingency plan. If he lost in common pleas court, he would seek an injunction against Sunday ball that would stymie all such attempts until the case went to circuit court. Robison and Wagner agreed that if the game were disallowed on Sunday, it would be made up in Washington. Judge Ong, whose decision on the Indians' case was anxiously awaited, reportedly had not ruled on the case because he was at a trotting meeting in Tiffin, Ohio, "doctoring his sick filly."[4]

Limping noticeably, Sockalexis took his place in right field for the first game of the Washington series on Thursday, July 8. Cleveland pounded out ten runs on fourteen hits in the first three innings, en route to an easy 10 – 5 win. Sockalexis had two hits in four at bats plus a sacrifice, scored two runs, and played errorless ball in the field, recording two put-outs. The *Cleveland Press* commended Sockalexis for his effort this way: "Sox went into Thursday's game with a lame ankle, but played fast ball."[5]

On Friday, July 9, Judge Ong delivered his decision in Cleveland, and Robison finally won the victory he had fought so strenuously to obtain. Ong found the law prohibiting Sunday baseball to be unconstitutional. He wrote: "Custom has opposed the law. This absolute law against Sunday amusement is unpopular and antagonistic to the desire of the people."[6]

The *Cleveland Press* of July 10 crowed in one headline: "Indians Pleased With Judge Ong's Decision, So Manager Tebeau Declares Will Play Winning Ball From Now On." Tebeau was quoted as saying the decision "delights every player" on the team. He added: "It gives the players a home. The cry of some towns: 'Where'll you be next year?' has had its effect on some of the boys. I venture the prophecy that the decision will have a good effect on the general playing of the team, and I know every man in Mr. Robison's employ is glad. He is fighter from the word go and when he goes into a battle he goes in to win. That is what the Indians are now trying to do."[7]

Under a subhead "Mr. Robison Talks," Cleveland owner Frank DeHass Robison offered this prideful and bombastic comment:

> I consider the verdict of Judge Ong not only able and just but the only verdict a court of justice could give. From the start I have contended that a law restricting the personal liberties of the people, a law with so mephitic an odor in the public nostrils that it was a dead letter the state over, was unconstitutional. I have fought the thing on this line single-handed and alone, and the decision gratifies me more from the thought that I was right than from any prospect of mercenary gain.[8]

Cleveland immediately announced that it would play the following Sunday games: July 11, with Washington; July 18, with Brooklyn; July 25, with Baltimore; August 15, with St. Louis; and August 29, with Louisville.

Robison told the media that four games originally scheduled for Sunday that had already been played on other days had cost the club at least $15,000.

Robison told the press that he would "pitch the first ball over the plate at League park Sunday afternoon and Earl Wagner will catch it—or try to." Robison predicted that the Sunday crowd would be somewhere around 7,500; while another Cleveland official, a Mr. Muir, estimated 10,000. A mention in the *Cleveland Press* on Saturday reported that John Powell would celebrate the court decision that relieved him from punishment for playing Sunday ball by pitching the first legal Sunday game in Cleveland.[9]

Sockalexis did not play (replaced again by McAllister) in Saturday's game, a 3–1 Cleveland victory over Washington, but he was in the lineup for the historic Sunday game with the Senators. On Sunday, July 11, 1897, nature almost halted what no courts or ministers could prevent in Cleveland. Wind sweeping across Lake Erie carried torrents of rain and "threatened to dampen Frank Robison's victory over Cleveland's ministers." At 1 P.M., when the gates were due to open, it was pouring rain. By 2 P.M., however, with dark clouds still hovering over soggy League Park, a "reasonable gathering of 1,500" fans saw umpire Hank O'Day signal for the first batter. Cleveland clobbered Washington pitcher Les German for twenty hits, taking the game by a 15–4 count.

Under the subdued headline, "An Orderly Game," the *Cleveland Press* reported in its account: "There was no howling, hooting mob at League park, Sunday, as some of the extreme opponents of Sunday ball had prophesied. The 1,500 people who braved the bad weather and took their chances of a game being played, were enthusiastic, but orderly and well behaved. The game was played in mud, slush and drizzle. The Indians played with the spirit and dash of '95 and made the game a one-sided contest."[10] Powell was treated to an easy victory, lifting his overall record to 5–1, and the contest added his name to baseball history as the winning pitcher on the day that playing baseball on Sunday became legal in Cleveland.

Sockalexis had two hits, scored two runs, and had two put-outs. Batting third in the lineup, he singled to center field in the first inning in the middle of an early rally for Cleveland. No reference at all was made concerning his injured foot or how it affected his play. The first press criticism of Louis Sockalexis for playing under the influence of alcohol came after his sixty-first contest, on Monday, July 12.

The league-leading Boston Beaneaters had arrived for a three-game series. A good weekday crowd of 8,000 expected to see an outstanding pitching duel between two prime league aces, Cy Young and Kid Nichols. The *Cleveland Press* blamed two "horrible" fielding errors by Sockalexis for allowing seven of Boston's eight runs. In one instance, according to the

Cleveland Press account, he "misplayed" Jimmy Collins' hit into a home run; however, the *Boston Daily Globe* did not report the play as an error. "Through no fault of his own," Young trailed 5–0, claimed the *Cleveland Press*, and ultimately he lost his tenth decision of the year, 8–2.[11] Sockalexis did have two hits in two at bats plus a walk, but after he committed his second error, Tebeau took him out of the game and replaced him in right field with McAllister. The *Globe* said Sockalexis was replaced after reaching first base and reporting to Tebeau he was "too lame" to run.[12]

Focusing on the fans' anger with umpire Jack Sheridan over a disputed play that cost Cleveland two runs, the *Cleveland Press* said, "The score of the game should have been: Cleveland 2, Boston 1, and would have been but for the wretched efforts of the crippled Indian to play right field, the lack of a regular fielder in center, and Sheridan's inexcusably wretched umpiring.... Young gave way to [pitcher Henry] Clarke after Sox's horrible errors had virtually lost the game."[13]

Reserve outfielders Harry Blake and Jimmy McAleer were no longer with the team, and utility player Jack O'Connor, normally a catcher or first baseman, apparently had to be pressed into service to play center field. McAleer, said to be sensitive to criticism about his playing, had quit the team and gone home. Blake had been demoted to the minors because he was unable to hit a curve ball. After the 1897 season ended, McAleer wrote a letter saying that he wanted to buy the team from Robison because he and his business partner were doing so well with a furnishing goods store in Youngstown. Either business declined or baseball's allure was irresistible since McAleer rejoined Cleveland, as a player, in 1898.

Under the headline "A Wooden Indian," a reporter from the *Cleveland Plain Dealer* was apparently the first newspaperman to suggest that Sockalexis had a drinking problem in a story on Tuesday, July 13, saying that he "acted as if he had disposed of too many mint juleps previous to the game.... Sockalexis was directly responsible for all but one of Boston's runs.... A lame foot is the Indian's excuse, but a Turkish bath and a good rest might be an excellent remedy."[14]

The *Boston Daily Globe* account of the game was significantly different. Under the headline "Two Home Runs, Nichols And Collins The Heroes At Cleveland, Easy Victory For The Boston Team For A Starter," a final subhead charged: "Sockalexis Plays Like A Very Weary Indian."[15] In the box score, Sockalexis was the only Cleveland player charged with committing errors, a total of two. The box score also showed that of Boston's eight total runs, three were determined to be earned runs, meaning that Sockalexis's two errors were responsible for five runs, not six or seven. Sockalexis had a hit to center field in the first inning, but Cleveland failed to score. In the second, Boston scored a run on a triple by Stahl and a single by Collins.

Sheridan's first problems as umpire came when he called Young out at first base after second baseman Lowe fumbled his grounder and then apparently threw quite late to first. According to the *Boston Daily Globe* account: "The ball reached first a couple of seconds after Young, but Sheridan called him out. The decision nearly caused a riot. Play was stopped for five minutes, while the Cleveland players surrounded the umpire and the shouts of the spectators were deafening. After the game the Bostons themselves said the decision was unfair." That same inning Childs and Sockalexis followed with singles, but three outs were recorded without any scoring, largely because Young was called out. In the fourth inning, Duffy led off for Boston by grounding out to shortstop McKean. Stahl singled to left field. Collins popped up to second baseman Childs for the second out. The Boston paper reported: "Then Lowe pushed up a sky scraper which [center fielder Jack] O'Connor and Sockalexis both ran for and neither got. 'Sox' ought to have nailed it." Stahl scored the first run of an inning that should have ended with the catch of Lowe's fly ball. Instead, with Lowe on second, Begen doubled to center, scoring Lowe and the second run of the inning. Nichols followed with a home run that careered through the gap between center and right fields, scoring Bergen and himself before the ball could be returned to the diamond. That would make four unearned runs, if Sockalexis were to be charged with an error on the play. Cleveland led at that point, 5–0. In the Boston fifth, Tenney led off with a single "which he stretched into a three-bagger because Sockalexis let the ball go through his legs." Long popped out to shortstop McKean for the first out. Duffy singled, scoring Tenney with Boston's sixth run. Stahl lined out to O'Connor for the second out. Collins "then duplicated Nichols' hit of the previous inning, making the second home run of the game and sending Duffy in ahead of him."[16] Those last two runs made Boston's final count of eight for the game, but the *Boston Daily Globe* description hardly sounds as though Sockalexis "misplayed" this ball into a home run.

The *Globe* story continues: "It was raining pretty hard now, and Nichols suggested that umbrellas were in order. Sockalexis was given a base. The Indian, who all through the game had been playing like a cigar sign, said he couldn't run, so McAllister took his place at the bag and the next moment was forced at second."[17] Cleveland got its two meaningless runs in the bottom of the seventh inning.

On Tuesday, July 13, Sockalexis came out of the Cleveland lineup, not to return until July 24. His replacement in right field for the next two games was, strangely enough, the young pitcher Henry Clarke. Thereafter, until

Sockalexis returned to the lineup on July 24, it was Lew "Sport" McAllister who filled the post. McAllister was a versatile utility player who could play all nine positions, including pitcher.

Diplomatically phrased charges of "indifferent playing" and failing to "behave himself" leveled at Sockalexis clearly had nothing to do with concerns about how he was recovering from a foot injury. A *Boston Daily Globe* story stated: "Sockalexis has been laid off by Cleveland for indifferent playing. The players demanded that the captain play some one else in right field. Tebeau admitted the justness of the complaint and said he had tried every means to make Sox behave himself. Thus it was that Clarke played right field Tuesday."[18] The charismatic Sockalexis still had believers. Writing in *Sporting Life*'s "Cleveland Chatter," Elmer E. Bates commented:

> Sockalexis is nursing his badly sprained foot, and is urging Patsy to let him stay out of the game until he can play in his old-time form. In this the Indian will probably be humored. His hitting is needed, but he can only give an imitation of the way he played right field early in the season until he recovers from his lameness. The red man is a mark for more or less humorous writers the country over, and much of the stuff regarding his dalliance with grape juice and his trysts with pale-faced maidens is purely speculation. Sox is a natural-born ball player and Patsy has already tipped him to lead the League batters next season.[19]

Cleveland was in the midst of a lengthy home stand that lasted through the rest of July. After the three-game series with Boston (July 12–14), Brooklyn was the next team to oppose the Indians on Thursday, Saturday, and Sunday (July 15, 17, 18). To the red-hot young hurler Jack Powell went the honor of pitching that second Sunday game in Cleveland, and he responded with another victory, upping his record to 7–1. The team was now in fifth place in the league standings, with a record of 39–30. During the weekend, the Louisville Colonels announced the purchase of shortstop Honus Wagner's minor league contract.

Of Sockalexis's dramatic fall *The Washington Post* observed: "Alack for poor Sockalexis! Two months ago, his pedals were as active as the underpinning of a jackal and the cathode glint of his lamps penetrated the pill of horsehide e'en to its very rubber vitals. And now Sock's moccasins are charged with possessing the celerity of a Philadelphia messenger boy, and he can't see e'en through one of Dad Clarke's gags." (Dad Clarke of the Giants was often characterized as an easily hittable pitcher who was better known as a comic than a hurler.).[20]

From July 19 through 21 Cleveland split a two-game series with Baltimore, while a third contest was rained out. Sockalexis returned to the

Cleveland lineup and right field on Saturday, July 24, as the Indians began a two-game series with Philadelphia.

What an unusual game that turned out to be, a game that Cleveland ultimately won on a forfeit. In an apparent last-minute change, National League president Nick Young assigned umpire Bob Emslie to Cincinnati, leaving the Cleveland–Philadelphia contest without an umpire, so players were selected to umpire Saturday's game in Cleveland. The Indians chose a Philadelphia player with the optimistic-sounding nickname "Honest Jack" Boyle, while Philadelphia selected Cleveland's new substitute, Tom McGinty, who had not been with the team long. Behind the pitching of Jack Fifield, Philadelphia led the Indians and Cy Young 4–3 after eight innings. The trouble arose in the ninth inning when McGinty awarded Indians' catcher Chief Zimmer a base on balls. After McGinty called ball two on Patsy Tebeau, the Phillies objected boisterously. A delay ensued. When play resumed, McGinty called two strikes and then another ball, setting off more protests from the visitors. When McGinty called ball four to Tebeau, issuing another Cleveland walk, the Philadelphia team refused to continue. According to the *Cleveland Press* account of the game: "Finally, when Tebeau took his base on four bad ones, the Quakers rushed at the substitute umpire as if they would eat him up. They would not return to their positions." [21] After waiting a few minutes, McGinty awarded the game to the Indians, by the official forfeit count of 9–0, much to the delight of the 3,000 fans in attendance. For the July 24 game, the box score for Louis Sockalexis, who was dropped to eighth in the batting order, was a curious duplicate of his July 12 game: two hits and two errors in the outfield. Young won the victory, improving his record to 13 wins, 10 losses.

Third-place Baltimore (behind Boston and Cincinnati) came to town the next day and won, in extra innings, the third game ever played in Cleveland on a Sunday. Attendance was the big story. The *Cleveland Press* headline for the story read, "A Monster, The Crowd At The Base Ball Park, Over 13,000 People See The Indians Lose, All Local Records Put Far In The Shade." According to the story: "The audience filled every chair, every aisle and every inch of space in every stand and extended entirely around the field. There was not the slightest suggestion of disorder or of boisterous conduct. Good plays were liberally applauded and the defeat was accepted good naturedly." [22] Other accounts of the game set attendance at around 15,000. Sockalexis was back in right field for his second consecutive game and moved up to sixth in the batting order. He had one hit, a triple, in four at bats in the 6–5 loss and recorded one put-out in the field with no errors. According to John Phillips, one Cleveland newspaper offered this assessment of Sockalexis's inept play during one of those two games: "'Take that bat out of his hand and put a bunch of cigars in it: he'd look better in front of a cigar store, Tebeau,' a fan yelled in Cleveland the other day when Chief Sockalexis took three falls out of the atmosphere....' Sockalexis doesn't know when to quit drinking and call a cab."[23]

The very next day, Monday, he was out of the lineup again for the July 26 matchup against Amos Rusie and the Giants. McAllister replaced Sockalexis in right field, as the Indians lost to New York 6 – 5. The July 24 edition of *Sporting News* reported about a bar fight involving Sockalexis that allegedly took place in Chicago in late June, about a week before the infamous July fourth weekend, when Sockalexis "tried to clean up a saloon. A hanger-on at the place had Socks by the neck with one hand and a big cheese knife in the other when the police interfered."[24] Sockalexis did not return to the Cleveland lineup until Friday, August 13. This time a formal announcement explained Sockalexis's absence from the field, and the reason had nothing to do with the injury to his foot.

"Sox Under Discipline" read one of the subheads under the account of Cleveland's 8 – 2 loss at Cincinnati on Friday, July 30, in the *Cleveland Press*. The story reported that "Sockalexis is under discipline. President Robison claims to have indisputable evidence that the Indian has repeatedly violated the club rules in regard to drinking and has levied fines aggregating $175 on him and suspended him until he can bring a physician's certificate that he is in condition to play."[25]

The baseball and sporting world at large quickly picked up on the story. A *Boston Daily Globe* account carried the lengthy title: "Sockalexis Unmanageable, Fined $25, $50 And $100 In Three Assessments, And Suspended Without Pay Until He Gets In Condition." The brief account reported that President Robison had levied fines on July 30 for three instances of drunkenness and concluded, "Threats and coaxing, it is said, have proved unavailing with Sockalexis, and he has persisted in going his own way."[26] *Sporting Life* framed the news with a more subtle but perhaps more humiliating perspective: "Sockalexis has been fined by the Cleveland club various sums aggregating $175 for dissipation and has suspended him without pay until such time as he shall come to his senses."[27]

Sporting News quoted the Cleveland owner more extensively on the matter. President Robison stated: "It was reported to me quite early in the season, soon after Sockalexis had been secured by the Cleveland club, that he had been in such a condition but pleaded extenuating circumstances and promised to abstain from then on. For a time I heard no more stories, but lately it has come to my ears that he has been drinking a good deal, and I received indisputable evidence today that he had been intoxicated two nights this week."[28]

Providing an overview of the league and its drinking players, author Luke Salisbury offered this perspective:

The 1890s have a reputation, doubtless enhanced by John McGraw's many years of talking to New York newspapermen, as the roughest, drunkest, brawlingest decade in the game's history. There's no question that the game was rough — ballplayers have always been a hard-drinking, and now a hard-drugging, lot — but judging from Sockalexis's disappearance from the Spiders lineup, when drink affected a man's performance, he didn't play. By August, Sockalexis was a disaster. It didn't take long for the press to gloat. After all, he was now living out the stereotype of the drunken Indian. No longer was Louis Sockalexis a natural man and country boy, no longer was he some Huckleberry Finn "noble savage" with a touch of Horatio Alger; he turned into Huck's gutter-drunk Pap before their very eyes, and it only proved what they'd known all along about Indians. A Providence paper summed it all up with a pun: "Curved balls are not the sort of benders that have kept the Red man down."[29]

In an unflinching editorial the July 22 edition of the *Cleveland Plain Dealer* said: "It is no longer a secret that the local management can no longer control Sockalexis and when that management once loses control of a player it is likely to be 'all off' between said management and said player. This is an unfortunate fact for the team and also for Sockalexis. When the Indian came here he was ambitious and his head was level. He was courted by a pretty lively crowd and then the troubles began. Discipline had no effect. When a player begins to realize that he is the whole thing nothing can stop him."[30]

The editorial concluded, "Manager Tebeau still has hopes that the great Indian will come to his senses, and it is to be hoped that he will. He is likely to see that his popularity depends upon his ability as a player, and will not last after that ability is gone. If Sockalexis takes proper care of himself, his baseball career is bound to be a most brilliant one. If not, he will soon find that he was a nine-days wonder and that the nine days have passed. It will not take many days to decide the fate of Cleveland's great find."[31]

After playing New York from July 26 to 28, Cleveland's long home stand concluded, leaving the team in fifth place. With a record of 43 wins, 34 losses, the team departed for Cincinnati and dropped two of three games with the Reds, July 30 – August 1.

When Cleveland departed for Cincinnati, the team called up Fred Cooke from the minor leagues and put him in Sockalexis's spot in right field. In Cincinnati, Cooke went hitless in his first game, had one hit in his second, and went hitless again in the third, prompting one unnamed pundit to offer this early, caustic observation: "Cooke is no Chief Sockalexis but he causes a lot less trouble. But then, who doesn't?"[32]

Cleveland moved on to Louisville, August 2–4, where the Indians lost three out of four to the Colonels. In the first game of a doubleheader on Wednesday, August 4, Cleveland forfeited the game after Jesse Burkett was thrown out in the second inning for arguing a strike called against him by an umpire with the colorful name of Chicken Wolf, who was a former top player himself. Burkett had a reputation for contentiousness. According to author Robert Smith, Burkett gained the nickname the Crab because "he used to trade insults with spectators who tried to heckle him."[33] Umpire Wolf declared the forfeit because, after waiting for five minutes, captain Tebeau still refused to send up a pinch hitter for Burkett. In the second game that day, the Indians played with lackluster disinterest behind another minor league pitching prospect, left-hander Charlie Brown from the Dayton club. In the ninth inning, losing 7–4, another heated exchange between Burkett and umpire Wolf led to the player's expulsion. When Burkett refused to leave first base, Wolf called two police officers, who forcibly removed Burkett from the grounds. McAllister was back in right field, and Sockalexis "sat on the bench as usual."[34] After losing a makeup game in Cincinnati on August 5, the Indians dropped three in a row to the Colts in Chicago, August 6–8, and then returned to Cleveland to open a series with Pittsburgh.

Umpiring remained a serious problem throughout the league. Jack Sheridan quit in early August, saying that he could no longer endure the abuse. Bob Emslie was hurt in Washington and feared he had serious internal damage. In Boston, Tom Lynch ejected Orioles players Joe Kelley and "Dirty Jack" Doyle for cursing him. When Doyle continued to berate him with "such an astonishing vocabulary," Lynch attacked him, and the police had to separate them. Tim Hurst, who earlier in the year was not afraid to wade alone into an angry mob at Cleveland and fight them all, was charged with assault in Cincinnati. Out on $300 bail, he traveled to St. Louis to work the Pirates–Brown game. During the first inning at Sportsman's Park, he was approached by two detectives who told him he was under arrest on a new charge: assault with intent to kill. Hurst apparently had "to beg" the detectives to let him finish the game, which they did. He was then arrested and held without bail. Even Browns' team officials could not secure his release. Hurst was to be sent back to Cincinnati, where he was accused of "crowning" a local firefighter with a beer glass. The man was reportedly in critical condition. In St. Louis, Hurst was released on $500 bond. He was ultimately found guilty of assault and battery and fined $100 and costs in police court in Cincinnati.[35]

League president Nick Young was reportedly sending out telegrams trying to find substitute umpires. Even after the season ended, the criticism did not: Washington manager Tom Brown argued that umpires should stop the practice of leaving home plate to call balls and strikes from behind the pitcher when there were runners on base.

Returning to Cleveland, the Indians swept three games from Pittsburgh, from August 10 to 12. In the third game Sockalexis was "back in uniform and on the coaching line. He is expected to play soon."[36] And so he did. On Friday, August 13, Sockalexis returned to right field, had a hit, and threw out a runner in the 6–5 home victory over the St. Louis Browns. One paper said, "Sox can still throw the ball as was shown when he nailed Harley at second after the latter's . . . single."[37]

Louis Sockalexis was out of the next day's lineup for the opening game with St. Louis, replaced in right field by handyman Jack O'Connor. He would not play again until Sunday, September 12.

Cleveland split the last two games with St. Louis (August 14–15), then lost on successive days to minor league clubs in Toronto and Buffalo (August 17–18), but the team managed to beat the Orioles in two games out of three in Baltimore (August 19–21). On Sunday, August 22, on a day off, manager Patsy Tebeau was quoted as saying that he did not want "to dump" Sockalexis and that the Indian "will stay if he finds some common sense or his thirst abates. Sox seems repentant."[38]

Cleveland churned through its August schedule on the road, losing two games to the Giants in New York (August 23–25), splitting four games with the Beaneaters in Boston (August 26–28, August 30), suffering another embarrassing exhibition loss (12–1) to a minor league team from Pawtucket in Providence (August 29), and losing three out of four games to the Grooms in Brooklyn (August 31–September 1).

Not until the team reached Philadelphia and beat the Phillies 7–5 on Saturday, September 4, did another report about Sockalexis finally surface. A Cleveland newspaper said, "His thirst satiated and his wheel mended, Chief Sockalexis is ready to reclaim his job from Jack O'Connor." The story also reported on Sockalexis's famous pitching challenger: "Although he's lost his thunderbolt fastball of old, Amos Rusie is winning by pitching scientifically. He's 22–8."[39] *The Washington Post* announced that Cleveland and Philadelphia had agreed on a trade at the end of the season that would bring star slugging outfielder Ed Delahanty to the Indians. The *Post* boldly predicted that Cleveland's outfield lineup for 1898 would feature Burkett, Delahanty, and Sockalexis.

Early September saw Cleveland split a doubleheader with the Phillies in Philadelphia (September 6), then lose a doubleheader in New York (September 7). In Washington (September 8) the team dropped a doubleheader, and then, on September 9 and 10, lost two more games in Washington before returning to Cleveland. The team's record fell to 57 wins, 59 losses, but Cleveland remained in fifth place.

Playing at home on Sunday, September 12, Sockalexis returned to the lineup and reclaimed his post in right field. Cleveland won an easy 15–4 victory, clobbering the St. Louis Browns with twenty-two hits. Batting eighth in the order, Sockalexis delivered two hits, including a double, and scored a run. He had one put-out in the field and committed no errors. One paper said, "Sox was the happiest man in town after the game. He had played ball again, and played well." [40] That happiness was to prove short-lived.

Sockalexis was in the lineup the next day, Monday, September 13, when Cleveland barely held off a late St. Louis rally to take a 7–6 victory, and the team evened its overall record, 59 wins, 59 losses. Sockalexis had one hit in four at bats and committed two errors in the field. A newspaper account reported: "The Indian hit the ball unluckily. He had but one fielding chance, the ball bounding away from him awkwardly. He still lacks his old speed." [41]

The game, Sockalexis's sixty-sixth, would prove to be his last league performance of the 1897 season. The next day, Cleveland concluded its series with St. Louis, taking an 8–1 victory that marked the end of Cy Young's personal losing streak and brought his record to 19 wins, 20 losses. The game account said: "Sox sat on the bench and he is lame again." [42]

More problems with that original foot injury, suffered back on the fourth of July, were blamed for ending Sockalexis's year. *Sporting Life* offered this bleak assessment, "The latest in regards to Sockalexis is that the joints at the ankle are becoming rigid and the Indian may be permanently disabled. His foot has been subjected to an x-ray test." [43] The view was far less devastating, however, in a follow-up blurb the next week in the national sporting publication: "Sockalexis had his lame foot x-rayed Saturday. No bones are broken but there is interior inflammation that must subside before he plays ball again." [44]

The reports are confusing. Clearly Sockalexis had an injured foot that had not fully recovered. He had also been suspended for drinking. Were Cleveland officials still trying to cover up Sockalexis's drinking problem using the injury as an excuse? The "permanently disabled" assessment was an overstatement. Sockalexis apparently played in a Cleveland benefit game at the end of that week.

After the St. Louis series sweep, the team was idle on Wednesday and rained out of its series opener with Cincinnati on Thursday, September 16. On Friday, Cleveland pounded the Reds, 14–3. In right field, Sockalexis was replaced by Ira Belden, a twenty-three-year-old sandlot player from Cleveland who delivered a single and a triple in the game and fielded well.

Cleveland swept a double-header on Saturday, September 18, that saw Cy Young serve a no-hitter, a feat not seen in the league since 1893. An error by shortstop Ed McKean and two miscues by third baseman Bobby Wallace allowed three batters to reach base, and Young walked one man. With those exceptions, the game was perfect, and the 6–0 victory also allowed Young to even his record to 20 wins, 20 losses.

Cleveland had no league game scheduled for Sunday, but a short item in the *Cleveland Press* on Friday, September 17, discussed plans for a game to benefit local coal miners that Sunday in which Sockalexis was scheduled to play. Tebeau invited a number of well-known amateurs to help fill the rosters of the two teams that were to play at the Indians' home park. The "Indians" lineup included Young (pitcher), Criger (catcher), Burkett (center fielder), Tebeau (third baseman), Cuppy (first baseman), McKean (shortstop), McAllister (right fielder), Belden (left fielder), and Gilman (second baseman). For the "Redman" squad, the lineup was Powell (pitcher), Zimmer (catcher), O'Connor (second baseman), Wilson (first baseman), Wallace (shortstop), Pickering (third baseman), Sockalexis (center fielder), Murray (left fielder), and Hamilton (right fielder). No game summary was published of this intersquad exhibition game, but reports about Sockalexis being "permanently disabled" or physically unable to play were clearly wrong.[45]

From the beginning of the home stand in Cleveland on Sunday, September 12, the Indians raced off on a hot streak and won 12 straight games, carrying them into a season-ending series with Pittsburgh on October 1–2. The team lost a double-header on Friday, as well as the season finale on Saturday. In the final game of the year, Harry Blake, the player Sockalexis had replaced at the start of the year, filled the Indian's position in right field. Blake was called back from the minors, where he had been learning to hit curve balls. With 69 wins and 62 losses, the Indians claimed a disappointing fifth-place finish in the 1897 league standings.

On Wednesday, October 6, Cleveland announced its reserve list for the next season: Young, O'Connor, Childs, Cuppy, McKean, Wallace, Wilson, Blake, Zimmer, Burkett, L. W. McAllister, Criger, Powell, J. McAllister, Belden, Jones, Pickering, "and L.F. Sockalexis."[46] That mysterious "J. McAllister," who never once appeared on the Cleveland roster of 1897, offers a fascinating, possible solution to a riddle that may never be answered. For, as author Phillips speculated, he might be the Jack McAllister who, according to the *Official Encyclopedia of Baseball*, played as "Andy Coakley," beginning in 1902.[47] Coakley is the author of the most famous and most repeated quote about how good a player Sockalexis was. Apparently first reported in Hughie Jennings's syndicated column of 1926, Coakley's stunning appraisal went this way: "Sockalexis was the greatest ball player I ever saw... [He] had a gorgeous lefthand swing, hit the ball as far as Babe Ruth, was faster than Ty Cobb and as good a base runner. He had the outfielding skill of Tris Speaker and threw like Meusel, which means that no one could throw a ball farther or more accurately."[48] Coakley, a Rhode Island native who wound up as the long-time baseball coach at Columbia University, was a stellar member of the outstanding pitching staffs of Connie Mack's powerful Philadelphia Athletics from 1902 to 1907. The only problem with the potential link is that, according to official records, Coakley was born in 1882, making him only fifteen at the time of Sockalexis's brief, shining moment in the national spotlight.[49] He was born on November 20, 1882 in Providence, Rhode Island.

On Wednesday, October 6, the Orioles beat Boston 8 – 3 in a "dull" Temple Cup opener. Baltimore clinched the league championship on Monday, October 11, behind Bill Hoffer's 9 – 3 victory.

The 1897 batting champion was Oriole Willie Keeler, who had an outstanding .425 average. In spite of one deep slump, Big Ed Delahanty hit .350, and was not traded to Cleveland in the off-season. After a brief suspension for "intoxication on the field," Sockalexis's fellow rookie sensation, Napoleon "Larry" Lajoie, ended his first season as Philadelphia's first baseman with an impressive .375 batting average. The league's home run champion was Hugh Duffy of Boston, who collected 11.

After the 1897 season, Texas native Lew "Sport" McAllister threatened not to return in 1898. McAllister wrote a letter about the printing office he ran in Fort Worth and said that he was "inclined to stick to it next year unless he gets more money." A columnist in *Sporting Life* wrote: "He deserves it. A pitcher, catcher, first, second and third baseman, short stop and right, centre and left fielder, is rarely combined in one man."[50] Lew McAllister did return to Cleveland for 1898 and played primarily as a pitcher.

It had been an up-and-down year for baseball drunks. After getting off to a stellar pitching start, Louisville lefty "Still Bill" Hill, said to be "suffering from bad encounter with Kentucky firewater," was "furloughed for a month to get himself in shape" without pay. Hill was the man who surrendered the first two hits Sockalexis collected in his major league career. Philadelphia fined "Brewery Jack" Taylor for intoxication and supposedly suspended him for the season. He pitched against the Senators, however, soon afterward and had one of his better performances. Boston pitcher and outfielder "Happy Jack" Stivetts, available and largely unwanted by any of the teams at the beginning of the year, had reformed and was said to be "taking good care of himself." After pitching one particularly good game and winning, he reportedly begged his manager to be allowed to have one beer. His pleased manager told him, "You can have two."[51]

The 1897 record book shows that in his first major league season Louis Sockalexis delivered 97 hits in 278 at bats, a .338 average in just sixty-six games. He collected 3 home runs, 8 triples, 42 runs batted in, and stole 16 bases. In the outfield, he had 117 put-outs, 10 assists, and had committed 17 errors, eight of those coming in his last ten games.[52] By the season's end, the *Cleveland Plain Dealer* called him "a broken idol." In summary author Luke Salisbury wrote, "Sockalexis excited the cranks in a way no other rookie ever had, but he disappeared into the Indian burial ground of the bottle, and remains, even now, a riddle."[53]

10
The Great Lie

ACCLAIMED AS THE league's hottest attraction after playing for only three months during the season of 1897, Louis Sockalexis appeared ready to become one of the greatest baseball players of his day. The once derisive reference to the Cleveland ball club as "Indians" evolved from caricature to respect. Former Baltimore star Hughie Jennings, who retired from the game to become a professional spinner of baseball tales and legends, wrote about the phenomenon in his syndicated column "Rounding Third" in 1926. Jennings claimed hyperbolically that "rarely a game passed that was not featured by spectacular exhibitions of hitting, base running or fielding by the Indian. I do not believe there was a day when his name was not in the headlines, for his big play generally decided the game."[1] Yet as quickly as the wave of excitement crested, it collapsed. Jennings attributed the "fall" to events in Chicago; he was not referring to the infamous drop from a second-floor window in the late hours of July fourth when Sockalexis hurt his foot.

"The turning point in his career came in Chicago," wrote Jennings, as the result of heroics in the opening game of the series. It was the top of the ninth, with Cleveland trailing 3 – 0. The bases were loaded, with two men out, when Sockalexis came to bat. In the fashion of the storybook hero Frank Merriwell for whom he is widely believed to have served as the prototype, Sockalexis hit a grand slam home run, and his team took the field with a 4 – 3 lead, Jennings related. In the bottom half of the ninth, with two men on base and two out, a Chicago batter smashed a ball on a rising line, apparently perfectly placed between the fielders. Playing shallow to cut off the tying run, Sockalexis had to race back and far to the side. At the last possible moment, Jennings recounted, Sockalexis hurled himself parallel to the ground and made a sensational, one-handed catch in midair. It saved the game.

Fans, well-wishers, and teammates alike "carried him off the field on their shoulders" and headed directly to a nearby bar to celebrate, Jennings wrote, adding that these fans coaxed the hero until Sockalexis "gave in and accepted his first drink. It was the first taste he ever had of liquor, and he liked it. He liked the effects even better, and from that time on Sockalexis was a slave to whiskey. He would never break free from his desire for liquor. He had to have it, and schemed and plotted to get it. The rise of Sockalexis was rapid, but not any more rapid than his fall. He was drunk practically all the time and was no longer any use to the Cleveland team."[2]

The story, excepting the elements concerning Sockalexis's tragic alcohol addiction, bears little resemblance to the truth. In a 1986 Society for American Baseball Research story "The Rise and Fall of Louis Sockalexis," Jay Feldman wrote, "Great tale that it is, there are only two small problems with Jennings's story: (1) Except for a single grain of truth, it's total fabrication; (2) from 1926 on, everyone who wrote about Sockalexis took the Jennings fable as gospel, and with subsequent embellishments this concocted incident became one of the cornerstones of the Sockalexis legend — the unquestioned beginning of his swift and irreversible slide — and in this form it has survived to the present day."[3]

In fact, not one of Sockalexis's three major league home runs was hit against Chicago, nor were any of them hit under circumstances even remotely like those suggested in the Jennings story. Feldman concluded that Jennings had confused events from a three-game series in St. Louis, where on consecutive days Sockalexis made a great catch in the ninth to preserve a tie, smashed a titanic home run (in a 12 – 4 rout), and then had four hits in five at bats, including a triple with the bases loaded, leading Cleveland to an 8 – 3 win.

There is one game that comes closer to encompassing all the heroics Jennings described: the Indians' 6 – 5 win over Chicago in Cleveland on May 7. In that game Sockalexis slapped three singles, a triple, walked, stole two bases, scored two runs, and produced five put-outs, among them "a one-handed running catch of a line drive with two on bases." That game victory was preserved for Cleveland with a "game-saving" catch in the ninth inning, but outfielder Jesse Burkett made it.[4]

Although specious, Jennings's story "explained" Sockalexis's tragic introduction to liquor and his subsequent abuse of it. Lacking a more authoritative story, Jennings's tale surfaced in articles about Sockalexis for more than a half century after the 1926 column appeared. Other writers failed to research the Indian's documented use of alcohol. Some sources claim that he was disciplined for drinking at Holy Cross; it is a matter of record that he was expelled because of it at Notre Dame. Further, one of his three Cleveland baseball contracts — perhaps even his first one — had a proviso forbidding drinking because it was already well established that he did imbibe.

Why do we not know the truth? It seems evident that the Cleveland club, particularly owner Robison and manager Tebeau, had tried to keep Sockalexis's difficulties with liquor private, and he was given repeated opportunities to reform during the course of the 1897 season. In his first official statement, reported on July 31 in newspapers around the country, Robison alluded to a first incident "early in the season" and said that "for a time" he heard no more before the rash of reports of intoxication that had led to the suspension.[5] Tebeau acknowledged repeated failed promises from Sockalexis because "he couldn't let the strong stuff alone."[6] Because of his playing talent and perhaps because he seemed genuinely contrite and persuasive about his willingness to change, Sockalexis received second, third, and fourth chances. This pattern would repeat itself several more times before Sockalexis left Cleveland for good.

Feldman speculated that "the foot injury, then, which forced him out of the lineup, was in all probability the catalyst for Sockalexis hitting the skids. When he was playing every day, he was able to hold his drinking to a manageable level, but sitting on the bench, he could no longer keep it together."[7]

Salisbury believes that Sockalexis "probably got hurt," but he points out that in the nineteenth century, reports of sports injuries were often less than credible. He writes: "It's difficult to learn about injuries from 1890s papers because of the use of euphemisms. If a man had 'malaria,' chances were good he actually had venereal disease. 'Pneumonia' frequently stood for what in Boston is still referred to as 'Irish pneumonia,' which means complications arising from alcoholism. Sockalexis probably did get hurt, and then the question is, why did he not recover? Drink is undoubtedly part of the answer. Something happened over the Fourth of July. Sockalexis may have gone on a spree and hurt himself. What effect the war whoops, foot stomping, 'ki-yi's,' and feathers had on him one can only surmise. We know he drank in college, and maybe he drank more when he saw the bright lights of the big league. He may have played while drunk and hurt. Sockalexis was either driven by demons, divinely indifferent to his talent, or sickened at some level he may not have understood by being so good at the white man's favorite game."[8]

Perhaps he really did wilt in the absence of genuine laughter and friendship, seeking it in bars and brothels instead. It is not clear how successfully Sockalexis fit in socially with the Cleveland team. There is never any mention that he had friends on the club, only the recurring reports that several of the players were jealous of him and even mocked him in front of rival players. Just a few years later, the great "Shoeless Joe" Jackson endured very similar treatment throughout his playing days in Chicago and, ironically enough, earlier in Cleveland. Jackson was routinely mocked for his illiterate Southern country-boy naïveté. Though universally admired for his playing ability, he found himself virtually friendless in the daily exercise of his profession. (In his first year in major league baseball, Jackson actually abandoned his team, "homesick" for his native South Carolina.)

During the 1897 season, on June 8, the *Cleveland Press* carried an account of an American Indian who graduated from Harvard College, where he played baseball, but ultimately decided that there was "no living" in the white man's world for the Indian. Under the headline, "Is Civilization A Failure? Then And Now," the brief account reported: "John Redbird is a Cheyenne Indian. He went to Harvard college and was graduated. He played lawn tennis and base ball. He wore golf stockings. In the Cheyenne uprising in the northwest, Redbird is prominent. He is living in the teepees of the Indians, as did his forefathers. He has become an Indian in reality again. Redbird says there is no living among white people for a man with Indian blood in his veins."[9] Perhaps at the end of the nineteenth century that was true for Sockalexis as well, just as his father had feared.

Perhaps athletic jealousy or racial ostracism on the part of his Cleveland teammates was a factor. One story, cited by John Phillips, even suggested "a conspiracy" on the part of Cleveland players to undermine Sockalexis.[10] The idea was attributed to Washington owner Earl Wagner, who allowed his players to be arrested in order to challenge Sunday ball playing in Cleveland. The team had apparently agreed to help Cleveland mount a second challenge before the matter was temporarily settled in court. Wagner and Washington players said they observed Sockalexis enduring miserable treatment from his teammates. In an account after Cleveland's victory over Louisville, 16 – 5, on Tuesday, August 3, Phillips quoted Wagner as saying, "It looks as if Sockalexis was the victim of a deeply laid plot and that the Spiders are bent on boycotting" him. Wagner added:

> When I was in Cleveland on the last western trip, I noticed that Jesse Burkett and Jack O'Connor mildly joshed the redskin whenever he came to the bat. O'Connor yelled from the coach line to [Washington pitcher] Doc McJames, "Say there Doc, give him a slow one opposite across the tops of his golf socks. Lob it up to him." Perhaps the notoriety the papers gave Sock is the cause of the ill feeling against the son of the Penobscots. They tell me that Sock has more mash notes from the ladies than any matinee favorite the diamond has seen, not even barring Lee Viau. If the players under Tebeau cannot get along without joshing the Poor Lo there is but one thing for Tebeau to do, and that is to release or exchange him.[11]

Perhaps Sockalexis covered up the treatment he received from Burkett and the others on the team, but in the one interview in which he acknowledged the reports of jealousy, Sockalexis made a point of saying that they were not true, noting that Burkett had encouraged Cleveland to sign him. In addition, Sockalexis had played for Burkett at Holy Cross and Notre Dame. It seems unlikely that jealousy or problems with other players on the team were an issue. After all, Sockalexis returned to a Cleveland comprised of many of the same players in 1898.

Perhaps it was Sockalexis himself who created the story to camouflage his drinking problem and to help set the stage for more exceptions and sympathy. Sportswriters did little research. They seemed to accept anecdotes from management and players without question, even embellishing them to help with grammar and stylistic polish. Some of the quotations attributed to players sound more like the words of literary masters than rough-and-tumble ball players. Few players in that era or for several more decades had a college education. Baseball was regarded as lowbrow entertainment, a carnival, where drinking and betting were part of the fun. There is almost no evidence of writers like Jennings or Cleveland's Elmer Bates checking the accuracy of the stories they reported. And they could be quite susceptible to a con. One example is the story told about Sockalexis attributed to umpire Bob Emslie about a July 12 game in Cleveland. Unfortunately, Emslie was overseeing a game in Pittsburgh on the Monday the incident took place in Cleveland. Still, Emslie's telling of the tale is engaging:

> Sockalexis is far from a finished artist in practicing deception, or the "shooting the bull con," as Dad Clarke [a comic pitcher of limited ability in the league] puts it. In Monday's game at Cleveland, there was a cluster of glad hands when Sock beat out a bunt. Then in a few innings, Chick Stahl shoved a ball into the redskin's reservation. Sock booted it, juggled it, hit it and kicked it, and Pat Tebeau yelled to him, "Just cut that out a minute till I send you a pair of boxing gloves and you can scrap all you want with it." Sock's juggling act cost two runs and the game. When Sock returned to the bench, his head dropped and he was as mute as Dummy Hoy [an outfielder in the league who was a mute]. Tebeau asked him if he was studying up an excuse. "Yes, my foot is sore. Can't I quit, Cap?" said Sock. It was the redskin's error that gave him a sore foot. Twenty minutes before he flirted with Stahl's hit, he beat out a bunt at a rate of 10 seconds per 100 yards.[12]

One message is clear from the aftermath of the 1897 baseball season: Story after story carried expressions of regret and contrition from Sockalexis while owner Robison and manager Patsy Tebeau expressed their optimism about the Indian's future.

On September 18, under the headline "Sox Is Fixture On The Team," the *Cleveland Press* quoted captain Tebeau saying that Sockalexis would be Cleveland's "regular right fielder" next season. "The red man is anxious to play ball and to let side issues alone, and Patsy believes in giving him a chance."[13] A further pronouncement came in the October 8 issue of the *Cleveland Press* under the headline: "Old Sox Promises Patsy He'll Be Good

Next Season." The story claimed that Sockalexis would play for the team the following season, citing the

> authoritative and somewhat triumphant announcement of Manager Tebeau, Friday. Patsy and Sox had just had a "session." The captain of the Indians told the red man that he wanted him on his team in '98; that he would pay him well, and that the salary limit was in his reach. Only the Indian must be good, reserving his hilarity for the long "between seasons" period. Sox promised faithfully. Patsy believes he will keep his word. "I shall not be back in Cleveland before Feb. 1, '98," said Tebeau. "I wanted to see just how Sox felt. I think he is truly penitent, and that we can depend on him now. He will be an immense help to us if he plays ball in '98 as he is capable of doing."[14]

A number of newspapers and sporting publications carried similar accounts. The October *Sporting News*, in a report about "star players" who ran into difficulty with drinking problems, offered this summary for Sockalexis, who was being included in the Cleveland team preview for the 1898 season and "planned on" for right field. Under the headline: "Went Against Booze," the story read: "Sockalexis, who started out Phaeton-like, to set the world on fire and did so, failed to prove the able lieutenant that Tebeau expected. Fire water, persons of the feminine gender and late hours were greater attractions for the Indian collegian than was the straight and narrow path of the base lines, and the result was that a valuable right fielder was lost to the team at the time when his services were most needed."[15]

In *Sporting Life* for the first week in November, Elmer E. Bates wrote: "President Robison's only bit of news when I called on him to-day consisted of a letter from Sockalexis, who six months ago was the most-talked-of player in the big League. It was not the need of advance money that prompted the red man to take his pen in hand. He wrote Mr. Robison to thank him for his kindness to him and ask that right field be reserved for him for next season. The Indian said he had enough of folly and next season would pay Mr. Robison and Captain Tebeau back for their favors to him, and help the team win the flag."[16]

Comparing in retrospect the impact and the outcome of drinking on the careers of Sockalexis and Baseball Hall of Famer Napoleon Lajoie shows the tragedy and triumph that are possible. *Sporting News* in early October carried an intriguing profile headlined: "Booze Did It, Experience Of Two Young Stars In 1897, Lajoie and Sockalexis Began Finely, But Fell By The Wayside." The article began: "Two young stars who entered the National League within the last 12 months with the most brilliant prospects have almost thrown away their fortunes by the excessive use of liquor. One is Lajoie of the Philadelphia club. The other is Sockalexis, the much talked of player on the Indian team. Both were recognized as players who had abilities to stay among the major stars from the outset. Neither could stand flattery and success. Probably they had the love of strong drink before they reached the goal of their ambition in the baseball profession, and their success among the top notchers set that love on a riot run." Under the subhead "How Lajoie Lost It," Philadelphia's problems were detailed:

> Lajoie, early in the year, was looked upon as a probable candidate for leading batsman of the profession. By his indiscretion he killed off any such chance which he might have had. His crowning offense was to appear upon the field in uniform in such a decided state of intoxication that every spectator in the stands recognized his condition. He was suspended indefinitely and fined. Then the Philadelphia club made the general mistake which, oft repeated, has done more than any one thing to encourage breaches of discipline in the profession. A few days later it found its team badly crippled by accidents and sickness. Lajoie's indefinite suspension was removed and he went back upon the team.

The second section, under the subhead "Became A Bad Indian," dealt with Sockalexis:

> The case of Sockalexis is almost as deplorable as that of Lajoie. He entered the big league under the most flattering conditions. His ballplaying, particularly his batting, surprised the veterans of the profession. Then the fact that he was a full-blood Indian, though highly educated and possessed of all the refinements of a white man, made him doubly a hero in every city where the Cleveland team played. Suddenly his heavy batting declined, his fielding became ragged, and his playing in general ranged from poor to bad. Finally he dropped out of the nine entirely. The real cause was for a while suppressed. A bad ankle was the excuse given the public but the facts cannot be strangled and the truth went abroad. Sockalexis had succumbed to the curse which had been the bane of his nationality ever since civilization in America put whiskey in the reach of the aborigines. Sockalexis admitted it himself and seemed to be determined to redeem his great error. What is the queerest part about his case is his claim that until he became a ballplayer he did not know the taste of whiskey. But when he rose to be a hero and a public pet his admirers surrounded him. They must do him homage. Mere flattery is not sufficient. More seemed to be required to show their admission for the young Indian ballplayer.

Then, under the subhead "Whiskey," the article concluded: "Indians instinctively like whiskey. Sockalexis was importuned to join us. His first refusals were soon broken down. A step was taken. All the national love of

106

firewater lying dormant in his soul flamed out and the famous new star of the baseball field went out like a meteor."[17]

The perspective of time allows us to appreciate the link between Sockalexis and Lajoie. Both came up as rookies in the same year, 1897. Both quickly created sensational records, climbing to the top of the batting averages, but drinking just as quickly threatened their respective careers. Sockalexis was ruined, but Lajoie overcame his problem.

Lajoie came to play for Cleveland, where the popular star and player-manager saw the team nicknamed the "Naps" in his honor (Napoleon "Nap" Lajoie) following a fan contest in 1903. After a long and illustrious career, Lajoie left Cleveland in 1914 to finish out his Hall of Fame career in Philadelphia, where it had begun in 1897.

Impoverished and sick, Sockalexis died in 1913 and did not live to see the Cleveland team adopt the nickname Indians in 1915, following Lajoie's departure. "Indians" became Cleveland's only official nickname, and its origins unquestionably rest with Penobscot Indian Louis Sockalexis. As a result, Cleveland is the only major league team nicknamed for a specific player.

Today Lajoie's likeness appears on a plaque in the Baseball Hall of Fame in Cooperstown, New York, whereas Sockalexis's likeness, if it is connected to him at all, is most often linked to a ridiculous grinning American Indian caricature called Chief Wahoo, who appears as the image of the Cleveland baseball franchise.

11
Good Intentions Drown

N SPITE OF the anticlimactic end to his baseball playing in 1897, Sockalexis continued to attract attention after the season. In January of 1898 *Sporting Life* sent an editor to Old Town, Maine, to observe Sockalexis in his role as "groomsman" at the marriage of two notable Penobscot natives. The playfully mocking headline read: "The Gallant Socks, A Prominent Figure In A Function Of Civilization, The Famous Indian Player Acts As Groomsman At The Wedding Of Guide John Ranco To The Indian Maiden, Josephine Newell." The story reported that 400 guests "reveled" at the wedding, adding, "It was exclusive in the highest degree. Sockalexis was the groomsman, Miss Fly Rod, the bridesmaid, and only the big chiefs and hunters and guides of real renown received invitations." Under the subhead "The Real Hero," the writer claimed:

> But although the bride was the handsomest maiden on the island, and the groom a redskin Phoebus Appolo [*sic*], the gaunt Sockalexis and his white partner attracted the lion's share of attention from the assembled braves and woodsmen. The distinguished right fielder was recognized as a son of the tribe who sailed forth among the palefaces and caused the name of Penobscot to be recognized on all the bleacheries in the continent. As for Cornelia T. Crosby — Miss Fly Rod — there was not a red man there who did not delight to honor her.

Sockalexis's sophisticated style of dress impressed the writer. "The marriage was solemnized in St. Joseph's Catholic Church, Oldtown, by Rev. Father Cleary, whose priestly vestments added another note to the incongruity between the picturesque forest garb of the bridal pair and the irreproachably urban dress of Sockalexis — a flowing frock coat and accessories which looked as if they might have been made by a Fifth Avenue tailor." That the guests admired Sockalexis was evident in the text of a section with the subhead "Socks The Social Lion." It noted,

> Many were the questions with which Sockalexis, the real hero of the occasion, was pressed, and his old comrades refused to be satisfied with narratives of his exploits on the base ball field and his adventures in far cities. In the dancing, that was one of the best features of the reception, the tawny right fielder and Miss Fly Rod were frequent partners, and a more graceful pair never flitted over a waxed floor than the man of savage blood, with a civilized exterior and

education, and the daughter of civilization who elects to spend her days in the wilds with rifle and rod.

The writer explained the fame of Maine's legendary guide "Fly Rod" Crosby, under a subhead "A White Friend." It read: "Cornelia T. Crosby attracted a great deal of attention during the Sportsman Exposition at Madison Square Garden, last spring. She had charge of the Maine camp." Of her, Sockalexis was quoted as saying: "Her face is white, but her heart is the heart of a brave."[1]

Before the 1898 baseball season, Sockalexis had assured the press and his team that he had beaten his drinking problem. It would take only twenty-one games and a paltry .224 batting average to show that his promises were empty. He would never play more than four consecutive games during the entire season.

Before Sockalexis boarded the train for spring training in Hot Springs, Arkansas, his drinking problem surfaced anew. Several days before the team left Cleveland, Sockalexis disappeared and then missed the train south. He arrived two days late. A *Cleveland Plain Dealer* article on March 14 quoted his apology to playing captain Tebeau, "'I did it again, Cap,' said Sock to the manager sadly. 'A crowd got hold of me and before I knew it they had loaded me. I had not taken a drop in so long that I did not know my capacity, and before I knew it they had me. I am through for good now. My friends in Cleveland are my worst enemies, I fear, even though they don't mean to be. After this I will defy anybody to get me started.'"[2] The refrain, however, was wearing thin with the papers. On April 1, the *Plain Dealer* sniped, "All this talk by Sockalexis would have more weight had not the Indian told the same story before on several occasions."[3]

Curiously, Sockalexis didn't seem to be trying any harder on the field than he did off it. This was apparent even during spring training at Hot Springs. He was in a battle for his position in right field with old rival Harry Blake and 1897 late-season replacement Ollie Pickering. Though neither could approach Sockalexis's ability at the plate, both were clearly out-hustling him and jeopardizing his very place on the team.

The writer for the *Cleveland Plain Dealer* attacked: "There may be an excuse for a fielder dropping a ball, but there is no excuse for his shirking it, and the Indian shirks. He is the only candidate for the right field position who seems to think that the team could not get along without him. Blake and Pickering are working like nailers. The former's fielding is as near perfect as fielding can be and the latter not only fields well but keeps up his good work in getting to base on apparently impossible chances."[4]

The fans, too, were fast losing patience with Sockalexis, waiting for the drinking to stop and the heroics to begin anew. The *Cleveland Plain Dealer* sharply contended that, in several additional ways, in 1898, Sockalexis was his own worst enemy: "The public seems to have a grudge against Sockalexis and will never be satisfied until he is driven out of the business. While there are no temptations put in his way here and he has shown no signs of another outbreak, the petting that did him so little good last season has already begun. His every move is 'jollied' by the crowds. A scratch hit by Sockalexis is the cause of more applause than a two-bagger by some other man. This would all be very well if it didn't affect Sockalexis, but it does. He is very susceptible to flattery, as Cleveland fans have observed, and it seems to make no difference whether the flattery comes from a few hundred persons at Hot Springs or from thousands on the league circuit. Sockalexis acts like a leading man in a cross-roads theatrical company…He poses in the field and seems to feel that all eyes are resting upon him; but worst of all, he does not play ball with his old-time vigor."[5] Tebeau apparently lit a fire under Sockalexis when he dropped him from the regulars' lineup in practice games, but listed him instead with the opposing group of rookies and bench players.

According to John Phillips, on the train north from spring training camp in Hot Springs to Cleveland, Sockalexis told a reporter:

> After wintering in the woods of Maine, it took the life out of me in a warm place like Hot Springs. I felt well but couldn't get ginger enough in my game. I am in good condition again and will play as well as ever. As to my falling by the wayside again, there is no chance for it. I made a fool of myself and I know it. Mr. Robison and Mr. Tebeau stuck to me longer than I deserved and I mean to repay them. When I get to Cleveland, I intend to get a place near the ball grounds to live at, and then I will not go downtown all the season. My mind is made up and it is no joke. I have a good future as a ballplayer and only have to take care of myself to keep in the game.[6]

Yet, according to an early June story in the *Milwaukee Journal*: "Sockalexis' thirst has not developed a leak since his painting red experience at Hot Springs. Unless Harry Blake's batting develops a slump Sock will act as an audience on the bench throughout the season."[7] Sockalexis's drinking was apparent to his team. Soon he was unable to hide it from the fans, who heckled him and were particularly merciless in their taunting about his fondness for "firewater." Worn down, perhaps from a combination of continuous drinking and his inability to stop, plus physical deterioration and the emotional toll from the taunting fans, Sockalexis played poorly and, seemingly, with indifference.

With the sinking of the U.S.S. *Maine* in Havana Harbor, the yellow journalism of Hearst's newspapers and others led inexorably to renewed patriotic fervor and cries for war. Even Sockalexis's patriotism was called into question, albeit jokingly. A column containing notes on professional baseball in the *Milwaukee Journal* of April 2 claimed: "Col. Sockalexis is now the title given to the Cleveland Indian. A yellow kid journal has wired asking him if he would enlist in case of war with Spain. Socks' patriotism does not seem to be very warm, for he replied that he would be if he could get command of a regiment of Penobscots and draw as much money as he is making out of baseball. He is of the opinion, however, that his tribe would be slow in putting on war paint and he prefers the ball bat to the war club."[8]

This specter of war made for a troubling national backdrop as the baseball teams prepared for the upcoming season. A preview in the *Cleveland Press* discussed two innovations that the twelve-team National League would unveil. For the first time, an additional umpire was to cover the calls on the bases (as suggested by Washington manager Tom Brown, for one), and sanctions were to be imposed to curtail foul language and the vulgar taunting of opponents. According to the *Press*:

> There are many innovations, this year, but none of them more important than the trial by the National league of the double umpire system — one man to judge balls and strikes behind the catcher, and the other to render base decisions. By the new rules, these umpires are regularly assigned to the cities in which they are to officiate, and are not to be changed on any ordinary pretext. The new blacklist resolution, calculated to put a stop to the use of sulphurous language on the ball field, is also in force, and many interesting complications are likely to arise.[9]

The attempt to control vile language was, of course, expected to cause concern for the rowdy and generally quite profane Cleveland team. Sockalexis playfully offered one solution: "I'll cuss the umpire in Penobscot. And if they call me I'll say that I was telling them that they are right and that you fellows are dead wrong in kicking." He reportedly also offered to teach his teammates Indian words to use on the umpires, including "hickehowgo" (robber), "kanylanyee" (green lobster) and others, presumably too vile to print. The appropriately nicknamed "Crab" Burkett, in particular, was said to have found the lesson purposeful.[10]

When Cleveland opened the 1898 season in Cincinnati on Friday, April 15, Sockalexis did not play in the 3 – 2 loss. Whether that decision resulted because his nemesis, left-hander Ted Breitenstein was pitching, he was being punished for misbehaving at Hot Springs, or because he was impaired is not clear. Blake took his place in right field.

The Cleveland team looked much as it had the year before. Young, Cuppy, Powell, Zeke Wilson, and Lew "Sport" McAllister (the versatile player who could play all nine positions) formed the pitching nucleus. Criger and O'Connor handled the catching. The infield was unchanged: Tebeau at first, Childs at second, Wallace at third, and McKean at shortstop. Burkett returned to his post in left field. The rumored trade for outfield slugger Ed Delahanty did not happen; however, Jimmy McAleer apparently overcame his sensitivity to fan criticism and returned to center field. Harry Blake played more right field than Sockalexis had ever intended. According to an April 22 anecdote from *Cleveland Press* sportswriter Elmer Bates, Blake's batting improved when he quit smoking: "Arguments against the use of the offensive cigaret lose none of their force when Harry Blake's case is considered. Since the Portsmouth boy cut out the penny pipes his batting has improved about 50 per cent."[11]

A game-by-game box score analysis by Society for American Baseball Research member Richard "Dixie" Tourangeau of Sockalexis's appearances during the 1898 season showed that he was in the lineup when Cleveland won the second game of the season-opening series with Cincinnati on Saturday, April 16. Batting leadoff and playing left field, Sockalexis had one hit in four at bats in the 3 – 1 victory. On Sunday, April 17, Cincinnati pounded Cleveland, 12 – 1, and Sockalexis again had one hit in four attempts. In the field he had three put-outs, with one of them culminating in an assist for a double play.

The team traveled to St. Louis, where its series with the Browns was plagued by poor weather. The games scheduled for April 18 and April 19 were cancelled because of rain.

A *Milwaukee Journal* note on professional baseball for April 30 probably explains why Sockalexis played during mid April: "Sockalexis has taken excellent proper care of himself. Burkett has left the team because of the death of child."[12] Sockalexis was installed in Burkett's usual left field position. The April 18 edition of the *Worcester* (Massachusetts) *Telegram* reported the death of Jesse and Nellie Burkett's infant (5 months, 26 days) son, John G., in Worcester, on April 17.[13] Burkett was out of the lineup from April 18 to April 22.

In an April 19 column for the *Cleveland Press*, Elmer E. Bates offered comments about players following their first series of games. Under the headline "Into Scraps, Sox Tore A Bundle Of Letters," Bates says:

When Sockalexis came down to breakfast, Sunday morning, the clerk at the Gibson handed him a bundle of what ball players term "mash notes." There were a dozen of them. Some were very delicate little things, with ribbons and monograms. The Indian grabbed the bunch in his left, and with his right paw tore them into fragments. "That's what old Sox thinks of you kind of people, this year," said the son of the forest, as he kicked the scraps of paper toward the grate. "I've chopped fire water, and I've chopped cigarets, and I guess I'm enough of a man to chop the kind of folks who write you friendly letters without knowing you. I'm working for Mr. Robison, now."[14]

Is it a true story? Was Sockalexis really trying to change his ways, or was this another public relations story planted by the team to ensure continued public interest in the Indian?

Later in the same column Bates writes: "Sockalexis is still a magnet. He is calculated to wheedle a good many extra dollars into the box office during the coming season. Hundreds of people come to the hotel every day to ask the red man if he will be in the game. The son of the Penobscots likes this patronizing display, and his good-natured bronze countenance wears one continual smile."[15]

Sockalexis was not the only player seduced by the allure of Cleveland's infamous "down town." As Bates notes: "O'Connor, Sockalexis, Blake and others are negotiating for 'stopping places' near the Dunham Avenue grounds. Jack [O'Connor] said last night, 'I'm not going down town once until the season is over. Then I'll probably stay three or four days; yes, maybe five.'"[16]

After two days of rain in St. Louis, Cleveland finally played again on Wednesday, April 20, and collected a 10 – 5 victory. Playing as a replacement for Burkett, Sockalexis was hitless in five at bats and made two put-outs in the outfield.

On Thursday, April 21, 1898, a special edition of the *Cleveland Press* trumpeted the news that war had officially begun with Spain. In St. Louis, rain kept Cleveland off the diamond again. Another *Cleveland Press* headline that day claimed, "Indians May Break Loose At Any Time," but the story had nothing to do with Cleveland baseball. Apparently troops from Fort Niobrara, Nebraska, had been redeployed to New Orleans, leaving only a corporal and five guards behind, yet "within 15 miles there are 1000 of the most warlike Indians in the world. The inhabitants of this section fear these bloodthirsty Indians if no troops are brought here." The account reported that a petition had been presented to the War Department, requesting that Third Cavalry troops, taken from Fort Meade to Fort Robinson, Nebraska, "be placed here to menace the Indians."[17]

On Thursday, April 22, Sockalexis had a big game as Cleveland defeated St. Louis 7 – 0. The outfielder had two hits in four at bats, including a double. He scored three runs and had one put-out in the field. This was the last game Burkett missed because of his child's death.

The game scheduled for April 23 was also rained out, and the team traveled to Louisville for an April 24 game, which would see Sockalexis absent from the Cleveland lineup, as he would be for twelve straight games. He did not play again until a May 9 contest at home against Chicago.

From April 24 to 27, Cleveland won three games out of four at Louisville, lost at Cincinnati on April 28, and then returned for a triumphant home opener with Cincinnati on April 29. The trip to Cincinnati proved anything but uneventful. The Cleveland players shared a train with a contingent of soldiers, on their way to deployment in the war against Spain. Sockalexis was apparently on his way to the smoking car to have a cigar. One of the new recruits mistook him for a Spaniard and heated words erupted into a brawl. The *Cleveland Plain Dealer* noted: "for about five minutes Uncle Sam's new candidates for military honors found in Socks the toughest proposition they ever tackled outside of a Missouri mule. He was simply chock full of fight and when the Rubes gave him the opening he was quick to take advantage of it." According to the newspaper, when Tebeau arrived to help separate the combatants, it was the soldiers who were the worse for the encounter.[18]

The team suffered a defeat to St. Louis on April 30, the same day that newspapers were reporting 400 deaths in the Philippines, which was involved in the conflict with Spain. Sockalexis played in only four of his team's twelve games during April, collecting just four hits in 17 at bats.

Cleveland had an open date on May 1 and was rained out on May 2, forcing a doubleheader at home with St. Louis on May 3, and the Indians swept it. A single game victory at home over Louisville on May 4 was followed by two straight rain-outs, forcing another doubleheader on May 7 that resulted in two more wins over Louisville.

The "Diamond Dust" column of the *Milwaukee Journal* for May 6 quotes Sockalexis about his response to fans' mock war whoops and jeering calls: "Sockalexis says that he doesn't mind in the least the war whoops, catcalls and yells that go up from the spectators every time he goes to bat. 'Had I cared they would have driven me out of the business long ago,' said Socks. 'I got it from the very first day I played. In fact, [teammate Jack] O'Connor got me used to it in practice. He used to get the other players to 'whoop it up' when we were training before the season opened.'"[19]

By the time Sockalexis returned to the lineup for a Monday, May 9, home contest with Chicago, the Cleveland club was off to an excellent twelve-win and five-loss start. Whether he was really ready to play or was merely pressed into service again, Sockalexis replaced center fielder Jimmy McAleer, who left the team to be with his pneumonia-stricken mother. Playing in center field and batting sixth, Sockalexis had one hit in four at bats and an uncommonly high seven put-outs in the field during an otherwise dismal 12 – 1 Chicago rout over Cleveland. The game on May 10 was rained out, but on Wednesday, May 11, Sockalexis keyed a 7 – 5 victory over Chicago, with three hits in four at bats, a run scored, and two put-outs in the field. The only reference to Sockalexis in the game account read, "Old Sox led at the bat with three fine singles." [20]

In the May 12 issue of the *Cleveland Press*, Elmer Bates took advantage of Sockalexis's fine showing the day before to offer an optimistic forecast about Sockalexis: "The red man is making a commendable effort to regain the confidence of his employers and the public. He is playing high class ball and is fighting shy of the alleged friends who were responsible for his slip-up a year ago." [21]

Sockalexis remained in the home game lineup as Cleveland smothered Chicago 12 – 4 on Thursday, May 12, followed by a 7 – 3 Cleveland win in Chicago the next day, Friday, May 13. He had one hit in five at bats in both games. For the second contest, in Chicago, he returned to right field, where he had three put-outs, one of them leading to an outfield assist and a double play.

Bates offered a charming story in defense of Sockalexis after the outfielder's catch and throw against Chicago:

> In Friday's game a very pretty young lady sat directly behind the reporter's box. At her side was a coarse, loudly dressed young man constantly demonstrating his ignorance by loud and inappropriate remarks. "Tell me John" said the young lady sweetly, "Do you think Sockalexis is a good player?" "Good?!" he shouted to attract attention. "Good? Why he's the rankest, four-flusher as a fielder on the diamond." And just then Sox scooted across the field like a flash, grabbed a line fly ten inches from the ground and shot it into [catcher] Criger's hands, completing a beautiful double play. In the uproar of applause that followed the pretty girl clapped her hands and shouted at her discomforted escort: "Isn't he a fine four-flusher, John? Say now, be honest, isn't he a four-flusher for your life?" But John had had enough. [22]

Rain washed out the game scheduled for Saturday, May 14. In another column about Cleveland players, Bates reprised his season-opening story about Sockalexis spurning "mash notes." Datelined May 14 from Chicago, Bates wrote, "There were a few letters in the 'S' bag when the Indians arrived at the Leland Friday morning. Most of them were delicately perfumed little things and all were addressed to 'Mr. Louis Sockalexis.' The writers had all their trouble for nothing. The red man tore them all into shreds and kicked the pieces from him vigorously. 'None of that for me this year,' he said as he bought a morning paper and went up to his breakfast." [23]

When Cleveland opposed Chicago for the fifth straight time, and won a 5 – 2 decision, Sockalexis was absent from the lineup. In the sixth contest with Chicago, on Monday, May 16, Sockalexis was hitless in two at bats and had no put-outs in right field in a 12 – 4 loss. He would not make another appearance until May 23, when he briefly entered the Washington game as a pinch hitter, and he would not play a complete game again until the May 28 contest at home with Baltimore.

If Sockalexis was repeating his bad behavior, the Cleveland team was likely to be far less tolerant of it, in part because they had heard the promises before, but primarily because with Sockalexis on the bench the team was off to a great start, challenging for the league lead. Captain Tebeau wanted to win games, and an impaired player could cost Cleveland a victory. At the time of Sockalexis's fifth appearance in six games with Chicago, on May 16, Cleveland had a record of 16 wins and 7 losses and held second place in the National League standings. Only Cincinnati, with a record of 17 wins and 4 losses, had a better record.

During Sockalexis's second lengthy absence from the lineup, Cleveland lost at Chicago on May 17; had a day off to return to Cleveland to start a three-team home stand (facing Philadelphia, Washington, and Baltimore) on May 18; was rained out of its first game of a series with Philadelphia on May 19; lost to Philadelphia on May 20 but won both ends of a doubleheader with the Phillies on May 21; and had no game scheduled for Sunday, May 22.

Starting with those doubleheader wins over Philadelphia, Cleveland enjoyed a seven-game winning streak. On Monday, May 23, Cleveland came up with a two-run rally in the ninth inning to beat Washington 4–3. Appearing briefly in the game's ninth inning, Sockalexis pinch hit during the rally but made an out. He then completely sat out the team's two victories over Washington on May 24 and May 25, and the team's first two games of the Baltimore series, which resulted in victories on May 26 and May 27.

He played his first complete game since May 16 in the third and final game of a Baltimore series on May 28. He had one hit in four at bats and one put-out in a 3 – 0 loss that ended Cleveland's seven-game winning streak and the home stand.

There was no game on May 29, and the team traveled to New York for a doubleheader on May 30 in which Sockalexis enjoyed one more successful outing against a truly great pitcher he had tormented before: Amos Rusie. Sockalexis did not play in the morning game, which Cleveland dropped, 6 – 2. He sat on the bench for the first eight innings of the afternoon tilt until Cleveland mounted a furious four-run ninth inning rally to break a 4 – 4 tie and take an 8 – 4 lead. Elmer Bates provided this description of the ninth inning: "When the Indians had the bases full with none out in the ninth, Tebeau sent Sox in to bat in place of [pitcher Jack] Powell. The red man drove in two runs and two more were soon chalked up." Once again Sockalexis had reached the star New York pitcher Rusie for a key hit in a clutch situation and came around to score in the inning as well. Unfortunately, in the bottom of the ninth, Cleveland was forced to rely on Cy Young, who had been too sick to start that very game, to pitch in relief of Powell. Young was pounded for five runs in the Giants' last at bat, giving New York a 9–8 victory. Several of the New York heroes of the game "were carried off the field" by celebrating fans.[24] Despite his fireworks, Sockalexis was back on the bench and did not play in Cleveland's 3 – 1 game over the New Yorkers the next day, May 31.

At the end of May, with 24 wins and 12 losses, Cleveland held second place in the league, trailing only Philadelphia but followed closely by Boston. Though the club was doing well on the field, Cleveland owner Robison was back on the Sunday game warpath. A magistrate had overruled the previous judgment allowing ball playing on Sundays in Cleveland. The irate Robison threatened to put his team on the road for the entire second half of the season. Aside from the Sunday ban, attendance in Cleveland was woeful owing to several factors that included the war, bad weather, and a union boycott of the team. Sockalexis had played in only ten of the first thirty-six games, with brief pinch hitting appearances in two others. He had 12 hits in 43 times at bat. Absent from the Cleveland lineup for most of the month of June, Sockalexis played in only one game the entire month and made pinch hitting appearances in just two other games.

On June 1, Sockalexis received a base on balls as a pinch hitter in the ninth inning of a 2 – 0 loss that completed the series in New York. The next day Cleveland traveled to Boston and bested the Beaneaters 6 – 1, but Sockalexis did not play. This series was a battle for second place. At the time Cleveland, which at one point in late May had pulled to within one game of first place, was still only two-and-a-half games behind league-leader Philadelphia. Games were rained out for three consecutive days, June 3 – 5. Sockalexis was benched again as the teams split a doubleheader on June 6, Boston won the morning game 9 – 5, and Cleveland took the afternoon game 2 – 0.

Sockalexis's only complete game in June opened a series in Brooklyn. He played right field and collected one hit, a double, in four at bats. In the field he recorded a put-out and made one error in Cleveland's 6–5 loss on June 7.

Sockalexis did not appear in the next seventeen Cleveland games as the team won the next three games at Brooklyn, June 8–10; won two games but lost four to Pittsburgh in contests in Pittsburgh and at home, June 11–19 (with one rained-out game and two days off); and lost two games to Brooklyn, then won the last two games of the series at home, June 20–23. While Teddy Roosevelt's Rough Riders were making their famous charge in Cuba, the Indians lost two out of three games to New York at home, June 24–28 (including rained out games on June 26–27).

When the team traveled to Boston and won a game on June 29, he was not in the lineup, but, for the first time since June 7, he made a brief appearance as a pinch hitter in the sixth inning in a 10–5 loss on Thursday, June 30. He failed to hit safely against Vic Willis. Though he did not play in the July 1 win over Boston, Sockalexis did garner another at bat pinch hitting in Cleveland's 8–1 win over Boston on July 2, but failed to get a hit against Beaneater hurler Ted Lewis.

After the team had a day off on Sunday, July 3, Sockalexis appeared in five consecutive games. On July 4, the one-year anniversary marking the start of his collapse in the 1897 season, Sockalexis played in both games of a double-header at home against Chicago. In the morning game he had one hit in five at bats and scored three runs. In the field, he made one play, but it resulted in two outs when he recorded a put-out and then an assist, throwing out a Chicago runner. Again in right field, for Cleveland's 4–3 loss to Chicago in the afternoon game, Sockalexis had one hit in four at bats and scored one run. During this doubleheader, fans threw firecrackers at Sockalexis, some reportedly exploding near his feet and obliterating him from view in the smoke. The local fans continued to badger him incessantly about his drinking.

He played right field in Cleveland's pair of one-run losses, 5–4 on July 5 and 6–5 on July 6, in a two-game series at Chicago. He was hitless in four at bats in both games, although he did record another outfield double play in the second contest.

Sockalexis did not appear in a three-game sweep of St. Louis at home, July 7–9, nor did he appear in the first three games (two wins and a loss) of a four-game series against Philadelphia. The end of Louis Sockalexis's playing season came in the fourth game of the Philadelphia series in Cleveland. He appeared as a pinch hitter, batting for pitcher Jones, and made the last out in a 1–0 loss on Thursday, July 14, the day Spain conceded defeat in the Spanish–American War.

Claiming Cleveland captain Patsy Tebeau as his source, Hughie Jennings reported that the end of Sockalexis's 1898 season came in this way: "One day the Indian was missing. Tebeau sent out several messengers to locate Soc, but could not find him. That afternoon, as the Spiders rode to the ball park in an omnibus, they saw Sockalexis. He was stretched out on the sidewalk in front of a saloon, hatless, collarless and coatless, dead to the world. Tebeau, that night, gave him his release."[25]

Sockalexis had played in only 21 of the 72 Cleveland games, through July 14. He had collected just 15 hits in 66 total at bats, and scored 11 runs. He made one error in the field.

Focused on playing for the league title, Cleveland had no patience for distractions, nor any need for a player whose primary role was drawing crowds. In August, after playing eighty-eight games, the team was still charging after league leadership. The National League standings put Cincinnati in first place, with 62 wins and 29 losses; Boston in second, with 57 wins and 31 losses, 3-1/2 games out of the lead; and Cleveland in third place, with 54 wins and 34 losses, only 6-1/2 games out of first place.

Louis Sockalexis had finally worn out his welcome with Patsy Tebeau and the Cleveland team. Strangely enough, though, he would be welcomed back one last time in 1899 after the players were moved en masse to the St. Louis team by owner Frank Robison.

In October 1898 Sockalexis apparently had already begun a campaign to win a third major league playing opportunity. The *Pittsburgh Leader* said, "Sock swears he hasn't removed the scalp from even one glass of foamy beer since last spring, when he whooped up a dance on Superior Street in Cleveland and was discovered the next morning by manager Pat Tebeau in the act of fastening a half-Nelson to a lamppost." [26]

12
The Last Whimper

THE MAJOR LEAGUE CAREER of Louis Sockalexis ended almost unnoticed. He was invited to play in Cleveland for a third year in 1899, but he stayed only two weeks, playing in seven games. He was released by what would prove to be the worst performing club in professional baseball history. The 1899 Cleveland team won only twenty games and lost an amazing 134.

The record for "worst ever" is an unassailable title. By comparison, the other contenders for the title would include the 1904 Washington Senators, 38 wins, 113 losses; the 1916 Philadelphia Athletics, 36, 117; the 1928 Philadelphia Phillies, 43, 109; the 1935 Boston Braves, 38, 115; the 1942 Philadelphia Phillies, 42, 109; the 1952 Pittsburgh Pirates, 42, 109; and the 1962 New York Mets, 40, 120.

How was it possible that a Cleveland team that had been so competitive during the 1890s and that had featured outstanding players like future Hall of Famers Cy Young, Jesse Burkett, and Bobby Wallace could have fallen so far and so fast? The answer is not about players but about the monopolistic practices of greedy owners.

By 1899, the only major league was the National League, which included twelve teams: the Boston Beaneaters, the Philadelphia Phillies, the Baltimore Orioles, the Brooklyn Superbas, the Cincinnati Reds, the Pittsburgh Pirates, the Chicago Orphans (or Colts), the New York Giants, the Louisville Colonels, the Washington Senators, the St. Louis Perfectos (or Browns), and the Cleveland Indians. This baseball monopoly had held sway since the American Association folded after the 1891 season.

National League rules permitted a syndicate system of interlocking team ownership that saw its most cold-blooded application during 1899. That winter before the 1899 season, the owners of the Baltimore Orioles, which also owned the Brooklyn Superbas, transferred most of Baltimore's stars to Brooklyn, hoping to boost game attendance because of the larger population there. When Cleveland's Robison brothers added the St. Louis franchise to their portfolio, the consequences of syndicate baseball would prove to be as disastrous for the Cleveland club as they had been for Baltimore.

Although the club was showing its age, Cleveland had been a strong franchise and had won the Temple Cup, a forerunner of the World Series, in 1895, defeating John McGraw and the Baltimore Orioles four games to one. By 1898, however, the club had faltered. Despite a pitching staff anchored by future all-time victory leader Cy Young, and assisted by Cuppy and young Jake Powell; an infield rated among the best in the game, featuring Wallace, who moved to shortstop from third base; and an outfield led by two-time batting champion Burkett, the team was getting old. After a good start in 1898, they ended the year in fifth place with a record of 81–68 and repeated their 1897 finish.

Lacking the attraction Sockalexis provided and unable to deliver regular wins, the team saw attendance drop. Team owners Frank deHaas Robison and brother, M. Stanley Robison, felt the decline in their pocketbooks. The Robison brothers were streetcar magnates who relied on baseball patrons to help fill their token boxes before and after they walked through their ball-park's turnstiles. Attendance for the 1898 season declined to 70,496, by far the worst in the league, despite the team's winning record.

The Robisons and the city of Cleveland continued to wrangle over the blue law prohibition of Sunday baseball, a cultural evolution that did not reach New York until 1916 or Pennsylvania until 1934. For their part, the Robisons infuriated local fans and press by putting the team on the road for the final two months of the 1898 season in retaliation for poor attendance. Schedule making in the late 1890s was still a capricious matter. Owners could transfer home dates to their opponent's ballpark, with league approval that was willingly given. Late in the 1898 season, the Cleveland press derisively dubbed the team the Exiles, a nickname even more appropriate in 1899. When Cleveland played a home game on August 24, 1898, one city news-paper took the opportunity to mock the team: "Cleveland people were treated to a decided novelty yesterday afternoon at the park at the corner of Dunham and Lexington avenues when a game known as 'base ball' was played by two teams.... The game, although practically unknown in this city, is not a new one."[1]

The situation in St. Louis was not vastly better, but the city had potential. The Browns, once a powerhouse team, had captured championships in 1884, 1885, and 1886 but were coming off a dismal 39 win, 111 loss season that put the team in last place, 63 games behind 1898 pennant-winner Boston. Even more serious, the team's financial situation put it on the verge of bankruptcy despite ticket sales twice those of Cleveland. The principal cause of the team's financial condition seems to have been its owner, the innovative but controversial Chris Von der Ahe. In the 1880s he had joined in founding the American Association, which had allowed beer sales at its games, a decision that offended rival National League owners. The Bill Veeck or Charlie Finley of his day, Von der Ahe used cheap tickets, beer sales, firework displays, and Sunday baseball to snare fans. When the two leagues agreed to merge, St. Louis came under National League jurisdiction. After Von der

Ahe's extravagant lifestyle forced him to declare bankruptcy, his team was placed in receivership. The league suspended the Browns for failure to pay its dues and assessments. Yet St. Louis was still an attractive city for professional baseball. It had a loyal fan base and a population of 575,000 (according to the 1900 census), nearly 200,000 more than Cleveland. Best of all, professional teams could play on Sundays. The National League was not about to squander that potential, and its owners were "damned if they weren't going to make sure who controlled it."[2] The league declared that the Browns' franchise was not transferable by the bankruptcy court. That meant that control of the team reverted to the National League, whose owners chose the Robisons to run it. A precedent for the decision had been established after Ned Hanlon was permitted to hold ownership of both the Baltimore and Brooklyn teams.

Early in 1899, *Sporting Life* speculated that a boycott by Cleveland fans would prompt the Robisons to move the team and named St. Louis as a possible location. "The faithful in Cleveland have reached the conclusion that if any championship games are played in this city this year, they will be played by a Western League [the forerunner of the soon-to-be-established American League] club…. Not the slightest move [has been] made by President Robison and [Reds owner and league powerhouse owner John T.] Brush expects to send the present Cleveland club to St. Louis."[3]

On March 14, 1899, Frank Robison purchased the St. Louis Browns at a sheriff's auction, taking the presidency of the club himself. Brother Stanley took control of the Cleveland franchise, at least on paper. Shortly afterward, the Robisons transferred Cleveland's best players to St. Louis in exchange for most of the Browns players. Indians' player-manager Patsy Tebeau was kept on at the helm of the St. Louis team, now nicknamed the Perfectos. Lave Cross, the only regular to hit above .280 in 1898, became the new playing captain of the Indians.

Eleven of the Indians — including Tebeau, Young, Burkett, Wallace, and twenty-four-game winner Jake Powell — became Perfectos. Nine ex-Browns were transferred to Cleveland; the balance of the team's roster was filled out with rookies and unpromising journeymen. With little help from the brothers Robison, Cross was still assembling his ragtag band less than two weeks before opening day. In addition to the other ex-Browns, the lineup included a motley mix of has-beens and never-will-be's. The *Cleveland Plain Dealer* called the resulting assemblage the Misfits; *Sporting News* labeled them the Discards.[4]

Cleveland was scheduled to open the season at home against the Perfectos, but the Robisons, eyes firmly on the financial bottom line, transferred the game to St. Louis. The Misfits and Discards suffered a 10 – 1 loss battling against their St. Louis brethren. Caustic criticism followed immediately. One newspaper said the game "was not up to National League standards." The *Cleveland Plain Dealer* headlined the game account "The Farce Has Begun."[5]

By the end of the season the Indians had used fourteen pitchers. At a time when rosters of twenty or fewer players were the norm, thirty-one players would appear for Cleveland. One young player who showed genuine promise in Cleveland, pitcher Wee Willie Sudhoff, was transferred to St. Louis one-third through the season. Sudhoff won three games and lost eight for Cleveland; he won 13 games, with 10 losses, for the Perfectos.

In mid May, the *Cincinnati Enquirer* complained about the arrangement that gave St. Louis not only Cleveland's best players, but gift-packaged wins against a far weaker team: "Robison's St. Louis team's easy victories over Robison's Cleveland team [are] liable to create some queer comments if St. Louis should land the pennant. Better for Robison and better for the game if Robison would unload his Cleveland end on to Cleveland people and not attempt to run two clubs."[6]

The season opened for Cleveland with consecutive losses to the Perfectos, and then the team had three days off. Looking for any help it could find, Cleveland announced on April 17 that Louis Sockalexis would return to the Forest City fold. Cleveland traveled to Louisville, where it dropped the first two games of a four-game series.

Varying accounts claim that Sockalexis spent most of the winter of 1898–99 in Cleveland, ostensibly for rehabilitation. One doctor claimed he had lumbago. Other ailments requiring care included an injured knee and leg soreness. The once fit 180–plus-pound player had ballooned to more than two hundred pounds and was clearly not taking care of himself. That winter, on February 25, 1899, his mother, Frances, died and was buried on Indian Island. Tebeau had had no interest in extending an invitation to Sockalexis to attend training camp for the new St. Louis entry featuring the primary stars of the 1898 Cleveland club. *Sporting News* of March 18, 1899, reported that Tebeau regarded it as "a useless expense." He ignored claims attributed to Sockalexis in the Cleveland newspapers that he had joined a gym and would "surprise Patsy" with his new fitness regimen and abstinence policy.[7] Apparently Tebeau saw the hopelessly out-of-shape and overweight Sockalexis and rejected him.

New Cleveland playing manager Lave Cross, however, really had little to lose on such a gamble. He knew all about Sockalexis and his off-field problems, but he needed someone with gate attraction and charisma who could play. Sockalexis began working out with the Cleveland team. He told

Sporting Life correspondent Elmer Bates in the April 29 edition, "I expect to be back in the game for good within the week. I have cut out the red stuff for good, and am feeling fine. With [veteran catcher Chief] Zimmer and I back on the team, it will help out the boys who have been playing out of form." [8]

The now twenty-seven-year-old Sockalexis was nowhere near the able physical specimen he had once been. Even the slow-footed Zimmer, in *Sporting News* for May 27, bluntly commented: "I can give him twenty yards and beat him in a hundred.... You would not know the big Indian if you saw him now." [9]

Sockalexis made his first official appearance of the 1899 season on Tuesday, May 2, during a rare Cleveland home game. He was unsuccessful in a pinch-hitting role during a 3 – 2 loss to Louisville in the morning game of a doubleheader. Sockalexis did not play in the afternoon contest, a 9 – 5 Cleveland victory over Louisville, and the only win the Indians would record during Sockalexis's two-week stint with the club.

From May 3 to 6, Cleveland dropped all four home games against Chicago in a matchup of the "Orphans" against the even more pathetic "Castoffs," or Exiles. In the second game of the series, on May 4, Sockalexis made his only appearance against Chicago. Sent in briefly to pinch hit, he failed to connect safely.

On May 7, Cleveland was rained out, and on May 8, at Chicago, Sockalexis did not appear in Cleveland's 8 – 7 loss. Reportedly, Cross did not yet dare to take Sockalexis on a road trip and left him back in Cleveland. Starting on Tuesday, May 9, Sockalexis played in five consecutive ball games. In Cleveland, he was in the lineup for Stanley Robison's inept Exiles for a four-game series opposing brother Frank Robison's St. Louis club as well as many of his former teammates. One can imagine the bench jockeying and barbs that were directed his way during the series.

In the first game, an 8 – 1 loss, Sockalexis had one hit in four at bats against the venerable Cy Young. He had two put-outs in the field. In the second contest, a 12–8 loss, he was hitless in three tries against a pretty good pitcher named Al "Cowboy" Jones, who had joined the Indians in 1898. He had one outfield put-out.

The third game provided a brief display of his former ability, a reminder of what he might have been. In this 8 – 6 loss, Sockalexis had five hits in five at bats, including a double against outstanding hurler Jake Powell. In right field he made a double play on his one put-out, firing the ball into third baseman Lave Cross to retire a St. Louis runner attempting to advance. He threw out another Perfectos base runner during the game as well; however, he also made two errors. According to the *Boston Daily Globe*, only

150 spectators witnessed Sockalexis's performance. In the final game of the St. Louis series, Sockalexis was hitless in five at bats against Zeke Wilson, as the Perfectos beat Cleveland 5 – 4. Sockalexis had three put-outs in right field.

Although he apparently regained some batting and fielding form, Sockalexis was described as committing a number of mental lapses and making embarrassing displays on the field during the course of this handful of games. In one game he had reached third base, but disorientation, disinterest, or daydreaming led to a late start from third on a clean base hit to the outfield, and he was thrown out at home. He was ridiculed for dropping easy fly balls and then fumbling haplessly in the attempt to recover them.

Just as his major league season in 1897 ended in Pittsburgh, his major league career ended there in 1899. Cross elected to take Sockalexis on the road and gave him a start in right field. On Saturday, May 13, Sockalexis went hitless in four at bats in a 6 – 0 loss. The *Boston Daily Globe* did not even acknowledge Pittsburgh pitcher Jesse Tannehill, reporting simply, "Cleveland was shut out by Pittsburg [*sic*] in today's game. There were no features."[10] The box score followed. Sockalexis had one put-out in the field. At the time Cleveland's overall record was 3 wins, 19 losses.

A more detailed assessment of the last game of Louis Sockalexis was offered in the *Pittsburgh Post* of May 14. It noted that Sockalexis "looked lost" at the plate and was so inept in the field that he fell down twice. Upon fielding one ball in the field, he "tumbled to the turf with a thud as he straightened to throw." The official scorer, the newspaper stated, "didn't know what to make of the embarrassing display" and ultimately decided not to charge Sockalexis with any errors. After one of his poor fielding plays Sockalexis was cheered derisively by the Pittsburgh fans; however, the newspaper reported, Sockalexis tipped his cap and gave "a funny little nod" as though he did not realize the cheers were meant as pure jest. The *Post* concluded that Sockalexis is "nothing more than a tobacco sign in right field. In fact, a tobacco sign could not have done the damage he did."[11]

The *Pittsburgh Dispatch* for May 15 sniped: "Standing out in bold relief all by his lonesome, among the offenders on the visiting team, was Sockalexis, the Indian. His socklets must have been heap full of dope, for his efforts to take care of things that wandered into right field were as funny as a cage of monkeys. He was about as fast on his feet as a cow, didn't get within a mile of the drives in his garden and seemed to be dreaming of better days."[12]

On Tuesday, May 16, exactly two weeks after his first playing appearance, the major league career of Louis Sockalexis ended ignominiously. The *Boston Daily Globe* reported, "Sockalexis, the Indian ball player, was arrested in the Lyceum theater last night at Cleveland. He had been indulging in fire water and was creating a disturbance."[13] After the team returned to Cleveland from

Pittsburgh, Sockalexis attended a local theater to see a sketch called "A New Year's Dream" but apparently fell asleep noisily in his seat. When his snoring disturbed other patrons, the theater manager summoned the police. The police brought him to the central station and booked him for public intoxication. Sockalexis spent the night in jail. The *Cleveland Plain Dealer* for May 17, 1899, caustically noted that, "The judge would not release him, but Lave Cross did."[14] Cross had had enough, and Sockalexis was released by Cleveland for the third and final time. Shortly after Cross himself left town. He escaped with a promotion to the St. Louis team when Bobby Wallace was moved from third base to begin his Hall of Fame career as a shortstop.

Because of Robison's decree, Cleveland did not play its first home game until early May. In response, the fans largely boycotted the team when it did play in Cleveland. Losing money, Robison cut the payroll to control costs. In succession, the team released Happy Jack Stivetts (another recovering alcoholic with a poor record of sobriety), Jack Clements, Sockalexis, Kid Carsey, and even the popular catcher Chief Zimmer, who had been hitting well. Louisville signed him after his release.

Among the corps of St. Louis players more or less sentenced to play in Cleveland after the transfer, several young prospects blossomed. In addition to Willie Sudhoff, young catching prospect Ossee Schreckengost was playing a fine, consistent game, both in the field and at bat. In his first forty-three games Schreckengost's hitting averaged .313. He played a leading role in Cleveland's only victory over St. Louis, collecting three hits in the June 25 contest, including the game winner. Frank Robison promptly shifted Schreckengost back to the Perfectos in midseason.

Sporting News reported that "the patronage of the St. Louis club is gratifyingly good, but the Exiles are making expenses." The grumbling around the league was growing. It was reported that Pittsburgh received "slightly more than $64 as its share of the gate from a three-game set in Cleveland, $75 less than the team's hotel bill."[15]

Frank Robison steadfastly denied rumors in *Sporting News* that Cleveland would transfer all its remaining home dates, but on June 26 his brother announced that after the current home stand ended on July 1, Cleveland would become the Exiles once more, taking to the road for the balance of the season. Cleveland finished June with a 3–21 mark for the month, 11–48 for the season.[16]

Cleveland's win-loss tally did not improve in July. The team won only 4 games, lost 26, and saw Ossee Schreckengost shipped back to St. Louis. *Sporting News* winced at this latest "act of larceny," and said: "The switching of players between the St. Louis and Cleveland clubs is censurable. It is unjust to Cleveland and unfair to the other clubs."[17]

From August 26 to October 15, the remainder of the season, the Exiles won one game and lost forty. Between late August to late September they lost twenty-four consecutive contests, still a major league record. Cleveland played only 41 games at home all season. They had 9 wins and 32 losses at home, and 11 wins and a numbing 102 losses on the road.

Syndicate baseball seemed to work for the Robisons. Despite finishing a disappointing fifth in the league standings, St. Louis made a $40,000 profit. By slashing the payroll and minimizing home play, even Cleveland probably made money. The highest-paid Exile received only $2,500 for the season, and the Robisons left Cleveland without issuing the final paychecks to players. When the National League cut back to eight teams for the next season, the Robisons gave up their interest in Cleveland for $25,000.[18] Even the owners had had enough of the sorrowful practice of syndicate baseball, and they outlawed the practice of multiple team ownerships.

The Perfectos became the Cardinals and never finished higher than fourth place for the Robison brothers. Frank Robison died in 1910, and his daughter took over the team and did not improve it. St. Louis would not win a National League pennant in the twentieth century until 1926.

As for Louis Sockalexis, his fleeting two-week Cleveland season in 1899 consisted of appearances in only seven games. He managed only 6 hits in 23 at bats, a .273 average. He had just one extra base hit, a double, and three runs batted in.

Struggling to hang on to his career, Sockalexis found one last man in professional baseball who was not ready to give up on him. A player in the 1870s, "Bald" Billy Barnie had been the manager of the Brooklyn club in the National League in 1897. Barnie doubtlessly remembered the sensation Sockalexis had caused and the 17,000 fans the Indian had attracted to the Brooklyn field on Memorial Day that year. Now the manager of the Hartford franchise in the eight-team Eastern League, Barnie hoped that Sockalexis might help improve his team and fan support. Perhaps believing that the Indian player would fare better closer to home and away from the glare of major league cities and press, Barnie offered Sockalexis another chance to play. After his release from Cleveland on May 16, Sockalexis went directly to Hartford.

The *Hartford Daily Courant* of May 21 considered the local team's prospects in a story headlined, "Eastern League Outlook, Toronto The Only Team Hartford Has To Fear." The story includes a colorful description of the behavior that ended Sockalexis's Cleveland career: "The acquisition of Sockalexis to the Hartford team will give the name of 'The Indians' to the aggregation. He is to play his first game with the team in Rochester to-day. It seems that Sock's release by the Clevelands was due to a snoring turn he did in a rear seat in the Cleveland Theater. Noodles Hahn and Pink Hawley were in the theater at the time and they said Lo snored so hard that the people in the house could not hear what was going on the stage. Lave Cross then allowed Socks to go to Rochester to join the Hartford team." Another brief item noted the "well known Indian ball player" had arrived in Rochester and was to play his first game with Hartford the next day.[19]

Despite the *Courant*'s boastful headline, Hartford suffered successive defeats opening the season in Rochester. Sockalexis made his debut in the second game of the series. The May 24 *Courant* story headlined, "Sockalexis Smote A Solitary Single Swat," reported Sockalexis's first appearance in the Eastern League as a member of the Hartford team. He replaced a player named McCarthy in left field and caught the only ball that came his way. In four times at the bat he connected safely only once in the first inning. "Sockalexis proved to be a great drawing card and the game was attended by over 1,000," according to the *Courant*, which later in the account referred to the team as "the Indians."[20]

In its edition covering games played on May 30, the three-cent *Hartford Daily Courant* raved about Sockalexis's performance in the afternoon game of a double-header sweep at Springfield. The paper's archly poetical description of Sockalexis's play reported:

> Then up to the plate stepped Sockalexis, with the odor of the forest, with the dew and damp of meadows, with the curling smoke of wigwams, with the rushing of great rivers; strong of arm was Sockalexis, he could throw ten baseballs upward, throw them with such strength and swiftness that the tenth ball left his right arm, ere the first to earth had fallen; he had mitts made all of deerskin, when upon his hands he wore them, dangerous skitterers were eaten up. [Patsy] Tebeau, known as a boaster, made a bat for Sockalexis, from a branch of ash he made it; then Sachem [Hartford manager] Barnie said to Sockalexis, "Go, my son, into the forest, where the has-beens herd together, and drive the pitchers to the bushes." And Soxy drove. He did this twice in the game yesterday afternoon and each time sent in two runs. This was the kind of hitting that counted, and although the Penobscot was given a great reception when he appeared upon the field it was nothing to the tumultuous applause that greeted his work with the stick.[21]

Batting fourth in the lineup, Sockalexis played left field and had two hits in four attempts, one put-out, and one error. In the top of the first, Sockalexis fumbled a hit grounded to left, allowing a Springfield runner to score. In the bottom of the inning, however, Hartford's first two batters reached on singles and were sacrificed into scoring position, to second and third. Sockalexis hit the first ball pitched to send in two runs. In the sixth inning,

Sockalexis singled in two more runs after two men were out, and Hartford went on to an 8 – 5 win.

In the earlier, morning, game Sockalexis also played left field and batted fourth in the lineup. He had one hit in three tries and made three put-outs in the field. The account of that game reported: "The game was full of brilliant plays. Sockalexis made a fine catch in the seventh that saved runs."[22]

The Springfield newspaper was not particularly pleased with the hometown Ponies when they lost their fourth straight game to the Hartford "Wax-figgers" as reported on May 31. Hartford manager Barnie was credited with wisely using a left-handed pitcher named Knell who was tough for Springfield to hit. Springfield collected only two hits and one of them was a gift from umpire Doescher. Sockalexis apparently made a phenomenal running dive to catch Shannon's line drive, but Doescher said the Indian dropped the ball, so Shannon gained a two-base hit. Sockalexis was hitless in two official at bats, but he scored one run. At the end of this Springfield account, the reporter cited a source close to the team who claimed that, "without reservation…the Ponies are not keeping themselves in condition. Mr. Daly calls no names, but makes no bones of saying that players who stay out until midnight and 2 A.M. cannot play baseball next day. That some of the Ponies are guilty of such misbehavior, and that the dissension is chiefly between the players who are taking good care of themselves and those who are not. It is a sad state of affairs, isn't it?"[23]

By June 18, Hartford had stumbled badly, especially in light of preseason prognostications. Toronto was in first place in the eight-team circuit, with a record of 24 –14. Then, in order of standing, followed Montreal, Rochester, Worcester, Springfield, Providence, Hartford, and in last place, Syracuse. Hartford had a record of 19 – 25.

Sockalexis, too, was stumbling. He was criticized for inattentiveness and for "being too slow for use." On June 17, Sockalexis made an embarrassing error on an easy fly ball to present a 4 – 3 gift-wrapped victory to last-place Syracuse. He was booed mercilessly, and Barnie released him after the game. On June 18, the *Hartford Daily Courant* carried a roundup of baseball news with a detailed note about the release of Sockalexis from the Eastern League:

> The poor showing of the Hartford team in the last four games was not due entirely to the team's being broken up and Manager Barnie has decided to release some of the men who do not improve. Sockalexis was released Saturday night. He was given a ten days' notice by President Robison of the Cleveland Club several days ago and Mr. Barnie decided that he did not have any further use for him. The Indian has not kept himself in good condition, which was the cause of his poor playing. The Penobscot kept bad hours and as a result when he went after a ball his movements reminded one of a messenger boy on an errand with a copy of "Nick Carter" in his hand.[24]

Sockalexis appeared in just twenty-four games for Hartford, delivered 18 hits for an anemic .198 batting average, and scored eight runs. He committed five errors, for a miserable .918 outfield fielding average.

Almost immediately Sockalexis resurfaced in the Connecticut State League. Having just drunk himself out of two leagues in two short months, he found yet another league willing to give him a chance. Playing its inaugural season in 1899, the league had teams in the state's six largest cities, not counting Hartford, of the higher Eastern League. Tim Murnane, a respected player who became a well-known Boston sportswriter and editor, helped organize the new league and served as its first president. "Orator Jim" O'Rourke, the comically glib former New York Giants star, owned and managed the Bridgeport club, which was aptly nicknamed the Orators. Another former Giant, Roger Connor, managed and played first base in his hometown of Waterbury. Sockalexis joined Bristol and played for player-manager John Gunshannon. Again he was released after a very short stay, barely three weeks. Connecticut State League teams played on average ninety-five games, starting May 15 and ending September 16. In 1899, New Haven finished in first place, with a record of 55 – 38, and Waterbury finished in second, with a record of 53 – 43.

On July 15, Waterbury Rough Riders manager Connor announced in the *Waterbury Republican* that he had signed Sockalexis to play center field for the team. A former National League slugging star, Connor was the league's top hitter, with a .392 average in 92 games (two other players finished with higher averages but played in only 27 and 14 games, respectively). He signed Sockalexis in Bristol, where Waterbury had just won an 8–6 decision over the home team.

The *Waterbury Republican* story describing the July 15 game concluded, "Sockalexis has been signed by Roger Connor and left for Waterbury tonight." A story about player personnel changes on the team quoted Connor saying that he had "secured" Sockalexis to play center field.[25] The Indian was to join the team in Waterbury the next day and travel to Meriden for a two-game series.

In the July 18 edition of the *Waterbury Republican*, Sockalexis made headlines: "Baseball, The Indian Boy, Sockalexis's Great Catch Saves The Game." In his first game for Waterbury, Sockalexis demonstrated his special flair for the dramatic. Batting in the third position in the lineup and playing center field, he had only one hit in four at bats, plus a sacrifice, scored a run, made two put-outs, and committed an error. This was hardly stellar, but one of the put-outs was, apparently, a superb running catch that ended the game and preserved Waterbury's victory over Bristol, Sockalexis's most recent employer. A melodramatic newspaper account described Sockalexis's play with two men out in the last inning.

At that time Waterbury was still three runs in the lead that had been reduced from five runs, and Bristol base runners were strewed carelessly and promiscuously about the bases to be transformed into run makers with the aid of a hit or two that would incidentally make Waterbury's lead fade like a morning mist before the rising sun. There was a chap at bat too, who had made no hit during the whole game and this is the sort of man that always is dangerous in a pinch. Everyone held his breath and we had drawn and anxious looks on our faces when at last Mr. Bristol batter soaked the ball with an extra heavy acting swing. It went careering far out to center field way out where the bicycle riders gather their forces for the wonderful sprint home. It was flying with an easy birdlike wing high in the air and every eye of the thousand odd eyes on the grounds followed its course. But as it went there ran rapidly under it on the ground a fleet footed Indian boy. One Sockalexis of the family of Hiawatha, and related by marriage to Minnehaha. And as the ball kept going even as fast did the alert Indian also course. And the crowd watched anxiously the result little heeding the rapidly circling base runners as they passed one after another around the bases. The ball was descending. It came down in jerks, one plunge toward the earth brought it within reaching distance of Mr. Sockalexis and the climax was obtained, the end of the play was at hand and the curtain rolled down with a very pleasant ending to the story. Waterbury had won the game. Bristol was beaten again. Waterbury moved up the line and Sockalexis saved the day.[26]

Revenge against the club that had so recently released him must have tasted sweet for the largely unwanted Louis Sockalexis. Further, there is conflicting evidence here that Sockalexis had not permanently forfeited his speed, as a number of other sources alleged after he left Cleveland.

Playing before his newest home fans for the first time on July 18, Sockalexis delighted Waterbury followers with his batting as he led Waterbury to a 13 – 3 pasting of visiting New Haven. The July 19 issue of the *Waterbury Republican* carried a league game headline that read: "Baseball, Our Indian Sets A Great Pace Again Yesterday, Splendid Baseball." The story said:

"You won't write poetry about your Indian to-day," called out Tom Reilly to the press box in the early part of yesterday's game when things began to look bright for New Haven and the Blues were dancing gleefully about the ball field. But Tom shouted too soon. Indeed, a few lines of verse are coming to the great chief of all Indian ball players. He fielded in great shape, and his hitting was the marvel of the day. Roger Connor seems to be good company for the Indian lad as he has struck a winning gait and is playing as good a game as when the whole country went wild over at the time he was one of the stars of the Cleveland National league team. He did excellent work.[27]

Indeed, Sockalexis had four hits in five at bats, including a double, and scored two runs. In center field, he had two put-outs and no errors.

With New Haven in the lead 3 – 2 as late as the fifth inning, Waterbury exploded at the plate for eight runs, batting completely around its lineup in the sixth inning, with several players batting twice. Sockalexis had two hits in that inning: "The Indian that Tom Reilly told us we couldn't write poetry about, opened the inning's program with a two-bagger.... Sox was up again and the crowd cheered him. 'Pooh,' said [New Haven shortstop] J. Ira Davis and then Sox hit the ball a stinger for still another hit. There [were] more runs coming in." In the eighth inning, Sockalexis collected his fourth hit of the day: "Sox again started the fun with one more single and the gang wondered why Mr. Gunshannon [the playing manager of Bristol] let him go." [28]

Perhaps the answer simply lay in management. Gunshannon, like Tebeau and all the others who attempted to manage Sockalexis, could not seem to manage his drinking problem. On the surface, it appears Roger Connor was successful during this brief period with Sockalexis. Connor was professional baseball's first great home run hitter, a man now enshrined in the Hall of Fame as one of the greats of the game. He had a long and distinguished career as a slugging first baseman. His 138 total home runs stood as the major league record for twenty-three years until it was eclipsed by Babe Ruth. When the Waterbury, Connecticut, native left the top professional league, he purchased his hometown team and remained as its owner and player for many years. Supported administratively by his wife and daughter and on the field by his skilled ball-playing brother, Connor turned the club into a highly successful family franchise. Described as a deeply religious and moral man, Connor may well have been able to reroute the path of the rapidly sinking star — at least until the off-season.

By late August, Sockalexis was still playing with Waterbury and still garnering praise. Part of the reason is apparent from the August 24 game account of an easy victory over Derby. The lengthy headline in the *Waterbury Republican* read: "Another Victory For Waterbury Over The Derby Team, Louis Sockalexis, He Plays A Very Fast Game — This Player Is Making A Splendid Impression By His Fine Work." After praising several other Waterbury players, the story discussed Sockalexis:

> Let us pause for a moment and discuss our Indian friend. The Republican sporting writer has from the first maintained that Sockalexis is a great ball player. He is a man who isn't brilliant in one particular and a dub in another. He is very liable to make a failure any time at bat or in the field. But the thing

about his playing that makes it valuable and helpful to any team is that it abounds in surprises. Sockalexis is the man the crank loves to see come up when a hit is needed. Sockalexis is the chap who is liable to make an assist from deep field that shuts off the fatal run. Sockalexis is the man who is ready in the emergencies of the game and to-day he is one of the best men in this State league. There is just as good quality in this young Indian lad as there ever was. He is not old, he has not gone back, he simply needs the iron hand of Roger Connor to guide him, and he is liable to regain every inch of ground he lost since the days when the country went wild over him. Sockalexis has been placed at the head of the batting list. He celebrated the honor by making three fine drives, one a two-bagger out of five times up. The patrons of the game in the grand stand are all favorably impressed with Louis, and indeed Roger himself is very well satisfied with the work being done by him.[29]

In this 10–3 victory, Sockalexis played right field and led the batting order, collecting three hits in five at bats. He scored one run, had three put-outs and committed no errors.

Sockalexis grabbed more headlines in another dramatic confrontation on August 31 with hostile Bristol and its jeering fans, coming up with a timely hit late in the contest to tie the game and ultimately pave the way for a Waterbury victory. The *Republican* headline blared, "The Indian's Hit Ties The Score In The Seventh Inning." Down by three runs, Waterbury had loaded the bases with one man out when Sockalexis came to bat. The *Republican*'s reporter was overcome with the drama of the moment when he wrote:

"How would you like to be Sockalexis?" shouted the boy with the yaller hair. The Indian let the first one go by; he offered at the next. It was low and close and he just missed it. The Bristol rooters who were intrenched in the grand stand in great numbers shouted in glee. "He is a dead one," some one shouted, "we had no use for him." The Indian shot a glance at the stand out from beneath his red cap, and watching him closely he could be seen settling with a crouch in his track. [Bristol pitcher] Herndon was being encouraged by his whole team. Everyone held his breath. The next ball came up, and the boy who made the baseball world ring with his praises two years ago, reached out after it. He caught it full and it went on a high line straight out over center field. When the ball dropped it was far behind [Bristol center fielder] McHale who had gone after it like a deer. He fielded it with wonderful quickness but not so quick that three runs which were making had any difficulty in being scored. It was a hit that stands out as one of the best of the year. The timeliness of a drive of that kind is what counts. A three-bagger with two men out and no one on bases is a three-bagger, but it may not mean anything, but with three spry, anxious lads dancing on the baselines a single is beautiful to see, and a two-bagger — and such a two-bagger as Sockalexis made had fringes on it.

A glance at the crowd along the first baseline showed a curious spectacle. In its excitement the crowd opened and expanded instead of drawing close together. Men and boys danced on the green sward while the bright sunlight was a shadow compared to their glowing, happy countenances.

"How'd ye like to be de Indian," again screamed the yaller haired boy and again the crowd hurrahed for Sockalexis.[30]

Batting leadoff and playing center field, Sockalexis had two hits in three at bats, recorded two put-outs, and made one error. If he had enjoyed the "revenge" catch to save a game earlier in the year against the team that had dropped him, Louis Sockalexis must also have felt considerable satisfaction turning the jeers to cheers in this special moment. In one brief but stirring visit to his glorious past, he had proved he was equal to the best in the game.

An early September issue of *Sporting Life* carried a column about the Connecticut league through August 26. It recorded New Haven, with a record of 47–29, atop the eight-team standings for the circuit. Bristol was in second place, 43–33, and Derby was in third, 40–38. Waterbury held fourth place at 41–39, followed by New London, Meriden, Norwich, and Bridgeport. According to the story, "The work of Louis Sockalexis with the Waterbury team has been of late about as good as that of any fielder in the league." In an ironic juxtaposition, the Connecticut league article was immediately adjacent to a story describing the successes of the St. Louis Perfectos, with Sockalexis's former teammates Patsy Tebeau, Cy Young, Nig Cuppy, and Bobby Wallace. The article noted that Jesse Burkett was leading the league's batsmen with an average above .400. Lave Cross, the player-manager at the start of the season for Robison's woeful Cleveland franchise (and the man who'd released Sockalexis after only seven games) had been transferred to the St. Louis team and was reportedly playing well and fielding "brilliantly." Napoleon Lajoie had been out of the lineup when St. Louis beat his Philadelphia team, but he had clearly mended the drinking problem that had been evident in his rookie season in 1897.[31]

As the stretch run for Waterbury unfolded in September, Sockalexis continued his fine, consistent playing. On September 12, Waterbury battled Norwich and trailed 2–1 until the top of the eighth inning. Connor knocked in a run to tie the score in that inning, setting up a game-winning, three-run home run by Sockalexis in the final frame. A brief newspaper account recorded it this way, "In the 9th inning a batter hit by a pitched ball, a base on balls and then Sockalexis knocked out a home run and the game was won. Norwich could not score in their half."[32]

On September 15 in the next-to-last game of the year, hitting and fielding by Sockalexis coupled with an outstanding pitching performance by Denny

Reardon, clinched Waterbury's second-place finish in the league. The *Waterbury Republican* game account read: "The ball game between Waterbury and Derby this afternoon was the fiercest contest seen on the home ground this season. It practically meant that whoever won the game was to finish second in the league race and wrangles, disputes and contentions marked almost every moment of the game until the spectators were worked up to a highly excited condition.... Sockalexis carried off the honors by a wonderful scooping catch of a low hard hit liner to deep center at a critical time. Also with men on bases and two out he made one of his long drives."[33]

The next day the *Waterbury Republican* ran a considerably longer and dramatically embellished account of the game. Under the headline, "Second Place Ours, We Defeat Derby In A Great Game...Sockalexis Hero of the Day." The tightly contested match was not resolved until the late innings. In the fifth inning, "The Indian made a beautiful two-bagger," but the Sockalexis double did not result in any scoring. "It was 2 and 2 in the last half of the seventh and every one was nervous. [Waterbury left fielder] Hanscombe opened with a stinging drive. He was sent to second on a neat sacrifice by [second baseman] Delaney. Reardon made his base on balls and then came Louis Sockalexis' turn. What did he do? Why, he sent the ball out with such speed that the center fielder could hardly stop it as he met it rolling on the ground. Hanscombe scored. In the eighth we touched up [Derby pitcher] McPartland for two singles, a double and a sacrifice and the game was ours."[34] Sockalexis had two hits in four tries in the game, plus five put-outs in center field without an error.

After raving about Reardon's pitching and Connor's managing and hitting, the Waterbury writer waxed eloquent about Sockalexis:

The noble Red man, Louis (sure-eyed-ball-driver) Sockalexis was once more the genius of the day. Louis stands to-day the greatest emergency hitter that ever transpired in the Connecticut league or any other old league. Louis used to be credited with a lot of luck when, with men on bases at a critical time in the game, he used to drive out a beauty hit that put everyone into frenzies of delight. But he has been doing the trick so regularly and often that to do it again yesterday, when everyone admitted he would be justified in striking out when he had so often been tried and found not wanting, to do it yesterday once more which makes the eleventh time without a slip, was the straw that broke the camel's back and the truest American of them all in this great American game had to bow to such an ovation as pale faces seldom tender Indians.

As though that was not enough he goes it one better by making a catch that lets us into the secret of his great popularity of two years ago. It was a catch made against a fierce low liner that seemed to have every mark of a splendid line hit. Louis took it in on a running scoop that leaves this catch the best made here this year. What ball this Indian is playing these closing days.[35]

Neither game account revealed in which inning the catch was made, or the state of the game when it occurred.

Sockalexis ended his fine season with Waterbury playing well in the team's final game on September 16. Under the headline, "The Last Game, We Won It — And Took Second Place," the game account noted that if Waterbury had lost that last game, it would also have lost possession of second place. Until the sixth inning, Waterbury trailed Meriden 2 – 0 and had not managed a run or even a hit. In the sixth inning, Eddie Hanscombe singled, then second baseman Mike Delaney sacrificed him to second. The next batter grounded out, the inning's second, leaving matters in the hands of Sockalexis. "Our great red man was to bat once more. He had slipped into so many emergencies of late that the crowd was sure of him and they sent up a yell of frenzied delight. And the confidence was not misplaced. He shot the ball out for left field like a streak, fooling the second baseman and first baseman of the opposing team, who were laying for him on the right of the diamond. It was our first score."[36]

Two more runs followed, putting Waterbury in the lead, 3 – 2. Meriden tied the score in the seventh and then went ahead by one run in the eighth, 4 – 3. In Waterbury's eighth inning, Delaney walked after being hit by a pitched ball. "Like the clever boy that he is," the account noted, Delaney stole second and third bases. The next batter, the pitcher Prentiss, made an out. The account continued, "There was one man out and this irresistible Indian was up once more. It was too much to expect that he would keep up his record, but hanged if he didn't do it. He drove a long fly that was caught, but before it could be returned to the plate, Mike Delaney had scored." With two out and a man on second, Waterbury third baseman Pete Kiernan ended the team's season on a happy note, rifling a base hit that scored the winning run. The Waterbury reporter rejoiced, "We had won one of the hardest games of the year and second place. The crowd was so pleased that a hasty collection was made for the Indian, which netted him a neat sum." Several other popular players also received gifts.[37]

Released by Cleveland, then by Hartford in the Eastern League, and by Bristol in the Connecticut League, Sockalexis ended his 1899 baseball season to the sounds of cheers and adulation. Sockalexis had played in a total of sixty-one games for the team. He had 85 hits and batted .320 (with a slugging average of .421), scored 35 runs, and had four stolen bases. He ranked twenty-first from the top in batting average, but eight men listed above him played in just thirty games or fewer. Though he would offer the occasional sensational play, his overall fielding, however, was a disaster: He ranked thirty-sixth and dead last in fielding percentage among the league's outfielders with a dismal .802.

13

Rock Bottom

A WAY FROM THE Waterbury team and the guiding hand of Roger Connor, Sockalexis's fragile sobriety again slipped away, quashing any opportunity for professional play in 1900. There is no record of his signing with the team of any league that summer.

On March 31, 1900, the Bangor Daily News carried the following report out of Hartford, Connecticut, under the headline: "Decline of Sockalexis/ Once Famous Baseball Player Now Haunts/ Hartford Saloons." It stated: "Sock hangs out in the ward. The saloons on Front street are his haunts, and his bed is where he happens to pitch his wigwam. There are those who remember the glamour of his reputation, and who consider it an honor to 'set 'em up' for the big brave, and thereby he is able to quench his thirst. Apparently he has lost all the love he ever had for his race. The other day he came upon an Indian of the cigar store variety. 'Oh you brute,' he ejaculated in his purest English, 'you sign and symbol of a lost race. Take that, and that,' and he gave the Indian two punches that would have sent him to the 'Happy Hunting ground,' had he not been fastened too securely to this earth. Then Sock called him 'the white man's burden' and ungratefully passed on."

On April 18, 1900, a *Holyoke Daily Transcript* article noted that a prize-fighter named Tom Sharkey would umpire a Patriots' Day (April 19) holiday baseball game. A team from Easthampton was to field an all-star team made up of "several prominent Holyoke players and re-enforced by Sockalexis, the noted Indian fielder for the Cleveland National league team last season. Sockalexis is now in the city and is in fine training for the game."[1]

On August 23, the *Transcript* carried a story headlined, "An Idol's Downfall, Sockalexis, The Once Great Ball Player, Sent To Jail This Morning For A Month For Being A Vagrant." The story reported that Sockalexis was "without a friend to help him" and had been sentenced to a month in jail for vagrancy, specifically "sleeping in barns and being idle." The article editorialized, "What a fall, as he was arraigned in the clothes in which he had slept for months, from the one time most envied player" in the major leagues.[2]

Sockalexis would be "remembered," according to the paper, as "the bright star of the game in this city which Sharkey claimed to umpire. He attracted really more notice and applause than Sharkey." The story also claimed that "his folks and tribe have disowned him because of his actions."[3] A more complete account in the *Holyoke Times* of August 24, 1900, said:

Louis Sockalexis, the once famous National League baseball player, appeared in court this morning on a charge of vagrancy and was given 30 days in the county jail. He was arrested last night by Patrolman Greaney, who found him sleeping in a tumbledown barn in Ward One. At the police station, Sockalexis presented a sorry appearance. His clothing indicated that it had been worn for weeks without change. His hair was unkempt, his face gaunt and bristly with several weeks' growth of beard, and his shoes so badly broken that his toes were protruding. In court this morning, he attributed his downfall to firewater. He said, "They liked me on the baseball field, and I liked firewater." For the last year or so, Sockalexis has been a hanger-on around the cheap saloons in Hartford and other New England cities.[4]

A very similar report of the incident appeared in the August 26, 1900, edition of the *Springfield Union*, which included a reporter's interview with Sockalexis: "Attired in clothes which no tramp would accept as a gift, and peering out into the big and airy reception hall from behind a massive barred and screened prison door, L. S. [*sic*] Sockalexis, the once famous National league baseball player, told a Union reporter the story of his life and downfall." This newspaper claimed just the opposite of the *Holyoke Daily Transcript*, stating that Sockalexis hoped to return home next spring, with no suggestion at all that he was disowned or unwelcome to return to Indian Island. The reporter also noted that he "was surprised to hear [Sockalexis] speak absolutely perfect English without a suspicion of foreign accent."[5]

The *Union* account quoted Sockalexis as saying "O, I've always played ball.... It comes natural, I suppose, like anything else. All the rest of the boys played and so did I." He noted he had attended the Catholic school, St. Mary's. "I wanted an education and I studied hard for it. That was in 1891." He then described how Mike "Doc" Powers had invited him to join the catcher at Holy Cross. "They always have a great team, so I was delighted and went to Worcester. There I took a special course in Latin and Greek and played on the '95 and '96 teams."[6]

Omitting his Notre Dame arrest, jailing, and Tebeau's timely rescue on behalf of the Cleveland team, Sockalexis is reported as saying, "In '97 the Cleveland National league team offered me a fine job, and as I like to play so well, I naturally accepted and left college. It was a big jump for an amateur to a National league team, and I was much surprised to get such an offer." Again, glossing over difficulties in the facts, Sockalexis disingenuously claimed, "I played for them for two years and then they 'farmed' me out to Hartford." In the *Union* story Sockalexis explained his "fall" in the following way:

I was with the Eastern league team for several months and played in Springfield. Then I left and played with the Waterbury [Connecticut] team for a while, but left on account of an injured leg. Since then I have had hard luck and have drank more or less. My mother died in February and now no one is left but my father and myself.

On Patriot's Day last I played in Holyoke with Sharkey as umpire. This week was the next time I came to Holyoke, and the police seemed to know me, for they were on the lookout. I was with a couple of fellows, and the detectives and a policeman stepped up and tapped me on the shoulder. "Why, hullo, Sock, old man! You're just the fellow we want," and with that they took me to the police station.

Oh no, I never tramp about the country, and I have never before been arrested, or at least I have never been taken for anything except having a good time with the boys. This is the first time I was ever shut up. I receive money from home every once in a while, so I am not a vagrant.[7]

In response to a question about his plans after his release, Sockalexis answered, "Guess I'll keep straight and take ball playing again." He said, "I'm rather glad I'm here. My leg is sore and here it will get the best cure and I will have a chance to rest and get in good shape once more."[8]

As noted before, his mother, Frances, died on February 25, 1899. Why Sockalexis suggested that his father was his only remaining family member is unclear. The ballplayer was reported to be close to his sister Alice and her family, whom he visited frequently. Ironically, his father, Francis Sockalexis, died on February 26, 1905, just one day after the anniversary of his wife's death.

A newspaper clipping in the Baseball Hall of Fame Library offers clear evidence that Sockalexis's problems continued well after Holyoke. By mid October of 1900 he had returned to Pittsburgh, where two of his three major league seasons ended ignominiously because of drinking. He was apprehended by the police and "brought up before Magistrate Kirby, and was a sorrowful spectacle…suffering from an extreme case of nerves."[9]

Sockalexis returned to Indian Island in 1901. According to a story attributed to Marion Foster, his homecoming was inglorious. En route to his home in Houlton, Arthur Putnam, who had played ball with Sockalexis on the Ricker team, recognized him at the Bangor train station. At the station, Putnam recalled, Sockalexis was drinking and having trouble with the conductor. He wanted to go home, to Old Town and Indian Island. Putnam interceded on his behalf, persuading the conductor to let Sockalexis get on the train and taking responsibility for him. The conductor consented, and Putnam helped Sockalexis off the train in Old Town.[10] There would be no more baseball until 1902.

14

The Last Hurrah

M OST ACCOUNTS OF the life of Louis Sockalexis suggest that he was finished as a professional ballplayer after his two failed attempts to return to Cleveland in 1898 and 1899. Some writers remember that although Sockalexis was dropped by both Hartford and Bristol, he became a hero with Waterbury and completed a successful season in 1899.

Few writers, however, recall his last hurrah in 1902 playing in the league where his career in professional baseball began. In 1895, Sockalexis played just one game for Lewiston in the New England League, the last game of the season. He had one hit in four at bats, scored one run, and played errorless ball in the outfield. Joining two Holy Cross teammates, Mike Powers and Walter Curley, Sockalexis spent the summer season playing for Warren in the Knox County League and switched to Lewiston for the last game of the year. Seven years later, his skills compromised by alcohol, Sockalexis returned to semiprofessional baseball and showed that he still had a flair for making exceptional plays, both at bat and in the field.

In 1902 he played more games in one season than ever before. As an outfielder for Lowell in the eight-team New England League, he worked in 105 games. He had 117 hits, batting a respectable .288, with 50 runs scored. He was erratic in the field, however, committing 29 outfield errors for a lowly .800 fielding percentage. In several games he was credited with making spectacular catches, some of them at critical junctures. At Lowell, Sockalexis worked for playing manager Fred Lake, who as a former Boston Beaneaters catcher had played against Sockalexis during the 1897 season when Cleveland came to Boston. After his stint with Lowell, Lake would eventually manage the Boston Red Sox for two seasons. As the season began, hopes for Lowell were high, not only because of Lake and Sockalexis, but because the team was playing in a brand-new field at Spalding Park.

The May 2, 1902, *Boston Daily Globe* headline for the opening league game proclaimed, "Sockalexis Once More, Great Batting and Circus Catches Features of Dover-Lowell Game." The thirty-one-year-old Sockalexis was the game's star, although Dover narrowly nipped the Lowell club 5 – 4. The *Globe* reported, "Dover won the opening New England league game on Spalding park in the presence of eight hundred spectators this afternoon."[1]

About Sockalexis the paper said, "The work of Sockalexis, the noted Indian player, was of the phenomenal order. Three of his catches were made after long runs, and were followed by somersets [*sic*]. His batting was a spectacular feature of the game. In five times at the bat he placed the ball safely four times. Coming from the field to player's bench he was repeatedly cheered by the hometown Lowell fans."²

On May 16, 1902, the *Washington Star* reported, "Sockalexis, the most advertised baseball player of his day, now with the Lowell New England League team, has evidently spiked himself to the water cart." The paper apparently believed Sockalexis was drinking only water. It noted that the Indian had singled in his first at bat in Lowell and then "repeated the performance three times thereafter."³

On June 5, Sockalexis smashed three doubles and stole two bases. His third double, coming in the eighth inning, led Lowell to a 5 – 2 victory over Nashua. Lowell's first game at home after a week of road games attracted quite a gathering despite a shower that preceded the contest. The *Boston Globe* said, "The rejuvenated Nashua team came here yesterday afternoon and while Lowell succeeded in defeating them it was any one's game until the eighth inning when Sock put an end to the doubt by banging out a two bagger that brought in two runs and practically won the game."⁴

The *Globe* story also commented on the Indian's improving physical condition: "Sockalexis who has been gradually approaching his old time shape, got the fans going by his great batting and clever base running, despite the fact that he is still somewhat stiffened up in the pins. Sock made three pretty two baggers which brought in nearly all of Lowell's runs."⁵

Lowell scored three runs in the first inning. The team's leadoff man singled and was sacrificed to second base. He then "came home on a two bagger to the left field fence by Sock." Sockalexis stole third base and then scored on a teammate's single. After scoring one run in the top of the first, Nashua narrowed the gap to one run, 3 – 2, in the second inning. Neither team scored again until the eighth. In that frame, Lowell's leadoff batter, Connors, reached on an error, and its second batter of the inning, Cassidy, also reached safety with a single, Connors stopping at second base. The *Globe* account said, "Then Sock who had previously made two baggers was called on to lace it out for another. But Sock was playing the game scientifically and with no one out started to sacrifice much to the disgust of the fans. He made two bad attempts and then had to hit it out. He certainly was equal to the occasion for he soaked the next ball pitched way out into right field for a two-bagger scoring Connors and Cassidy."⁶ In this game Sockalexis played right field and batted in the third position. His three doubles came in four at bats. He scored one run and played errorless ball in the field.

On June 18 Sockalexis snapped a seventeen at-bat hitless streak with a home run and gave Lowell its 4 – 3 margin of victory over Dover in an away game. The *Lowell Sun* headline on June 19 said, "Everyone Played The Game Yesterday And Sensational Plays Were The Order—Sock Makes Two Of The Runs With A Homer." The Associated Press game account appeared in the *Sun* and said, "Everybody on the Lowell team was alive to the occasion yesterday. Connors was in the game for fair and so was Moran, while old Sock made a home run that took the breath away from the Dover bunch.... The beautiful home run by Sockalexis was instrumental in winning the game."[7]

After collecting two runs in the second inning, Lowell added its second and final pair of runs in the third. With one out, left-fielder Cassidy drew a base on balls. "Then Sockalexis sent the sphere over the left field fence scoring Cassidy and himself."[8] Dover scored single runs in the fifth, seventh, and eighth innings to fall one run short. The home run was Sockalexis's only hit in four at bats. He played right field and batted third in the game. In the field, he had one put-out and made no errors.

That game put Lowell just percentage points out of first place in the New England League standings. Manchester topped the circuit, with a record of 26–13 and a percentage of .667. Lowell was next, at 26 wins, 14 losses, for a percentage of .650. Then came, in order: Dover (22–16), Lawrence (21–18), Haverhill (18–21), Concord (16–23), Fall River (15–26), and Nashua (13–27).

By the beginning of August, Manchester had established clear dominance in the league, with a record of 55 wins, 24 losses. Lowell, however, was slipping. The team, with a record of 42 wins and 39 losses, had dropped behind Haverhill and Dover into fourth place and was just a couple of games ahead of Lawrence and Concord.

On August 2, Sockalexis led the way at bat and in the field against the top team in the circuit. The *Lowell Sun* headline said, "Lowell's Victory Over Manchester Team In Hard Battle, Sockalexis Made Some Great Plays." In the 6–5 victory, Sockalexis had three hits, including two doubles, in four at bats and scored two runs. Then, with tying and winning runs on base, he caught the final out of the ball game, "Win Clark came up and sent the sphere out for a couple of bases but the side was retired when Smith sent out a beautiful fly to 'Socksie' in right field." A column that day praised the hitting of Sockalexis against Manchester and its tough pitcher, a man named Bishop: "The fans were just beginning to nail old Sock hard when up he comes against the celebrated North Carolina wonder and does some A1 hitting."[9]

By early September Lowell had slipped under .500, with a record of 53 wins and 55 losses. Only Nashua and Fall River trailed sixth-place Lowell as the season wound down to its conclusion. Sockalexis continued his fine all-around play. On September 1, Lowell lost a doubleheader to lowly

Nashua: "Nashua Showed Lowell How To Finish, Visitors Won Both Games After Victory Seemed Certain For Home Team—Sockalexis Puts Up Star Game" said the *Lowell Sun*. In the first game Sockalexis was hitless in two official at bats but reached base on walks and was hit by a pitch. He stole a base and threw out a runner on the bases. In the afternoon game, which Nashua won 4–3 in its last at bat, Sockalexis "put up" his "star game." According to the game account: "Sockalexis was Lowell's star player. He made a circus running catch and at the bat made two timely two baggers." Sockalexis "smashed out" his first double in the sixth and scored on a teammate's single and then, in the ninth, knocked in another run (but a potential second and tying run was thrown out trying to score).[10]

In the team's 7–1 loss to Haverhill the next day, Sockalexis collected two more hits in four at bats and had an outfield assist. Manchester pounded Lowell 12–1 on September 3, and Sockalexis continued hitting consistently, collecting two hits in five at bats, including a double. Lowell broke its September losing streak on the fourth, with a 7–5 win over Manchester in an abbreviated five-inning game. Sockalexis had one hit in three at bats. Lowell played a benefit game on September 5 for St. John's Hospital, against a pickup team of local star players. No box score was published, but Sockalexis was listed as a player in the contest.

The season came to a close on September 6, 1902, with a terrible 13–0 drubbing at the hands of Lawrence. The team committed eleven errors, five of them attributed to Regan, the second baseman. Sockalexis had an error, but also an outfield assist. At bat, he finished his season with two more hits in four at bats.

According to the *Lowell Sun*, the hometown team concluded its season with a record of 53 wins, 58 losses.[11] The *Encyclopedia of Minor League Baseball, 1997*, however, records the Lowell record as 52 wins and 59 losses. Since Sockalexis is credited with playing 105 games that season, he obviously missed only six outings and was not plagued by the distractions that had troubled him in the past.

In his last five games, Sockalexis averaged nearly two hits per game, with nine hits in twenty-three at bats (an average of .391). The *Reach Guide* of 1903 listed Sockalexis as the twenty-second best hitter in the 1902 league, at .288. Several of the players higher on that list did not appear in as many games. If only players with one hundred or more games are counted, Sockalexis would have moved up to the tenth highest average. Sockalexis had 406 at bats. If only those players with four hundred or more at bats are considered, Sockalexis rises to eighth position in the league. For Lowell, Sockalexis had the third highest average. One of the two players who had a higher average appeared in ninety-two games, but the other played in only fifty-five games.

Lowell's record is a bit confounding. According to both the *Spalding Guide* and *Reach Guide*, Lowell's final record is recorded as 53 wins, 60 losses (not 58 losses as reported by the *Lowell Sun*, or 59 losses as reported by the *Encyclopedia of Minor League Baseball*).

The *Reach Guide* credits right-fielder Sockalexis with playing 105 games, with 117 hits in 406 at bats. His hits included 100 singles, 15 doubles, 1 triple, and 1 home run. He had 137 total bases, scored 50 runs, and batted .288.

Sockalexis played the entire season and was playing well through the season's end.

The reasons for his failure to return to the league are a matter of speculation. One report has him playing semipro ball for Wheeling in Illinois' Central League in 1903, but league statistics do not list him.[12]

15
The Final Years

I N 1902 Louis Sockalexis was reported to be running the ferry between Indian Island and Old Town, Maine, a job he would fill periodically during the remainder of his life. In his last decade, Sockalexis worked at a number of vocations and avocations in Maine, many of them involving baseball.

Town semi-professional baseball had a boom period in the mid-1890s, but by 1905 it was "practically dead," according to the *Bangor Daily Commercial*. However, with an assist from Sockalexis, there was a brief resurgence in Bangor during the summer of 1907. Although there were only four teams still in the Maine League, and only two of them had participated for the whole season, Bangor defeated its arch-rival, Portland, for the league title. "The Queen City of the East has fairly and unquestionably won the baseball championship of Maine, We have beaten our dearest rival, Portland, to a frazzle," declared the *Bangor Daily News* on Sept. 2, 1907.

In a *BDN* article published 100 years later, historian and journalist Wayne Reilly quoted the original *Bangor Daily News*: "Ten years ago Bangor was leading the clubs of the New England league and was one of the hottest baseball towns in the country." Dubbed "The Millionaires," in recognition of the wealthy boosters who financed them, the Bangor club took the New England title in 1896.

Led by a new owner, Fred Paige, who had plans to rebuild the diamond at Maplewood Park (located inside the oval of the racetrack at present-day Bass Park) and deck out the players in new white-and-maroon uniforms, the team received more than 100 applications from players hopeful of joining the club. The signing of players was a hot news item. One was a Sock protégé, Henry Mitchell of Indian Island, who had played ball for the Carlisle Indian School in Pennsylvania. He was characterized as "the most promising Indian player since the days of the great Sockalexis," reported the *BDN* on March 22, 1907.

Then "Old Sock" himself showed up, much to the surprise and delight of all. At age 35, the legendary slugging outfielder was trying once again to regain a moment in the sun on the baseball diamond.

Paige said he thought the application from Sock was an April Fool's joke. Then he tried him out. "Outside of a little surplus fat he was sound in wind and limb and no trace of rheumatism," said the *Bangor Daily News* on April 2. "He is by no means an old man although many people get that impression because he is called 'Old Sock.' I believe he is worth taking a chance on anyway," Paige told the newspaper. "If he doesn't make good, it's back to Old Town for him."

Louis Sockalexis had not lost his ability as a crowd-pleaser. "Bangor fans would be mightily pleased to see old Sock swing his great war club as in days of yore and lambaste the leather over the standpipe," wrote the always enthusiastic, unnamed reporter. Sure enough, the fans cheered heartily when he made an appearance in the field or at bat. With Sockalexis and Mitchell on board, the *Bangor Daily Commercial* nicknamed the team the Indians and the Braves, at least for a few weeks.

But when the team suffered humiliating defeats at the hands of the University of Maine and Higgins Classical Institute, Paige replaced almost all of his original team members.

After the Maine League games got under way on May 24, Bangor gained supremacy. By June 17, the team had won 11 of 15 games against competitors from Lewiston, Augusta, Waterville, Portland and Manchester, N.H.

On June 17, the *Bangor Daily News* reported the team was in a crisis, $300 in debt and Paige was looking for ways to raise money. Sockalexis had been suspended on account of "indifferent playing." Still, he had made some good plays and had his share of hits. And he had lasted longer than almost all of the other members of the original team.

Just prior to the opening of the 1907 Maine League season the Bangor town team played two exhibition games that — considered with a modern-day perspective and sophistication — were not appreciated for the unique historical events they were. Members of an all-black professional team, a race barred until forty years later from playing Major League baseball, opposed a team featuring the first American Indian to break a color barrier and ever play at that level.

The author first learned about the exhibition games from Clark Thompson, Bangor historian. The Bangor club hosted the Philadelphia Giants, the reigning champions of the Negro League. One of the more youthful members of the Giants, John Henry "Pop" Lloyd, would be named posthumously to the National Baseball Hall of Fame in 1977.

A center fielder in those days, Lloyd, then 23, would earn his ultimate distinction as a stellar defensive shortstop with a sharp batting stroke, and the nickname "Pop" would come many, many years later when he was a veteran playing-manager and mentor.

The talented Philadelphia Giants were on a barnstorming tour, playing the best white teams from different regions around the country in their home ballparks. The black players would keep up a lively, humorous chatter and, for the most part, attempt to win without inflaming palpable racial prejudice and tensions. In 1910, in a 12-game series with the Detroit Tigers in Cuba,

Lloyd had 11 hits in 22 at bats, and Ty Cobb was said to be so embarrassed at his team's five losses in the series that he vowed never to play against blacks again.

Lloyd was in demand as an all-star player who went on tours to Cuba and the West Coast. His Negro League statistics, from 1914 to 1932, include: 477 games played, 1,769 at bats, 651 hits, 90 doubles, 18 triples, 26 home runs, and 56 stolen bases. His batting average was .368. He died in 1964.

The first game in Bangor was Monday, May 7, and the Giants won easily, 21-5. The 35-year-old Sockalexis started the game in center field – meaning he and future Hall of Famer Lloyd were swapping the same position in the field – and was Bangor's cleanup hitter. He was hitless in two plate appearances and was replaced by a man named McIntire. Sock recorded no putouts or assists in the field but was charged with one error. A man who batted from the left side, and who had trouble with lefthanded pitchers when he first encountered them in the Major Leagues, Sockalexis, no doubt, found a stellar performer like the Giants' McLellan, reputedly "the fastest colored pitcher in the country," a handful to deal with at the plate.

The second game between the Giants and Bangor resulted in a 10-7 victory for the Giants and was called after only seven innings because of fiercely cold temperatures and gale-like winds. There was no box score provided for this game.

Concerning Sockalexis in the second contest: "Old Sock got into the game yesterday with more signs of life than he has shown yet. He pulled down two high (flies) out of the hurricane and the one that he didn't get was on account of the wind. The Giants outfielders misjudged several of the high ones."

He played baseball briefly with Bangor in a semiprofessional league and then umpired semipro games. Still immensely popular on Indian Island, he organized and coached a juvenile team on the Indian reservation. He was photographed wearing his old Cleveland cap (with a big "C" on it) and uniform for a postcard that was sold to tourists who visited the island. The weathered lines in his face and puffy jowls in this photograph were a marked contrast to the sleek, athletic look of his Holy Cross portraits or the trim, athletic figure holding a bat in the photograph taken of him at Poland Spring. Only the somber, stoic expression seems comparable.

When he was a boy, writer Francis Hatch recalled watching Sockalexis play for the town team in Castine during the summers between 1905 and 1910. Hatch said Sockalexis paddled down the Penobscot River to stay for the summer with his uncle's family in a tent at the north end of town. Joe Sockalexis, his wife, and children made baskets as their summer trade. Hatch remembered Sockalexis as "mild-mannered, courteous and, of course, was 'the big attraction' on the ball field Saturday afternoons when he played first base." The uniquely situated baseball diamond, which still exists, was laid out on the parade grounds within the ramparts of Fort George, an eighteenth-century British compound. The league had some outstanding college players, including several from Harvard and Yale, as well as notable regional players.

Sockalexis still garnered top billing. "He was our hero," Hatch said, "and he never disappointed us. If the opposing pitcher tried to walk him, with an extra wide pitch, he merely stepped across the plate and slapped it over the right field embankment while the fielder, high on the rampart like Hamlet's father's ghost, made a futile gesture and scrambled out of sight down into the moat to retrieve it. The relay usually came in too late, though Soc had adopted a leisurely pace around the sacks."[1]

Noah Hooper, a pitcher and teammate of Sockalexis in the league, told Hatch that Sockalexis "was one of the nicest men I ever knew, never arguing or shouting or making fun of an awkward player. Now and then, in the heat of an argument, I would throw the ball out of the fort. But Soc never did anything like that. He had a way, when he was on first, of talking with a batter and getting him all balled up. He didn't raise his voice or appear to be working on the man. But somehow he got him confused to the point of striking out. As a hitter, even though his speed was gone, he could place the ball just where he wanted to without seeming to try."[2]

Walter Ranco, the longtime proprietor of a small store in Old Town and once a member of one of the juvenile teams that Sockalexis had coached on the island, added: "Soc taught us to get on base and not to worry about the extra base hit. He showed us all the tricks of working a walk from a pitcher. He told us if a pitch was too hot, just to dunk it. We were proud to play for him, because he could do anything we tried to do — and do it so much better." Apparently Sockalexis was an adept instructor, for five of his young players went on to play in the New England League, Ranco told Hatch.[3]

Several more remembrances of Sockalexis as a ballplayer and an umpire in his later years appeared in a 1965 *Bangor Daily News* article by Steven Strang. The piece featured stories about Sockalexis from two local men who had known him fifty years before. One was John Nelson, the Indian representative to the Maine legislature, who recalled that Sockalexis was "an umpire when I was playing. No one ever disputed his calls. He was a robust man, and he knew what he was talking about when it came to baseball. Sometimes the players would start to argue a call. Lou would put on his scowl. I can see him now with his finger pointing at the player. The only time the player said anything else was when he was walking away from Lou." Nelson said Sockalexis was generous with helpful advice: "He taught me how to throw a curve the way the pros threw it." Nelson also recalled seeing Sockalexis play a few times: "If he made an infield hit, he'd take two bases.

The infielder wouldn't expect him to try for second, so he'd dash down without even looking at first."[4]

According to Nelson, the legendary throwing exhibitions continued in Sockalexis's later years. Nelson smiled as he recalled the day two Old Town merchants offered Sockalexis a prize if he would throw a baseball across the Penobscot River from Indian Island. Recalled Nelson, laughing, Sockalexis "threw it over to the other bank all right." The merchants offered him a second prize if he could throw the baseball back to Indian Island, and he did. Nelson also mentioned another of Sockalexis's skills, singing in his church choir: "People used to come from miles around to hear him sing. He had a beautiful bass voice." According to Nelson, "Lou has a nephew named after him here on the island. His name's Lou Sockalexis, too. The last of the line, I guess."[5] After the ballplayer's nephew and World War II veteran Louis Sockalexis died in the late 1980s, the name Sockalexis disappeared from Indian Island.

Sockalexis was playing for a Bangor town team in 1907. According to a *Bangor Daily Commercial* article in May of 1907, he batted cleanup and played right field for the team: "Sock continues a great favorite with the stands and is getting back to his old game every day." The fans even had a jingle to sing in praise of him, called "Songs of Sockalexis."[6]

William "Chic" Baker of South Brewer, Maine, told Strang that he had played against Sockalexis in a Maine semipro league in 1909 or 1910. Baker remembered that Sockalexis had "square shoulders and was close to six feet tall. He had a slim waist, deep chest and weighed about 190 pounds. A baseball uniform really showed up his build. He was very graceful in the field, and had a great stance at the bat. He was very particular about what pitch he hit. The first two times up to bat, he went down on called strikes. He didn't even move his bat at any of the pitches. The last two times up, however, he smashed two hits on the first pitch. During that game in the Eastern Ball Park he made an outstanding catch while playing first base. The batter lifted a high fly down the right field line. Socks turned and ran back about 50 feet, never looking up at the ball, turned, and speared the ball with his glove. It was a terrific catch. He had good judgment."[7] Baker laughed:

> Sockalexis wasn't always serious on the ball field, however. He pulled a trick play one time. I think it was during that same game. The batter hit a slow grounder to third base. The throw to Socks was late and the runner was safe. Socks walked away from the bag and rested both his glove and his free hand on his knees, and looked ready to field for the next play. The runner naturally led off first, and was standing in front of Socks. Socks reached down and took the ball from out of a secret pocket on the inside of his right pants leg.

Of course he tagged the runner out. I've never seen any ball player with a secret pocket like that before or since.[8]

Baker found Sockalexis was always ready to help young players improve their game. "I was only 16 or 17 at the time. Socks was umpiring with our team then. He came over one day and gave me some advice on how to swing. His advice made me a .300 hitter most of my ball playing days." Baker remembered Sockalexis as "kind of a reserved fellow. He'd say what was necessary, and that's all. He was interesting, though. I guess you could say he was sort of my hero," Baker sighed in conclusion.[9]

On February 16, 1909, *The Washington Post* carried a story datelined Worcester, Massachusetts, reporting that Sockalexis "is to return to the game. Though rumor has had the old Indian dying of rheumatism in diverse places many times, he is on deck again and has asked for a chance to play in the outfield of the Holyoke club of the Connecticut League. He says he feels better now than he has since he quit the diamond. Holyoke will give him a chance."[10] Holyoke, Massachusetts, is close to Worcester and Holy Cross College, where Sockalexis was legendary; the fan attraction possibilities might have been enticing. However, Holyoke was the town where he had been arrested for vagrancy in 1900. Apparently the tryout, if there even was one, did not go well; there is no record of Sockalexis playing in the Connecticut League in 1909.

In September of 1910 Sockalexis shared headlines with Napoleon Lajoie on the same day. The 1897 rookie batting stars who fell from grace because of drinking directed their lives and careers along two very different paths. While Sockalexis's major league career was falling permanently overboard, in Philadelphia, Lajoie righted his ship and was en route to becoming one of baseball's greatest players. In mid September of 1910 both of them were in the news once again for very different reasons.

The Cleveland team carried the nickname the Naps in honor of the team's manager and star player since 1903. Lajoie was riding a hot batting streak in 1910 and took the American League lead in hitting from Detroit's Ty Cobb. According to a story in the *Bangor Daily News* of September 14, 1910, Lajoie surpassed Cobb with an average of .363, while Cobb's average was listed at .359. The popular Lajoie would ultimately win one of the closest and most controversial batting titles in baseball history that year against the controversial Cobb. The pivotal moment came on the final day of the season when the third baseman on the team opposing Cleveland played so deep that Lajoie was given gift bunts, so that he, rather than Cobb, would be sure to win the free car given to the winner of the title. (Determining the true winner of the 1910 batting title has challenged researchers for decades. For a time Cobb was believed to be the victor; however, one researcher eventually determined that he was inaccurately credited with two hits in a regular season game.)

On September 14, 1910, the *Bangor Daily News* column from Houlton contained general news from that northern community town and reported that thirty-three hoboes had been "run into jail" late Sunday night and early Monday morning, but in the "excitement of Monday's election" (gubernatorial, national, and state legislative races), thirty of them "broke jail Monday night."[11] The *Bangor Daily Commercial*, in its Tuesday, September 13, 1910, "News From Up In Aroostook [County]" column reported that thirty hoboes who were locked up on Sunday "for vagrancy" and who would not be tried on election day, "escaped from the lockup Monday night."[12] The September 14 issue of the weekly *Aroostook Times* carried a similar item, adding an editorial aside, "Thirty hoboes were locked up on Sunday for vagrancy, and who would not be tried on election day, escaped from the lockup, thus saving the county the cost of feeding and trying them. Doubtless they will make tracks for other parts."[13]

The *Brockton* (Massachusetts) *Enterprise* for September 13 linked Sockalexis with the incident in a story headline "Home Run By Sockalexis, Once Noted Indian Ball Player Breaks Jail With Other Hoboes." The story said: "At Houlton, Me., 27 hoboes broke jail last night. Professional hoboes have been numerous for past month and Sunday the police rounded up 30 and placed them in the jail to await a hearing Tuesday, owing to Monday being election day. With a cold-chisel the nuts were removed from the door and the bunch walked out. Three refused to walk out and will be discharged Tuesday morning. Among those who escaped was Sockalexis, the noted Indian baseball player."[14] It is a mystery how a newspaper in Massachusetts knew Sockalexis to be a member of the hobo group and why two Bangor newspapers and one in Houlton failed to mention him if he was there.

Another former Cleveland player made the Brockton newspaper's sports pages that day. The Spiders star left fielder and batting champion, Jesse Burkett, was apparently still living up to his argumentative nickname, the Crab. At a banquet in Worcester for his New England League players, Burkett announced his retirement as their manager after many years, saying it was time to move on "to a new field" of endeavor, but did not say what that would be. Burkett reportedly hesitated a moment in the face of beseeching requests for a speech. He reluctantly went ahead after someone in the audience suggested that he "just meet it!" as he had done so successfully on the baseball field for so many years. He acknowledged that he had been ejected from the game thirty-nine times during the past season and that he had "made it a particular point not to get put out the 40th."[15] Burkett subsequently returned to managing.

The *Aroostook Times* for Wednesday, September 21, carried an item called

"Hoboes" with the parenthetical notation that the story had been "omitted from last issue." It read:

> The Houlton police, dressed in citizens clothes, made several trips to the vicinity of the Cold Spring and the Horseback, Sunday, and rounded up 28 hoboes, and landed them in lockup. Thomas Hay, night baggageman at the R. & A., brought 5 during the night and placed them with their chums. This class of men has been exceptionally bold, and the gardens, the chicken roosts, and even the potato fields between the R. & A. yard and Cary's Mills have suffered seriously, and the danger from fires is great with this irresponsible class of the traveling herd. A mere warning to leave town has no effect, as many will hang around hoping to get a winter's free board with the county. They should be set at work on the roads or at a large wood pile, and made to pay for their keeping.[16]

Louis Sockalexis was not mentioned among the men arrested, and the story did not describe the group's escaping jail.

A portrait of what was likely to have been the last meeting between Jesse Burkett and Sockalexis comes from a story by John J. (Magnate) Haley, with R. H. Collins in an August 7, 1949, edition of the *Portland Press Herald*. Haley explained that he had seen Sockalexis only once in his life, after the Penobscot's ball playing days were long over. Burkett had come to Portland, Maine, to manage his Worcester club against the local New England team. Haley, then a youthful baseball lover, had "picked a spot on the sidewalk outside of a Congress Street hotel to watch the Worcester team assemble for the game."

As the players were leaving the hotel, a few of the younger ones surrounded a figure near the front entrance and began making derogatory remarks, "Suppose he can give us a war dance" and "Let's hear your war cry, Chief." They were followed by "youthful but coarse laughter when Burkett pushed his way through the thickly knotted ring of players."

Haley described Burkett's eyes as being "like hot coals and his voice was thick with scorn as he faced his charges." Burkett, according to Haley, then said, "Why you whelps.... There isn't a one of you fit to carry this fellow's shoes. You're looking at the greatest ball player who ever lived." Then Burkett threw an affectionate arm around the shoulders of Louis Sockalexis and said, "Come on, Sock." And together they walked down Congress Street, leaving the crestfallen and embarrassed group of Worcester ballplayers behind them.

Haley said he really had not noticed Sockalexis until Burkett arrived. He described Sockalexis as "wearing a visored University of Maine freshman cap, a faded blue coat, almost colorless dungarees and rundown shoes. Yet, one could almost sense a note of rediscovered pride in the Indian's walk as he strode off arm-in-arm with his former teammate."[17]

By 1912, Sockalexis was again reported to be running the ferry across the Penobscot River from Indian Island to Old Town. When his second cousin, Andrew Sockalexis, finished second by only 35 seconds in the 1912 Boston Marathon, Louis Sockalexis served as the host of a special reception for the marathon runner after his return to Indian Island. The *Bangor Daily Commercial* of Thursday, April 25, reported that "the feature of the evening was the presentation to the audience of Andrew Sockalexis, the famous Marathon runner, and popular favorite with all his tribesmen, by Lewis [*sic*] Sockalexis, the old Cleveland baseball star." The reception was preceded by a concert and dance. Displaying his noted singing skills, Louis performed a solo, "Everybody Has Their Eyes on Me."[18] This is one of the rare instances when Louis and Andrew Sockalexis shared a public appearance. When Andrew Sockalexis married Pauline Shay in early November 1913, just two months before Louis Sockalexis's death, the old ballplayer was not mentioned among the list of guests.

The *Bangor Daily Commercial* published a profile of Sockalexis, "Once Deerfoot Of The Diamond, Now Charon Of The Penobscot," on Saturday, July 20, 1912. Much of the story was repeated verbatim in the *Bangor Daily News* obituary of Sockalexis in December 1913. It was penned by an unnamed writer who came "north," possibly former ballplayer-manager Tim Murnane, who was the sports editor at the *Boston Daily Globe* and the organizer and first president of the Connecticut League in 1899. He had traveled to Indian Island on at least one earlier occasion and had written the poignant story "The Dreamer" in 1908.

The story begins, "Up on the Penobscot river, near the village of Old Town, Me., Sockalexis, [at] one time the pride of all baseball, is running a little ferry. The writer found him there, straining his eyes in the light of a full moon to read the account of a big league game in which Chief Meyers had starred. He is not Sockalexis, the steel thewed [*sic*], his step is not firm, though there is still that hint of steel spring muscles that gave him once the name of 'Deerfoot of the Diamond.'"

After recounting Sockalexis's career and life and his concerns about "what might have been," Sockalexis tells the reporter, "Like me the sun has come home to rest. Soon will come the shadows." The reporter noted that Sockalexis "asked me then if they spoke of him 'down there.' What would you have me tell him. I had to lie."[19]

The *Bangor Daily Commercial*'s "Up In Old Town" column for Friday, September 13, 1912, mentioned a championship baseball game in which the All–Old Town nine would be traveling to South Brewer Saturday "to try and get the scalps of the Easterns." Manager Dorr selected players from the nines of the Inter-Village league. "A red hot game" was expected and "a large number will probably accompany the boys from the city." The account noted: "Louis Sockalexis will umpire and the game is called for 3 o'clock."[20]

Celebrating the marathon running feats in 1912 and 1913 of Andrew Sockalexis, who was the fourth-place finisher at the 1912 Olympic Games at Stockholm and who took second place again at the Boston Marathon in 1913, the *Old Town Enterprise* briefly played the "what-might-have-been" game with the life of Louis Sockalexis in this brief commentary, first published in the *Kennebec Journal* on August 2, 1913: "If Louis Sockalexis had followed the line of conduct he has handed to Andrew Sockalexis to let John Barleycorn alone, he would have been a fixed star in the baseball world instead of only a meteor. It is good news that the Holy Cross and Cleveland player is on his good behavior in these days. It was a treat in the old days just to see Louis run out a hit. Billy Sunday, Jimmy Callahan and the lamented Mercer had nothing on the Old Town Indian in going down to first."[21]

In July and August of 1913 there were newspaper accounts of two players Sockalexis had known and about baseball. After "retiring" from managing that city's team in 1910, Jesse Burkett was back in Worcester, Massachusetts, guiding the town entry as manager in the New England League. Wee Willie Sudhoff, one of the few stars of the 1899 Cleveland Exiles (who was moved by owner Robison to his more successful St. Louis franchise), was reported to be "violently insane." Sudhoff, thirty-eight years old and said to be suffering from an old head injury as a beanball victim, had to be forcibly removed from his home by two police officers. Washington's Walter Johnson won his thirty-sixth game of the year. The Chicago White Sox had "balked" and then refused to play an exhibition game with the Mohawk Giants when it was discovered that Wickware, the team's star pitcher, was a "colored twirler."

In August a *Worcester Telegram* headline asserted, "Sockalexis Back As League Umpire, Famous Indian Is Holding The Indicator In Games In The Eastern Maine League." The story reported:

> Louis Sockalexis, who in the late 90s was famous as a Holy Cross baseball player, and who afterward broke into professional ball and startled all balldom with his brilliant and phenomenal playing, and whose name is destined ever to remain in the category of the greatest players in the history of baseball, after a lay-off of many years is back on the diamond again. But no longer is Sock chasing the little pill over the lot and smashing the ball out with the bullet like drives that made his name so famous. He is an umpire in the Eastern Maine league. Every so often some Holy Cross man manages to run across the path of the famous Sock, and the great, full-chested Indian swells with pride when tales of Holy Cross are recited to him. If there is one thing left in life that brings joy to the heart of Sockalexis, whose achievements are now but history, it is to meet a Holy Cross man.[22]

Walter McManus, a Holy Cross pitcher, encountered Sockalexis while playing in the Eastern Maine League. McManus claimed Sockalexis was "proving as great a favorite as an arbiter as he did a ball player." McManus related that "for the past few years he has run a ferry across the Penobscot river" but that "few [visitors] who passed over that ferry knew that the great, melancholy, full-chested Indian whose long limbs and wiry muscles testify to his former speed, is the once famous Indian ball player. But the present summer Sockalexis has forsaken his ferry and taken to the diamond." [23]

The *Worcester Telegram* story concluded that Sockalexis "was regarded as the greatest ball player in the college world. His batting was wonderful and his speed enabled him to steal bases at will. Everywhere crowds went wild over him. Even now, when the winds whistle through the trees up over the crest of Mt. St. James legend says it is the echo of cheers which the student body sent ringing across the campus for Sockalexis...years ago." [24]

Sockalexis reportedly did well as an umpire only a few months before his death. In its issue for the week of August 23, 1913, the *Old Town Enterprise* carried this local story: "Louis Sockalexis as umpire for the Maine and New Brunswick League is considered a great success and fills a long felt need." [25]

Just three months before Louis Sockalexis's death, the great Carlisle Indian athlete Jim Thorpe, triumphant after winning gold medals at the 1912 Olympic Games in Stockholm, made his "first full game" big league baseball debut for the New York Giants in a game at Boston on September 29, 1913. Giants manager John McGraw, who had played against Sockalexis in 1897 as a member of a stellar Baltimore club, reportedly had Sockalexis's ball-playing abilities in mind when he offered Thorpe the opportunity to play. At the time, McGraw's Giants had already clinched the National League pennant and were playing out the schedule with reserves. According to a game account, Thorpe "poled a home run into the center field bleachers and also made a single" in a 5–3 New York victory. He also "pulled down several difficult flies" in the outfield.

Ironically, Thorpe experienced a meteoric rise and fall in big league baseball very much like that of Sockalexis, but for an entirely different reason. Thorpe turned out to be a far less talented hitter than Sockalexis had been. According to Stephen Thompson, Thorpe was easily the most famous American Indian ever to play major league baseball, but he was far from the best. From 1913 to 1915 he was with the Giants, returned from the minors to play with the Reds and then the Giants in 1917, and closed out his baseball career with the Braves in 1919. He was, according to Thompson, "never more than a part-time player." [26] The only time he appeared in more than one hundred games was 1917, when he batted only .231 in 308 at bats. His lifetime average was a mere .252. After his legendary track-and-field career and subsequent mediocre baseball career, Jim Thorpe did prove his skills as an outstanding professional athlete playing football.

Stating that Sockalexis was "the first Indian to reach the major leagues, or at least the first to have any significant impact," Thompson notes that a number of fine American Indian ballplayers quickly followed Sockalexis. John T. "Chief" Meyers served as a star catcher with a highly respectable lifetime average of .291 playing for the Giants, Dodgers, and Braves between 1909 and 1917. Albert "Chief" Bender earned a place in the Hall of Fame after pitching for the Philadelphia Athletics from 1903 to 1914. A little later, "Indian" Bob Johnson, Moses "Chief" Yellowhorse (who appeared in only thirty-eight total games), slugging first baseman Rudy York, and pitching standout Allie "Big Chief" Reynolds, a member of the Creek nation from Bethany, Oklahoma, were among other American Indians to play in the major leagues.[27]

A February 23, 1934, issue of the weekly *Old Town Enterprise* featured Sockalexis in an account describing the careers of five great American Indian athletes. Written by Jim Hurley for the *New York Daily Mirror*, the *Enterprise* published only the portion about Sockalexis. The story was part of an effort to collect donations for a memorial fund that would pay for a more fitting memorial on Sockalexis's grave. The five American Indians whom Hurley cited were Sockalexis, Sac and Fox nation member Jim Thorpe, Chippewa nation and Baseball Hall of Fame member Charlie Bender, Onondaga nation member (from Ontario) Tom Longboat (a legendary long-distance runner and winner of the 1907 Boston Marathon in record time), and John Meyers, the great catcher of the New York Giants from the Cahuilla nation of Riverside, California. Bender, who was born in 1883 and died in 1954, was from Brainerd, Minnesota, and compiled a major league pitching record of 204 wins and 129 losses. He appeared in five World Series and was the top pitcher in 1911, winning 18 games and losing only five with a no-hitter included among his victories. Hurley asserted: "Those [five] names were household words in America at various times from 1895 to 1915.... The career of Sockalexis was the most dramatic of the five. His flash across the athletic horizon was more colorful than the rest and at the same time the briefest, ruined by early success and the glamor of the throngs." After detailing that rise and the fall, Hurley wrote: "Then, like hundreds of stars before and since, he passed on forever into the great sea of the forgotten. Stark tragedy dogged him for a few years during which he was a complete down-and-outer, but he finally drifted back to the reservation of the Penobscot, where he awaited his twilight days running a little ferry."[28]

16
Death and Continuing Misconceptions

WRITER FREDERICK JOHN and student chronicler Trina Wellman both have claimed that Sockalexis married when he returned to Indian Island for good, but offer no name, no shred of documentation. There is really no evidence he ever married, and there is no record of a state marriage certificate in his name in Maine. Just who, if anybody, was the great love of his life is a secret that rests with him.

John described Sockalexis later in his life as "just one of the fat, smoky, care-free Indians of the little village."[1] He continued to serve as the island's ferry operator in the days before a single-lane bridge connected the reservation to the mainland. During the winter he worked for $30 a month as a woodcutter at a logging camp in Burlington, just north of Old Town.

Only the unreliable Hughie Jennings offers any biographical details of Sockalexis's life in Maine. Jennings imagined that "Sockalexis' downfall had broken his heart…. In the evenings he would bring out his trunk and read over the clippings that he had saved during his big league career. These clippings were the chapters that told the story of his greatness. He would read each one over and over, memorizing each word."[2] As touching and theatrical as this sounds, Jennings offers no source for his knowledge of such nights, no evidence that he himself saw or talked with anyone who was with Sockalexis in the last days of his life.

Jennings was no stranger to difficult times and tragedy. Extraordinary ironies exist that may tie the two players as kindred spirits. An outstanding player as a youth, Jennings too made a rapid rise to the major leagues. He began as a catcher and moved to first base but ultimately made the unusual transition from those positions to shortstop, so that his manager could take advantage of his speed. Described as a complete player, Jennings was a stand-out as a hitter, fielder, and base runner. On Baltimore's pennant-winning teams of 1894, 1895, and 1896, Jennings hit .332, .386 and .397, respectively. In his book *History of the Detroit Tigers*, Fred Lieb describes Jennings as enthusiastic and bright. His enthusiasm, it is said, inspired the nickname, "The Ee-Yah Man." As a coach, Jennings jumped up and down on one leg, flung his arms in the air, and screamed a piercing "Ee-yah! Ee-yah!" to encourage batters from the third-base coaching box. Proof of his intelligence, Lieb suggests, was demonstrated in that, "unlike many of his fellow players of the gay nineties, Jennings didn't spend his winters sitting on his seat swilling up a lot of beer. He managed to pick up his share of schooling in the coal country," attending St. Bonaventure College and later Cornell's law school.

Although Jennings contracted tuberculosis later in his life and died of meningitis in 1928 at the age of fifty-eight, for a time he seemed "to have as many lives as a cat," Lieb noted. On June 28, 1897, just a few days before Sockalexis's crossroads Fourth of July jump from a building's second floor, Jennings nearly died after a fast ball struck him in the head under the left temple. The pitcher that day was Sockalexis's arch foe, Amos Rusie. For several days Jennings hovered between life and death and then pulled through. Apparently Jennings had a hard head, literally speaking. Some years later he was working out in the Cornell gym and intended to finish with a swim. The place was poorly lighted, and Jennings was unaware that an attendant had drained the pool. So, yes, he dove in head first into an empty pool. Again, it was feared he would die, but again Jennings pulled through. Later, during his Detroit days, Jennings was driving with some friends over one of Pennsylvania's slippery roads during the winter off-season. The car went over the side of a mountain. Two people died and another was seriously hurt, but Jennings escaped with only a few bruises.[3] It is possible that Jennings's problems with accuracy and memory of the Sockalexis story are attributable to a physical condition resulting from the traumatic incidents he suffered.

Louis Sockalexis was not so fortunate. Two months after his forty-second birthday, on Christmas Eve, 1913, Sockalexis was missing when his shift came back to camp at the end of the logging day. One of the crew members found him dead. Jennings claimed that "the ravages of rum and worry over his failure had destroyed his health. He became a shadow of the once great athlete.... He was stricken with heart disease. Chronic alcoholism was cited as the cause of death."[4] The *Bangor Daily News* reported that Sockalexis had suffered a heart attack.[5]

There are actually several different versions concerning Sockalexis' death in the lumbering community of Burlington, and the role that Moore's Tavern did or did not play in the last minutes of his life.

In a letter to the author, Alan H. Hawkins, then Superintendent of Schools in Cape Elizabeth, said he'd heard stories in the early '60s and '70s at a time when he was "most interested in the small town of Burlington, Maine, located on the Passadumkeag River and a well-known entry to the lumbering areas east of Burlington in the Nicatous [Lake] area." In 1977 he published the history of the town.

Hawkins wrote: "During my early days of research Moore's Tavern, located at the intersection of Route 88 and the road from Lowell, was in its last days but was still owned and operated by Norris and Elvie Moore. They had been there as early as 1908. I remember several times when I went to dinner there with Stewart M. Lord, the local town clerk and historian. Norris always regaled us with stories of lumbering days in the area. I well remember sitting in front of the fireplace one evening and he was telling about the exploits of Louis Sockalexis, not only as a baseball player but as a lumbering man and, unfortunately, as a drunk. He said that Louis stayed more than once at the Tavern to sleep off days of drinking. One night, a very cold one, Louis was found lying out front and was carried into the Tavern and laid in front of the fire to warm up. Unfortunately, it was too late, and he died lying there. Now I am not sure of the whole truth of that story but do know that Louis was well-known in the area."

In the winter of 1979, Norris B. Barker of Enfield, published the following letter on the editorial pages of the Bangor Daily News: "As a young boy I lived in Burlington. One day a few of us were playing ball in the schoolyard when a tote team on its way to a lumber camp in the Nicatous Lake region came by. An Indian jumped off the wagon and joined our game. After a few minutes of play, he ran down the road and climbed back on the wagon. I saw Louis Sockalexis again on a cold December day. He had leaned against a tree in front of the Burlington Hotel, but was now slumped down in the snow. A man standing nearby told me that he was dead. I am now past 80, but I still remember a man who stopped his journey long enough to spend a few minutes to play ball with a bunch of kids."

And, finally, there is this statement from Fern Cummings, long-time Burlington town official and curator: "Sockalexis fished and hunted at Nicatous. He had a heart attack and they were driving back to Bangor. They stopped at the Tavern because he was not doing well. He died there. There was no 'tavern' at that time for drinking. In fact, the tavern did not have drinking publicly – the townspeople forbade it in the 1800s."

Jennings claimed that when crew members removed Sockalexis's blue flannel shirt, they found a wad of newspaper clippings in one of the pockets. They were accounts, Jennings maintained, of his great ninth inning against Chicago. Jennings even created a headline for the report of this mythical game, After repeating the point that his greatest moment resulted in his greatest fall, Jennings concluded, "Yes, he might have been the greatest player of all time. He had a wonderful instinct and no man seemed to have [had] so many natural gifts as Sockalexis." [6]

Jennings is a talented teller of tall tales, but as Society for American Baseball Research member Jay Feldman comments, "Given Jennings' track record for accuracy, this may well be hyperbole. Even if it is a bit of an exaggeration, though, it says something essential about Sockalexis; the man had some ineffable quality that caused people to idealize and romanticize him and his exploits — he thoroughly captured the popular imagination." [7]

On Thursday, December 25, 1913, the *Bangor Daily News* carried this headline on the front page, "Unexpected Death Of Louis Sockalexis, Famous Penobscot Indian Baseball Player's Meteoric Career A Notable Chapter In The History Of The Diamond." The accompanying story reported that Sockalexis "dropped dead of heart disease this morning while working at Sibley's lumber camp in Burlington, about 35 miles from here." The story asserted that when the "great Book of Baseball" is ultimately written, "there will be a chapter on 'Sockalexis, The Greatest Player Who Might Have Been.' In all of baseball history there has been no more lamentable chapter than the rise and fall of 'The Abanaki Adonis,' as one writer called him."[8] Much of the obituary's text was taken from an account in the *Bangor Daily Commercial*, word for word, run the year before. It summed up Sockalexis's last years this way:

For a few years he drifted about in the minors, with Hartford, of the Eastern League; Lowell, of the New England League; Bangor, of the Maine State League. He was just an ordinary player, but just the same, pitchers who faced him were often surprised at the way he would cut in on a drop or shoot for a triple or home run when least expected. And the pity of it all is that had Sockalexis played out his game, he might have retired a wealthy man, or even spent his last days as a big league umpire. For the past ten years or so "Sock" has umpired hereabouts, in Aroostook and elsewhere and it can be truly said his average work has been exceptionally good. He was never known to make a mistake in the interpretation of the rules and his judgment on balls, strikes and base plays was rarely questioned. The most rabid [umpire-baiter] was always at a loss to "get to" Sockalexis. There was a quiet dignity about him which offered no opening. He rarely talked back or said much to the players, but when he did there was never any doubt as to what he meant. His last work as umpire was as official umpire in the last games of the season in the New Brunswick and Maine league and at South Brewer in the 1913 season. Personally Sockalexis was much like the typical Indian, taciturn and inoffensive. He was a voracious reader particularly of sporting news and had a vast fund of information on baseball for many years past. The name of Sockalexis is yet magic with the old-time fans who remember him in his palmy days and some of them cannot be convinced that the Indian had all the physique and skill to have risen to baseball fame — as high and mighty as "Ty" Cobb or any of the great outfielders of those and former days.[9]

The *Old Town Enterprise* for the week of December 29 had this headline: "The Death Of Louis F. Sockalexis, Indian Ball Player Of National Fame." The account said: "The death of Louis F. Sockalexis of Indian Island took place in Burlington Wednesday morning. He went to work for the winter for a Mr. Sibley, lumberman. He has always been considered to be in rugged health and left last Friday morning, Dec. 21st, 1913, for that place where he died." Accompanied to the station by his sister, Mrs. Thomas Pennewaite, his closest relative, he reportedly complained of a pain in his left side. His sister wanted him to stay at home. But Sockalexis "thought it would not amount to much" and continued on to the lumber camp.[10]

The *Enterprise* obituary makes a surprising assertion about Sockalexis's father's alleged love of and "reputation" for playing baseball. Francis Sockalexis was the man supposedly so infuriated at the thought of his son leaving the island to play the white man's game that he paddled to Washington, D.C., to seek a presidential decree making his son chief of the Penobscots. The obituary claimed, "Louis Sockalexis was the son of the late Francis P. Sockalexis who as a young man had quite a local reputation as a ball player so Louis came rightly by his ability for playing base ball." The obituary distilled Sockalexis's career in baseball, explaining simply, "For the best part of twenty years Lewis [*sic*] F. Sockalexis has been a well known figure in baseball circles in spite of himself."[11]

His later years were described this way: "Since leaving the leagues some years ago he has coached local teams, umpired as his services were desired and his work was always very satisfactory. He knew base ball from A to Z, and all lovers of the game were always glad of an opportunity to talk base ball with Sockalexis. He was always pointed out when at a game as the only Sockalexis of league fame. He was always quiet and gentlemanly and made many friends."[12]

Describing his modest wake, the paper said, "As he lay in his plain and modest casket supported by two kitchen chairs in the humble home of his sister, his hands folded across his manly breast, with fingers bent and crooked, the result of many a hard battle on the diamond, we could not help moralizing a little and thinking how different the surroundings might have been had he followed the course of his colleagues, say McGraw, Mack and others of his day. While his career in the national league was short but meteoric his name will have a place in base ball history of the last two decades. His funeral took place from the church on the island today, Saturday, Dec. 29th 1913 and was largely attended."[13]

The *Bangor Daily Commercial*, for December 28, 1913, carried a photograph, the headline "The Last Of Sockalexis, Once Famous Indian Buried Beside Departed Tribesmen In The Island Churchyard," and the following account:

Practically every man, woman and child on Indian Island, a number of Old Town citizens and others attended the last rites for Louis Sockalexis held Saturday morning in St. Anne's church, on the island, which he had attended regularly all his life. The sudden end of the once-famous ball-player who dropped dead on Wednesday while at work in a lumber camp at Burlington seems to have made a profound impression among the tribe.

Perhaps no other resident of the island was so well posted on general current events as he. None were ever so much in contact with the outside world and he retained a deep interest, particularly in sporting events and was looked to as an authority. He was a voracious reader and his home was always full of books and papers. As he rarely left the island for any length of time he will be greatly missed especially by the younger generation with whom he was a great favorite.

The service was impressively conducted by Rev. Mgr. Trudel's assistant, Rev. Paul Von Buhrer of St. Joseph's church in this city [Old Town]. After the conclusion of the mass, the funeral cortege passed slowly along the main street to the cemetery. At the grave there was a brief service, Fr. Von Buhrer speaking at some length of the life and career of the dead tribesman.[14]

The bearers were Francis Sockalexis, Louis's uncle and the father of marathon runner Andrew Sockalexis, Mitchell M. Francis, and Stephen Sockbesin, all tribal members.

In Cleveland the death of Louis Sockalexis received passing attention. Three of the city's four daily newspapers carried the story. The *News* contained one paragraph. Both the *Cleveland Plain Dealer* and the *Leader* printed the same wire service account, and the *Plain Dealer* story included the former ballplayer's picture.

The *Leader* also carried a brief accompanying story, featuring an interview with a former teammate, shortstop Ed McKean. McKean was quoted as saying of Sockalexis: "He was a wild bird. He couldn't lose his taste for firewater. His periodical departures became such a habit he finally slipped out of the majors. He had more natural ability than any player I have ever seen, past or present."[15]

The testimonials that followed Sockalexis after he left the playing field and, indeed, for many years after he died, leave little doubt about his extraordinary ability and unfulfilled potential.

Hughie Jennings, a great player who eventually managed Ty Cobb for fourteen years from 1907 to 1921, wrote: "Louis Sockalexis had the most brilliant career of any man who ever played the game. At no time has a player crowded so many remarkable accomplishments into such a short period of time as Sockalexis. He should have been the greatest player of all times — greater than Cobb, Wagner, Lajoie, Hornsby, or any of the other men who made history for the game."[16]

Jennings and immortal baseball manager John McGraw both expressed the sentiment that, had Sockalexis stayed in the major leagues for five years, without drinking trouble, he could well have become the greatest of all time, including Cobb, Honus Wagner, and Ruth.[17]

Writer Francis Hatch cited the remarks of Spiders' shortstop McKean: "Old Soc was a wonder when he joined us in '97. I can't recall any ball player of recent times, with the possible exception of Joe Jackson, who attracted so much attention. He was a remarkable hitter, a man of amazing speed, and a fair outfielder."[18]

The oft-quoted Andy Coakley, who pitched for the Athletics in the days of Waddell, Bender, Plank and Coombs, called Sockalexis the greatest ballplayer he ever saw: "He had a gorgeous left-hand swing, hit the ball as far as Babe Ruth, was faster than Ty Cobb and as good a base runner. He had the outfielding skill of Tris Speaker and threw like Bob Meusel, which means no one could throw a ball farther or more accurately."[19] This remark seems to have originated with the famous wire service sportswriter and author Harry Grayson.

Coakley's manager on the Athletics, Connie Mack, had had an eleven-year playing career from 1886 until 1896, mostly as a catcher with Washington, Buffalo, and Pittsburgh. Then, from 1901 until 1950, he built a distinguished managerial record that led to the Baseball Hall of Fame. Mack wrote of Sockalexis: "He was a huge fellow who looked like an Indian on the warpath and who scalped the great pitchers of his day. He swung his bat with the power of a tomahawk.... When he appeared at the bat the fans broke out in vociferous war whoops. His throwing arm was the wonder of the times. Standing erect in deep center field, he could throw a ball like a shot from a gun — straight over home plate as perfect as a strike. His feet were as fleet as those of a Maine deer. He could do a 100-yard dash in ten seconds."[20]

According to *Bangor Daily News* sportswriter Bud Leavitt, Maine-resident William Carrigan, who managed the Boston Red Sox to American League pennants in 1915 and 1916, declared that Sockalexis belonged with baseball's "very select company." Carrigan, who left baseball for banking in Lewiston, Maine, said: "I don't remember ever seeing a quicker bat or a stronger arm. Among the moderns, possibly the one player worthy of comparison is that young man Joe DiMaggio. He has a trace of Sockalexis' stuff. But I don't believe he can run or throw with the Indian."[21] Even Babe Ruth's boss, New York Yankees general manager Ed Barrow, weighed in with this irreverent assessment: "Sockalexis was the greatest outfielder in history, the best hitter, the best thrower, the best fielder and also the best drinker."[22]

At first, Louis Sockalexis was buried in a remote corner of the reservation, his grave marked only by a wooden cross with his name burned into it. After seeing this humble grave site, Holy Cross classmate Joseph H. Powers wrote the verse "Sockalexis," which was published in *The Purple* of Holy Cross.

The Penobscot reservation,
In Old Town, down in Maine,
Within a lonely graveyard,
I saw a marker and a name;

And the name was Sockalexis,
On a mildewed stone, so bare,
Nothing else, just Sockalexis;
Nothing else was written there.

Fond memories of the nineties
Gripped me in nostalgic haze,
As I gazed upon that marker
Of that star in college days.

Tall and bronzed and handsome,
I just saw him there once more
Out upon that upper diamond
Mid the crowd's tremendous roar.

He was to all, the greatest idol,
Yes, baseball's shining light,
And Holy Cross, his Alma Mater,
Built his pedestal of might.

His star shone on so brightly,
And in rapid strides, he rose,
A world's outstanding fielder
In a baseball world of woes.

His career, a shining stardom,
Then — a shining star no more,
Just an aged and weary body
The years had called his score.

Yet, he died with all his spirit,
All his tribesmen told me so;
He was loved by all his people,
Yes, by all the world, I know.

Once more, I read that marker

But I read it with a sigh;
Then one more prayer to heaven
For that gracious Indian boy.[23]

In 1934, *Penobscot Times* editor Tom Wadsworth spearheaded a drive to erect a more fitting memorial to Sockalexis. Describing the campaign thirty-eight years later, sports broadcaster and columnist Curt Gowdy wrote, "The Cleveland Indians organization was asked for and responded with a $100 donation" to start the ball rolling, and the subsequent fund-raising culminated in a formal ceremony, held by State of Maine and Indian Island officials. Gowdy added, "Money started pouring in from baseball fans all across America and soon the large stone monument was a reality. It has crossed bats with a baseball above them in bronze."[24]

Gowdy also described a second memorial, a wooden marker in the shape of a baseball diamond, positioned behind the stone monument. That marker was eventually removed, but according to Gowdy the text of the marker read, "This is the grave of the famous Louis Sockalexis who was the first Indian to become a major league baseball player, following graduation from Holy Cross College at Worcester, Mass. He joined the Cleveland team in the American League. He was a talented and spectacular player and colorful in all his actions. Soon after he joined the Cleveland team it was renamed the Cleveland Indians, the name it still carries today."[25]

The Gowdy column itself featured several significant handed-down errors about Sockalexis. Citing his "good friend, Bud Leavett [*sic*], the outdoor editor of the Bangor News," as his companion in discovering the legend of Sockalexis, Gowdy stated that he and Leavitt had learned about the famous Sockalexis's "brothers." In fact, Sockalexis had a famous second cousin, Olympic marathon runner Andrew Sockalexis. Gowdy revives the fanciful assertion that Sockalexis could "hit a baseball the length of the reservation, which is some six hundred feet." He also says that Cleveland fans were responsible for giving the team its official nickname, the Indians, a misconception still widely accepted today.[26]

A *Boston Herald* editorial on May 18, 1934, commented, "A tragic little episode in baseball is recalled by the efforts of the Penobscot Indians of Old Town, State of Maine, to raise $400 for a tablet on the grave of their tribesman, Louis Sockalexis." The editorial quoted Sockalexis as saying after his arrest for vagrancy and public drunkenness, "They liked me on the baseball field, but I liked firewater." The editorial concluded, "Add 'ring' to baseball field and the list of Caucasians about whom the same epitaph might be written would go back to the earliest days of pugilism, come down to the present and receive additions day by day."[27]

Headlines from the sporting pages today need to include "drugs" in the alcohol category and "football," "basketball," and other games in the sports category. Sadly, the names of the many, many more who made the same rise and fall as Louis Sockalexis would also have to be added.

The new monument erected over Sockalexis's grave was officially dedicated on Sunday, June 24, 1934, at a 2:30 P.M. service attended by a large crowd. The inscription on the monument reads: "In memory of Louis Sockalexis whose athletic achievements while at Holy Cross College and later with the Cleveland major league baseball team won for him national fame. Born Oct. 24, 1871 – Died Dec. 24, 1913. Erected by his friends."

Describing the dedication, the *Old Town Enterprise* said, "The Long, Long Trail has been reached, the monument has been erected and unveiled, it is now a matter of past events.... The mighty ball player, Louis Sockalexis, has a monument worthy of his achievements erected over his grave and his fellowmen of the Penobscot Tribe can point with pride and honor to this beautiful shaft of granite which marks his resting place." [28]

The 152nd Field Artillery Band played before the ceremony started. At 2:30 P.M., the Rev. Morris H. Carroll, pastor of St. Mary's Church in Old Town, the man who had arranged the program, served as the master of ceremonies and delivered the opening address, thanking all those who made contributions on behalf of the committee. The main speaker was Raymond A. Grady of Bangor, the state deputy of the Knights of Columbus, identified as the largest contributor to the fund. Grady discussed his own acquaintance with the great baseball player. [29] A number of people associated with Holy Cross attended the ceremony, including writer and translator John A. Fitzgerald, who had composed a commemorative ballad that was declaimed during the ceremony.

> Louis, we've gathered here today
> Tribesmen and sportsmen, we all attend
> To mark the spot where your mortal clay
> Came to our universal end.
> More than one epitaph's been penned
> Of the player that never had peer,
> But here's your mead, for an old-time friend:
> "He was loyal and brave, and his heart sincere."
>
> We could write: "At the start of the season's play.
> When the Bruins brown were all set to rend.
> You 'stole' six times on that Patriots' day.
> — A record that none can tie or mend —

And cracked a homer its way to wend
Through their chapel window, from out the clear,"
But no! 'Tis a finer tribute to send:
"He was loyal and brave, and his heart sincere."

As a batter, no pitcher could say you nay,
You straightened whatever they could bend;
And on Giant-Indian opening day,
The Gotham fans came in crowds to tend —
"Rusie will fan him!" So they intend,
But — "the first ball a homer, into the Clear!"
What a line! But a greater one, old friend, "heart sincere."

Louis, with saddened hearts we send
This tribute to one who had no peer,
To one of the few who met his end
Loyal and brave, and his heart sincere.[30]

In January 1956, Louis Sockalexis was the individual who topped the list of those elected to the newly established Holy Cross Athletic Hall of Fame. The *Old Town Enterprise* reported that, "His name will be placed first on the roll of athletic greats at the second annual Varsity Club dinner, Saturday evening at Kimball Hall, Worcester."[31] Ralph Ulmer, the president of Old Town's city council, represented Sockalexis's hometown and accepted the honor on his behalf. Selecting Ulmer to receive the award for Sockalexis proved controversial. As Penobscot tribal governor Albert Nicola explained to the *Bangor Daily News*, "When an Indian gets in trouble, he's from Indian Island, but when he does something great they say he's from Old Town."[32] Members of the Penobscot nation were angered that Holy Cross would invite a white official from Old Town to the ceremony instead of a representative of the Penobscots.

Long after his death, honors continued to come to Sockalexis. In 1969, Louis was made a charter member of the Maine Baseball Hall of Fame. In 1978, the commissioners of Cuyahoga County, Ohio, proclaimed May 30 to be "Louis Sockalexis Day." Part of their resolution read: "Sockalexis is, indeed, the father of the Cleveland Indians, and deserves a tribute befitting that honor."[33]

On June 2, 1985, the Maine Sports Hall of Fame belatedly inducted Louis Francis Sockalexis into its ranks. Maine's Joan Benoit Samuelson, a 1984 Olympic gold medal–winning marathoner from Cape Elizabeth, may have been the catalyst to bring Louis Sockalexis this long overdue honor.

After Benoit Samuelson won the first-ever woman's marathon in the Olympic Games during the summer of 1984, she was nominated to the Maine Sports Hall of Fame, even though her career was far from over. Comments about Benoit Samuelson led sportswriters to rediscover Andrew Sockalexis, whose marathon performance at the 1912 Stockholm Olympics had gone unrecognized. Andrew Sockalexis was then nominated to the Maine Sports Hall of Fame and elected with Benoit Samuelson in 1984.

Discussion about Andrew Sockalexis led to the realization that Louis Sockalexis, too, had been ignored. The omission was corrected a year later. At the induction ceremony, Edwina Neptune of Indian Island, a niece born many years after Sockalexis's death, represented the Penobscot baseball star.

The Sockalexis name disappeared from Indian Island on June 16, 1987, when the great baseball player's nephew and namesake, Louis J. Sockalexis, died at age seventy-two. The son of the ball player's uncle, Edward and wife, Olive (Tomer), he was born on Indian Island on July 2, 1914, six months after his famous uncle's death.[34] In a 1978 newspaper interview, Sockalexis said, "My whole family is gone," adding that his five brothers and two sisters were all buried in the Indian Island Catholic cemetery.[35] A handyman skilled at lumber work, carpentry, and plumbing, Sockalexis was noted for his expert woodcarvings, a skill he had practiced since his youth.

In 1994, the *Bangor Daily News* reported that the headstone on Louis Sockalexis's grave had been selected as one of "61 Don't Miss Places in Baseball" by *USA Today's Baseball Weekly*. Other baseball memorials on the list included Pierce Oil in Northborough, Massachusetts, the former Sunoco station where Detroit Tiger pitcher Mark Fidrych worked before he was named American League Rookie of the Year in 1976; Gate to Heaven Cemetery in Hawthorne, New York, the burial site of Babe Ruth and Billy Martin; the original "Field of Dreams" built for the movie in Dyersville, Iowa; and Mickey Lolich's Donut and Pastry Shop in Lake Orion, Michigan.[36]

On April 22, 2000, Louis Sockalexis and Andrew Sockalexis were inducted into the American Indian Athletic Hall of Fame, in Lawrence, Kansas, in ceremonies held in Tulsa, Oklahoma. Representing the two athletes were Steve Padovano, the husband of Ann Padovano, a great-great niece of Andrew Sockalexis, and Angelo Quito, a great-great nephew of Andrew's. Also present for the induction ceremonies were Butch Phillips, a Penobscot tribal elder, and this book's author, who initiated the petition for consideration of both Penobscot athletes for the Hall of Fame.

17
Sockalexis's Cleveland Indians

O VER TIME, the question of the Cleveland Indians' nickname and its relation to Sockalexis has caused debate. One issue that can be easily resolved concerns whether Sockalexis's arrival in Cleveland in 1897 brought a change in the team's nickname. Clearly it did, despite claims to the contrary by Don MacWilliams, a Portland, Maine, sports broadcaster and the author of a book about the state's most famous athletes. Until Sockalexis arrived, Cleveland's sportswriters called the team the Spiders. The evidence in sports pages makes it clear that the arrival of Sockalexis prompted the newspapers to use the nickname the Indians. MacWilliams was mistaken in his belief that the team was already nicknamed the Indians before Sockalexis came on the scene because he failed to see that the nickname emerged during the exhibition season of 1897, spurred by the presence of Sockalexis. The second and more complex question concerns whether the adoption of "Indians" as a permanent nickname in 1915 was the winning choice in a fan contest and whether the choice was a tribute to Sockalexis.[1]

Cleveland's major league baseball team has a long and colorful history of nicknames. In 1869, Cleveland's first professional baseball team was known as the Forest Citys. They were called the Spiders from 1889 to 1897. Then Louis Sockalexis caught the attention of sportswriters, who referred to the team as the Indians. In 1899, the team was stripped of its best players and hosted few home games, which is when sports pundits rechristened Cleveland "the Exiles" and "the Misfits" (see Chapter 12). Reconstituted as an American League team in 1900, Cleveland also began wearing bright blue uniforms that won the appellation Blues or Bluebirds from 1900 to 1901. Feeling the need for a more forceful nickname, the Cleveland players renamed themselves the Bronchos for the 1902 season. When the team discarded the blue uniforms in 1903, the *Cleveland Press* held a name contest for the fans. The winning selection, "Napoleons" or "Naps," honoring the arrival of the team's new manager, Napoleon Lajoie, led the popular selection by eighty-four votes.

In March 1903, the *Cleveland Press* asked readers, "What Would You Call the Bronchos? New Nickname to be Selected by 'Press' Readers This Week." The story said,

> The Bronchos are to be Rechristened . . . . That title was fitting when [manager] Armour's aggregation was composed of untamed Indian ponies, but it hardly applies aptly to his present stable of probable derby winners.

Something more fitting is needed. The Press thinks so, and President Kilfoyl is of the same opinion, but neither the Press nor the Cleveland Ball Club Co. desires to provide the name.

"Put it up to the public," said President Kilfoyl. "Let Press readers vote as to what nickname we shall give the team, and whatever name the voters select shall be the team's official sobriquet."

And that's the plan. Every reader of "The Press" is entitled to vote, and he may select any name he desires. The name receiving the highest number of votes will be chosen.[2]

The account noted that readers were expected to give a reason for their preferences, but that votes would be counted whether a reason was provided or not. "The name should be fitting, however," the newspaper cautioned.[3]

Then, "for the guidance of voters, a few suggestions as to names are given herewith, but voters are not restricted to these names. On the contrary, the contest is conducted principally in order that an original and especially apt nickname may be produced." The list of suggested names included: The Napoleons, in honor of their captain, Napoleon Lajoie; The Armour-clads, in honor of their manager William R. Armour; The Metropolitans, because Cleveland is the metropolis of Ohio; and The Buckeyes, because the Clevelands represent Ohio in the American league.[4] "The Emperors, also in honor of Napoleon Lajoie and because the original Napoleon was an emperor." The contest was to accept entries for the period of one week, and end on Saturday April 4.[5]

On March 31, *The Press* ran essentially the same notice headlined, "How Does 'Cyclops' Please Your Fancy? That's One of the Names Suggested as a Nickname for the Bronchos." The fan's reasoning was, "Would you call them the Cyclops, because they are all giants."[6] The headline for April 1 read, "Napoleons, How Would That Do As A Nickname For The Bronchos?" By way of explanation the accompanying story said:

> Napoleon once won a pennant or two. Of course, that wasn't what they called his victories, in those days, but what he did was equivalent to winning a pennant, to say the least. But be that as it may, Napoleon was quite a fellow, no less so, perhaps, than his successor in the base ball world, Napoleon Lajoie. Perhaps that's why so many fans are voting to have the Bronchos rechristened the Napoleons. It is true that the original Napoleon came to a bad finish, but before he did that he placed to his credit several performances not at all to be sneered at. Therefore, it seems that Napoleon isn't bad for an official nickname for Cleveland's possible pennant winners. But Napoleon isn't the only name that is receiving votes. Emperors finds favor, and so do Metropolitans. Giants is another suggestion, but the New Yorks are known as Giants, whether rightfully or not, and it would be like stealing another's

thunder to name our team similarly. The Buckeyes, the Invincibles, the Birds, the Superlatives and the Viceroys are names that have been suggested.[7]

April 2 brought more urging for votes and additional suggestions for names: "Hundreds of votes are being received. Napoleons, Emperors, Lajoies, Buckeyes and Giants are names that are receiving many votes. Thoroughbreds, Eagles, Cyclops, Birds, Selects, Excelsiors, Superlatives, Thistles 'because they stick,' Armour-clads, Monarchs, Invincibles, Braves, Homers and Commodores are some other suggestions. One voter suggests Spikes, because "they'll nail the pennant," and another offers Somarlas, as a contraction of Somers, Armour, and Lajoie."[8]

The April 4 headline read, "Last Day, Broncho Voting Contest Result Will Be Announced Monday." Among the newest offerings were: Terrors, Dachshunds, Majestics, Midgets, Tip Tops, Crackerjacks, Hornets, Iroquois, and Prospectors, among others. It was noted that "Napoleons continues to find favor and so does Buckeyes."[9]

On Monday, April 6, 1903, a *Cleveland Press* story, headlined "Napoleons, That's The New Official Nickname Of The Former Bronchos — Many Votes Cast," stated:

> Farewell, Bronchos, And Welcome, Napoleons! Almost 5000 votes were cast in "The Press" contest to decide what should be the official sobriquet of the Cleveland team, this year, and Napoleons has won by a safe margin from Buckeyes and Emperors, names that had a close run for second honors. Metropolitans, Giants and Cyclops were nicknames that found considerable favor, but the fans sought to honor the greatest living ball player, and succeeded in so doing by casting a plurality of the votes for Napoleons. Following is the record of votes cast for all names that received more than 100 votes each: Napoleons 365, Buckeyes 281, Emperors 276, Metropolitans 239, Giants 223, Cyclops 214, Gladiators 191, Imperials 174, Armour-clads 114, Red Devils 109. Consequently the Bronchos have become the Napoleons. Here's hoping they carry the name with distinction.[10]

Wasting no time, a *Cleveland Press* story that day about an exhibition game in New Orleans headlined a Cleveland victory story, "Napoleons Outclassed The Pelicans, Despite Listless Playing — Moving North Now."[11] In Cleveland the team was known as the Napoleons thereafter; however, in other cities references to nicknames from the club's past appeared frequently. As late as 1907, the *Boston Daily Globe* used Indians as the Cleveland nickname in a headline noting the team's final appearance in Boston that season, "Last Indian Game Today."[12]

In Cleveland newspapers, Napoleons or Naps was the prevailing nickname for the team from 1904 through mid January 1915. Following the team's poorest showing since 1899, however, its star player-manager was eclipsed, and a new nickname was needed.

Franklin Lewis, in his *History of the Cleveland Indians*, concludes that amateur baseball was more popular in Cleveland in 1914 and 1915 than the Naps were. Toledo was only fifth in the American Association, while the Naps wound up eighth in the American League. "Disinterest in the Naps reached such proportions in 1914 and 1915 that amateur baseball in Cleveland boomed miraculously." In 1914, a reported 80,000 people watched the Telling Strollers beat the Hanna Street Cleaners in a city championship game. The next year, a "legendary" 100,000 fans saw the Cleveland White Autos beat the Omaha Luxus for the world amateur championship. White Autos' star pitcher, Louie "Big Six" Crowley, was said to be more popular in the city than any player on the Naps or with Toledo.[13]

At the end of the 1914 season, Cleveland owner Charley Somers released Lajoie to the Athletics (where he had started his career and where he played two more seasons, finishing with a lifetime batting average of .338). Somers fired new manager Joe Birmingham early in the 1915 season, saying, "My reason for dismissing Birmingham is because I felt the Cleveland fans demanded a change in managers." Lee Fohl, a former catcher, replaced Birmingham as the manager of the Indians, and the team finished seventh, in next-to-last place in the league standings. Said to be desperate for cash, Somers even sold the legendary Shoeless Joe Jackson to Chicago that year. According to Lewis,

> With Lajoie gone from Cleveland, there was speculation in the daily newspapers about a new nickname. The usual slang-touched and colorful names were introduced. But one was outstanding — Indians. So the Naps became the Indians and now, more than 30 years later, modern fans don't recall any other name for the home favorites. . . . There is a story, still heard frequently, that the Indians were named after a real Indian known as Sockalexis, a wild slugger who joined the National League Spiders in 1897. Sock was strong and fast, and there was fire in every movement. But there was fire in his throat, too, and it needed extinguishing. Between remedies for this and the discovery by enemy pitchers that left-handers who threw curves could baffle the redskin, Sock enjoyed a rapid demise as a big leaguer. However, his presence caused many persons to refer to the Cleveland team as Indians, and this interlude in nicknames was brought to the attention of the 1915 newspaper readers when they were voting on an alias to succeed Naps.[14]

The story of a fan contest and of the selection of a name honoring

Sockalexis springs from Lewis's account. The newspapers of the time reveal a different story. On January 5, 1915, the Napoleon Lajoie era ended in Cleveland when the Rhode Island native (who was also nicknamed "The Woonsocket Wonder") was sold to Philadelphia.

Searching for a way to revive interest in the team, Cleveland owner Charles W. Somers created a committee of sportswriters from the city's four newspapers to select a new nickname. Fans were encouraged to provide suggestions to the committee for two weeks, but the final selection would be the decision of the committee, a decision not necessarily based on the popularity of any particular name. Some of the suggestions included: Leafs, Barons, Hustlers, Foresters, Bears, Lions, Youngsters, Kids, Grays, Climbers, Bruins, Blues, Royals, Minors, Tip Tops, Buckeyes, Settlers, Vels, Lakedgers, Originals, and Terriers. One suggestion was Some Hams, a not so flattering merger of the first four letters of owner Somer's name and the last three letters of short-lived manager Joe Birmingham's name. Another fan suggested the Scraps, because "That's all that's left of 'em." Recalling the team's horrible 51-win and 102-loss last-place finish of 1914, a fan named E. H. Kramer wryly concluded that the team should be called the Sleepers.

Although the name Indians was selected on Saturday, January 16, 1915, by the committee, the new nickname was not adopted officially. The team decided to allow a waiting period in order to decide whether the name seemed to fit, caught on with fans, and would be appropriate year after year.

Whether the idea for the name was submitted to the committee or originated with its members is unknown. Legend, largely springing from the unattributed assertion of team biographer Franklin Lewis, says the suggestion came from a fan who wanted to pay tribute to Sockalexis and the Indians nickname from 1897.

On January 17, 1915, page one of the *Cleveland Plain Dealer*'s sports section carried a huge cartoon that made light of the new nickname. The cartoon was followed by a story headlined "Baseball Writers Select Indians As The Best Name To Apply To The Former Naps." The story reported:

> With the going of Nap Lajoie to the Athletics, a new name had to be selected for the Cleveland American league club. President [Charley] Somers invited the Cleveland baseball writers to make the selection. The title of Indians was their choice, it having been one of the names applied to the old National league club of Cleveland many years ago.
>
> The nickname, however, is temporarily bestowed, as the club may conduct itself during the present season as to earn some other cognomen which may be more appropriate. The choice of a name that would be signifi-cant just now was rather difficult with the club itself anchored in last place. . . .
>
> While picking a name for the Cleveland A. L. team, the committee also

agreed that the Cleveland A. A. team owned too many names and that while they were at it, it might be well to agree on just one name for the erstwhile Bearcats. Consequently, the other old nickname of the Cleveland National leaguers was adopted and henceforth all the local papers will call the A. A. club the Spiders.

So there you are — Indians and Spiders.[15]

The *Cleveland Leader* on January 17 reported the same news:

The Indians are with us! That's what will greet the Cleveland American League club when it hits a rival city this year, as the Naps have been officially laid to rest. In place of the Naps, we'll have the Indians, on the warpath all the time, and eager for scalps to dangle at their belts.

At a meeting of local sport writers yesterday afternoon, this was decided upon. The Association team will be known as the Spiders in the future.

Now, if the Naps get going good, and many here think they will, we'll have the old Indians on the warpath, mowing down their opponents in whirl-wind fashion, but, if they follow in the footsteps of the 1914 Naps, we'll have the Indians getting licked most every day.

But the name should prove a good one and may be a mascot which will aid the locals in more ways than one. Ball players as a rule are superstitious and the change in name may work wonders with them. The old "Naps" seemed to imply lack of speed and fight and the new one shows just the opposite.

The fans, who have heard of the new name, were loud in their approval of it, many stating that it would stimulate interest in the club among the fans, as a new name implies that something new will be shown. That's what Manager Birmingham wants to do, show the fans a fighting team, one which never quits.

The Association team will not be labeled Bearcats or Bruins in the future. Spiders being the name agreed upon.[16]

The January 16, 1915, *Boston Daily Globe* announced the name change this way: "The Naps are Dead; Call Them Indians Hereafter." The story, datelined Cleveland, said:

"The Naps are dead! Long live the Indians!" The Cleveland American League baseball club will in future be known as the "Indians." The team was given its new nickname by a committee of local sporting writers at a meeting this afternoon.

The name is a good one, in that it recalls the old fighting days of the early American League period, when the Cleveland players of those days were often referred to as the "Indians" in other cities of the circuit. And that's just what Manager Birmingham has promised the fans the forthcoming season — a "fighting" team.

The old nickname "Naps" became obsolete when Napoleon Lajoie was sold to the Philadelphia Athletics.[17]

Some of the thinking that led to the choice of "Indians" was explored in *Sporting Life*'s "Cleveland Chapter" column on January 23. Writer Ed Bang reported:

> With Lajoie going to the Athletics, it devolved upon the sporting editors of the four Cleveland papers to get together and decide on a new nickname for the team, as "Naps" became obsolete immediately Larry was disposed of to another team. It was back in 1902 [the Contest was in 1903] that Cleveland fans held a voting contest in an effort to arrive at a nickname for the American League club and the rooters voted almost 10 to 1 [*sic*; in fact, Naps topped the next selection by only 84 votes] to call the team after the great player who had just then joined the local outfit. "Naps" was taken from Lajoie's first name, Napoleon, and "Naps" it has been through all the years Larry has been here, whether he was manager, captain, or simply a private in the ranks. The Cleveland sporting editors wrestled for a long time with various nicknames, including Blues, Grays, Bucks, Buckeyes, Eries, Euclids, Raiders, and finally agreed on Indians. In the early days of the American League the Cleveland team was known as the Blues in some cities, and the Indians in others. The newspaper contingent decided that Indians would be far more appropriate than Blues, and thus Birmy's [Birmingham] 1915 outfit will be known as Indians, instead of Naps.[18]

Commenting on the change of nickname, *Sporting News* said:

> While there is no particular reason why the name Indians should have been adopted, the same name was worn by the Cleveland National League team prior to the entrance of Charley Somers into the national pastime. The choice is but temporary, however, but will be made permanent if no better cognomen is thought of before the season is over, it being the wish that the team would go out and make a name for itself.
>
> At their meeting the scribes also decided that it would be better if all the papers get together on one name for the Cleveland American Association Club. As a result of that decision, the name of Bearcats was cast into the discard and that of Spiders selected.
>
> Thus, both Cleveland teams will be known during the coming year by nicknames that were applied to the old National League club that was led by Pat Tebeau.[19]

A *Cleveland Plain Dealer* editorial on January 18, 1915, explained the new nickname this way:

> Many years ago there was an Indian named Sockalexis who was the star player

of the Cleveland baseball club. As batter, fielder and base runner he was a marvel. Sockalexis so far outshone his teammates that he naturally came to be regarded as the whole team. The "fans" throughout the country began to call the Clevelanders the "Indians." It was an honorable name, and while it stuck the team made an excellent record.

It has now been decided to revive this name. The Clevelands of 1915 will be the "Indians." There will be no real Indians on the roster, but the name will recall fine traditions. It is looking backward to a time when Cleveland had one of the most popular teams of the United States. It also serves to revive the memory of a single great player who has been gathered to his fathers in the happy hunting grounds of the Abenakis.[20]

The editorial makes it clear that in adopting the nickname Indians, the committee understood that the name arose in 1897 because of the presence and impact of Louis Sockalexis on the Cleveland baseball club.

18

Who Is an Indian

So, just who is and who isn't an Indian? That simple question actually proves quite complex to answer. In a talk he gave at the Baseball Hall of Fame in June of 2009, on the topic of how Major League Baseball and the Baseball Hall of Fame can best attempt to recognize who is and who isn't deserving of recognition as a Native American pioneer player, author Joseph Oxendine used some of the following background and criteria. Oxendine, a member of the Lumbee tribe of North Carolina and former chancellor of Pembroke State University, wrote the book American Indian Sports Heritage in 1988. A former professional baseball player himself for three years, Oxendine earned a doctoral degree at Boston University.

Oxendine traced the history of the identification process as follows:

For many years the U.S. federal government, through the Census Bureau, categorized citizens into "White" and "Negro" and "Other" groups. Such a designation included Indians in the "Other" category.

More recently (2002) the Census Bureau has assumed a more "social" definition of race, including the following designations: (1) American Indian and Alaska Natives, (2) Asian, (3) White, (4) Black/African-American, and (5) a combination of two or more of the above groups. (Note is made of the fact that Spanish/Hispanic/Latino may be of any race).

Reviewing American Indians who have played major league baseball requires a careful look at Indian identification, Oxendine stated. Unfortunately, there is no succinct, universally accepted statement or judicial definition of an "Indian." Within the U.S. federal government different agencies which provide services for Indians have varying criteria for determining which citizens are eligible for benefits.

The Bureau of Indian Affairs (BIA) is the principal federal agency for dealing with recognized Indian tribes. In identifying an Indian, the BIA places emphasis on (1) one who declares himself or herself as an Indian, (2) is an enrolled member of a tribe or agency, and (3) is regarded as an Indian in the community in which he or she lives.

A specific blood quantum is not a universal requirement for tribal membership or Indian identification, Oxendine noted. Individual tribes may establish their own standards for membership and this includes the matter of blood quantum. A given tribe may require that member be one-half blood, one-fourth, one-sixteenth, or some other designation. Some tribes have no specific statement regarding blood requirement.

Conversely, Oxendine added, there are citizens who have substantial blood quantum, but are not recognized as Indian. For example, one may have a father or mother, or both, who are Indian, but are not themselves so recognized because, as he stated, "they have no cultural affiliation with the Indian community." Such persons may have moved away and disassociated themselves from the Indian community, "often believing that in an era of racial discrimination there were significant disadvantages to being recognized as an Indian," Oxendine concluded.

For his book on Native American athletes, Oxendine stated that he contacted some professional athletes who reported to have had some Indian heritage but found that some declined to verify any Indian connection.

Aye, there is the rub, for those of us concerned about "the search" by baseball historians and the Society for American Baseball Research (SABR) to identify anyone, with any trace of Native American blood, and replace Sockalexis with him merely because they can prove "blood."

So, there is James Madison Toy, dealt with in detail in Chapter 4... and Joe Visner (also known as Joe "Vezina," 1859-1945), a catcher and outfielder from Minnesota who played in 1885 and again from 1889-91...and, according to SABR researcher Peter Morris, there is also the now definitive "first American Indian" Tom Oran (1847-1886), an outfielder who moved from his native California to St Louis and played 19 games for the St Louis Red Stockings in 1875.

One or two or all three of them might have had some Indian heritage – but if any one of them did he (1) did not claim it outright so it appeared in print at the time he played, (2) was not an enrolled member of any particular tribe, and (3) was not regarded publicly as an Indian in the community he lived in. Toy and Visner, matter-of-factly stated, "looked white" in the photos that exist of them, especially because of prominent facial hair, and did not make any claim that has yet been found in print about being Indian while they played.

There are, apparently, no existing photographs of Oran, but articles about him at the time he played are exactly like those of Toy and Visner, offering no identification of an Indian background. Morris can't find a definitive census identification for Oran, weakly suggesting that "a guess" by one earlier researcher that a certain "Thomas Indian" might be Oran will have to suffice. Further, all documentation that Morris offers maintaining Oran was identified as an Indian or a "half breed" come in articles well past his playing days.

There is simply no proof that any opposing player, any fan or any member of the media writing about baseball knew, at the time, that Tom Oran, Joe Visner or James Madison Toy had a Native American background. Contrast this with all the sensationalism attending his very presence in Cleveland's spring training camp, all the racist banter in the newspaper headlines, and all the vile racist behavior directed at him by opposing players and fans in almost every game of the 1897 season, and isn't it obvious Louis Sockalexis earned the right to be called "the first-known American Indian to play Major League baseball"?

19

The Dreamer

THE FOLLOWING STORY was written by Timothy Hayes Murnane for the May, 1908, inaugural issue of the monthly publication *Baseball Magazine*. Murnane, a native New Englander (born in Naugatuck, Connecticut), was a big league player who became a manager, and then a *Boston Daily Globe* sports editor. He played big league baseball for Boston and Providence, from 1876-78, and for Boston again, in 1884, playing a total of 229 games in four years as a first baseman-outfielder. In 1899 Murnane organized and was the first president of the Connecticut League, where he would have seen Sockalexis play. Murnane was still sports editor of the *Boston Daily Globe* when he died in 1917 at age sixty-four.

This fictional tribute to Sockalexis, unabashedly respectful and spiritual, makes compelling mention of his unparalleled ball playing skills and his fatal weakness. The reference to Sockalexis's brief return to glory may well be based on the Penobscot's success at Waterbury in Murnane's Connecticut League in 1899. And it is possible Murnane came up to Indian Island at a later time to lure Sockalexis back into playing; it was rumored, as late as 1909, that Sockalexis was going to make a comeback in the Connecticut or New England leagues. Note the suggestion of an epic canoe trip for Sockalexis to make to return home — it sounds something like the legendary trip that some sources credited his father Francis with making to try to stop his son from playing baseball.[1]

    The night was crisp and cold, and the stars sparkled in a clear dark blue sky, high over the headwaters of the Penobscot. The playing of a dying flame from a few loose embers across small windowpanes, gave warning that the little cottage was inhabited, and the stranger approached cautiously, across a thin carpet of a new fallen snow.

    A sharp rap at the door brought the response: "Come in," and the Big Noise pushed back the door with a "Hello neighbor." There was no answer from the man who sat on a low bench close to the fire with a crutch at his side.

    Approaching, the stranger asked: "Isn't this my old friend Battle Ax?"

    The name caused the invalid to straighten up and open his eyes. Then, throwing a few sticks of woods on the fire he was soon able to recognize the features of his caller.

    "Are you glad to see me, Ax?"

"Indeed I am, but I'm all done up with the rheumatism."

"I came down to see if you would go out next spring and play ball for me."

"Oh, how I would like to; but I don't think I will ever play another game."

"Yes, I played several years in the National League, and was considered one of the great players, I can almost hear the ringing applause as I hit the ball on the center, or when I made a long accurate throw. But my popularity was my undoing, I dallied with the 'Red Water.' It was come and go with me, and I found it difficult to keep away from the merry-go-round of civilization. Ah, yes, I was a favorite with the public but weakened; the pace was too fast for a boy developed by Nature. But I believe if I had one more chance I could win the battle against myself."

"Say Ax, I'll take a chance, take care of yourself, and in the spring come and join us."

With the spring came a message from the Indian, saying: "I will come, but with a weak ankle." The answer went back, "Come on, I will plow up center field so that the going will be easy."

With renewed spirits the Indian came and made good, was the sensation of the day and once more became the idol of the fans. But soon the "Red Water" commenced to show its work, and Battle Ax found himself in the same old condition, Broke!

He went to the Big Noise and said: "Kind master, I find myself short on change, and would like to return to my people under the sparkling stars on the upper Penobscot." The Big Noise smiled, he was happy, for an idea struck him full on the brain and he spoke slowly but with full knowledge that the Indian was a weak one with the paddle.

"Battle Ax," said he, "Get a birch canoe, follow the coast after you leave the Merrimac until you come to the Bay of Penobscot, then hug the shore until you find the river. Then, with the help of the great spirit, you will have nothing to fear until you hit Bangor and have to shoot the falls."

The return of the great Indian to the old town was never headlined in the daily papers and the stars once more twinkle high over the little cottage. The snow will never be broken again by a base ball manager looking for some one for a headliner, for Battle Ax has added other troubles to his rheumatism and sits the long evenings through gazing into the blazing logs, until the colors of the rainbow seem to reflect on Angel's wings, and the wild hurrahs of the howling fans awake the once great ball player to real facts of what might have been.

A Gallery of Photographs

(Photos from the National Baseball Hall of Fame Library are credited to NBHFL; those from The College of the Holy Cross Archives, to CHCA; those from the Penobscot Nation, to PN.)

Jesse Burkett, two-time batting champion and Baseball Hall of Fame member, who coached Sockalexis at the College of the Holy Cross and was a teammate of his in Cleveland. (Photo: NBHFL)

Roger Connor, professional baseball's first great home run hitter and member of the Hall of Fame, helped stop Sockalexis's slide through the Connecticut League. Perhaps it was his Christian values and iron hand, in watching over Sockalexis as his playing manager in Waterbury, that led to one special glory moment in baseball following the Penobscot Indian's final fall from grace in Cleveland in 1899. (Photo: NBHFL)

Napoleon *"Larry" Lajoie*, second
baseman who was a player-manager with the Cleveland team. His
presence led fans to vote for the
nickname "Naps" in 1903. The
nickname stuck until 1914, when
Lajoie left Cleveland to close out his
career in Philadelphia. Lajoie
began playing professional baseball
in 1897 but, unlike Sockalexis,
managed to check an early drinking
problem and went on to a Hall of
Fame career. (Photo: NBHFL)

Hughie Jennings, shown doing his
famous "EEEEE-Yah!" cheer
from the coaching box, played against
Sockalexis as a member of the Baltimore
Orioles and later wrote a column about
Sockalexis in the 1920s that helped
promote his fame but also led
to a myriad of myths.
(Photo: NBHFL)

John McGraw, one of the most famous managers in baseball history, played third base for the Baltimore Orioles team that faced Sockalexis in 1897. According to Hughie Jennings, McGraw thought Sockalexis would have been one of the greats of the game if "he could have stayed up five years." McGraw was said to have pursued Indian athletic legend Jim Thorpe, believing he might be as skilled player as Sockalexis had been. (Photo: NBHFL)

Amos Rusie, one of the first great pitchers in baseball history, gave up the most famous home run Sockalexis ever hit, on the Penobscot Indian's first at bat in the Polo Grounds in New York City. (Photo: NBHFL)

Bobby Wallace, Hall of Fame short-stop for his sterling fielding, was playing third base for the Indians in 1897 when Sockalexis joined him as a teammate. (Photo: NBHFL)

Cy Young, the legendary pitcher with the most career wins (511) of all time, was the top Cleveland pitcher when Sockalexis joined the team in 1897 and was en route to a stellar Hall of Fame career. (Photo: NBHFL)

186

John Montgomery Ward, Hall of Fame player, urged Cleveland to sign Sockalexis out of the College of the Holy Cross, predicting he would be a great player.
(Photo: NBHFL)

Mike Powers, teammate of Sockalexis in a Maine summer baseball league, urged the Penobscot youth to join him at the College of the Holy Cross, where Sockalexis would be a star for two seasons and ultimately be named to the Holy Cross Athletic Hall of Fame. (Photo: NBHFL)

Louis Sockalexis from a formal portrait taken in 1900. (Photo: NBHFL)

Louis Sockalexis, as a member of the Lowell club in the New England League, in 1902. (Photo: NBHFL)

Oliver "Patsy" Tebeau, *player-manager of the Cleveland team in 1897, went to Notre Dame and signed Sockalexis to a professional contract. Tebeau said he tried everything he could to lure Sockalexis away from drinking in 1897, even with the offer of an increased bonus, but ultimately had to release him from the team before the end of the season.* (Photo: NBHFL)

James Madison Toy, *the man Baseball Hall of Fame historian Lee Allen claims was "the first man with an American Indian background to play major league baseball." With his impressive handlebar moustache and obvious Caucasian features, it's very questionable whether his peers and the fans knew about his Native American heritage...if, indeed, he was Native American.* (Photo: NBHFL)

The College of the Holy Cross baseball team in 1896. TOP ROW: *Sockalexis, Cavanaugh (manager), Kelly, Finn (secretary);* CENTER ROW: *Gaffney, W.H. Fox, Pappalau, Powers, Maroney, W.J. Fox, McTigue;* BOTTOM ROW: *Garvey, Lavin, and Curley.* (Photo: CHCA)

Coach Louis Sockalexis, standing at top left, joins his youth baseball club from Indian Island for a team picture, taken around 1906. (Photo: PN)

*This grave site memorial to **Louis Sockalexis** was unveiled in 1934. A campaign spurred by a local newspaper editor and Sockalexis's friends at Holy Cross College raised funds to replace the original wooden cross with this more substantial monument.* (Photo: Ed Rice)

*While **Louis Sockalexis** was playing stellar ball for the Warren team in Maine's Knox County summer league, he was seen by an opposing manager, writer Gilbert Patten, and reportedly became the model for Patten's fictional baseball hero, Frank Merriwell. The three Holy Cross players for Warren were Louis Sockalexis, front row at left; Curley, front row third from left; and Powers, seated behind Curley.* (Photo: CHCA)

Louis Sockalexis, many years after his playing days, as he appeared in his old Cleveland cap and uniform, on a postcard sold to tourists on the Penobscot Indian Island Reservation just outside Old Town, Maine. (Photo: PN)

Andrew Sockalexis,
Louis's second cousin, who took 2nd place in the Boston Marathon in 1912 and again in 1913 and 4th place in the Olympic Games of 1912 in Stockholm, Sweden. He is wearing his U.S. Olympic singlet and running on Indian Island shortly after his appearance at the Olympic Games. (Photo: PN)

Louis Sockalexis in 1894 *wearing a Poland Spring team uniform and standing in front of the famous Poland Spring Inn.* (Photo: PN)

Louis Sockalexis wearing his Holy Cross baseball uniform. (Photo: CHCA)

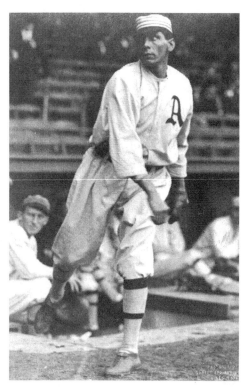

Hall of famer **Charlie Bender** of the
Chippewa Nation played for the
Athletics.(Photo: NBHFL)

John Meyers, the great catcher of
the New York Giants(Photo: NBHFL)

Jim Thorpe is perhaps the greatest Native American athlete. A member of the Sac and Fox Nation, he was the first Native American to win an Olympic gold medal for the United States. He also played professional baseball, football, and basketball. (Photo: NBHFL)

Augusta Baseball Club, 1893. **Louis Sockalexis** *is to the left in the front row, wearing his catcher's mitt.* (Photo: ER)

195

Afterword

THERE ARE NO ILLUSIONS of fame or pecuniary advantage resulting from this book, only the fervent dream that there will be a copy available to everyone interested in Louis Sockalexis's remarkable story. This manuscript largely grew out of my work in libraries over the course of eighteen years. At times, I experienced excitement not commonly associated with library research. Those moments, in which something completely new or unexpected about Louis Sockalexis was revealed to me, left me nearly unable to restrain a desire to shout out loud.

I hope those moments of discovery never stop, although it is discouraging that in this "information age," so many stories are still being lost. Far too many people who knew Louis personally or had stories about him died without sharing their anecdotes.

Over the past five years or so I have visited the grave of Louis Sockalexis from time to time, mostly to apologize. I guess I had begun to personalize my relationship with him, and I even began to imagine that he was growing impatient with me to finish and publish this book. I hope with this account to create the most complete record about him ever penned.

I know there are things about Sock I believe might be true but can't prove, so I left them out of the text of the book. For instance, I doubt anyone really used the nickname "Chief" for Sockalexis in a complimentary way; if it occurred it was meant as the vile, racist identifying tag intended to demean and denigrate a race of people, a culture considered "primitive" and "savage." The nickname was applied to almost all the pioneer Native American players (Bender, Meyers, et al) and pretty much all those identifiable-for-their-race players who followed, right through to Allie Reynolds into the 1950s. It is important to note that many players in history with authenticated Native American heritages but no identifying physical features deliberately eschewed public acknowledgement they were Native American; racism was that virulent. Think about it this way: No one would think about dubbing contemporary players like Jacoby Ellsbury, Joba Chamberlain and Kyle Lohse with this nickname even though they are all known to have Native American backgrounds; that term was never meant respecfully. I believe the nickname should be stricken from all these players' biographies wherever they appear. Further, I believe Sockalexis just might have been baseball's first "five-tool" player (hits for power – meaning exceptional home run capability, hits for exceptional high average, exceptional fielder, exceptional throwing arm, and exceptional speed that can be used to steal bases at any time) but, of course, the professional game was in its infancy and no such labels or sophisticated appreciation of the game would have been offered at the time. And, finally, I believe Louis Sockalexis is an obvious Jackie Robinson-figure, a man who showed remarkable grace and scintillating ability – albeit for only three months – in the face of the worst verbal taunts and flagrant racist behavior from teammates, from opposing players, from fans and from the media. However, unlike Robinson who is revered for experiencing all this, Sockalexis continues to get no credit and no appreciation for what he was forced to withstand. It remains wrong, to this day, that our national museum to celebrate the history of the game, the National Baseball Hall of Fame in Cooperstown, New York, still fails to acknowledge Sockalexis and the game's other American Indian pioneers while offering exhibition tributes to pioneer blacks, Hispanics and women in baseball.

As both a passionate journalist and teacher of journalism for more than a quarter of a century, I was fascinated by the life of Louis Sockalexis and the early days of baseball as depicted by American sporting journalism. Unfortunately, I came to understand that the journalists of the late nineteenth- and early-twentieth centuries would not have fared well in my class. There is a discouraging lack of respect for grammar and spelling. Reportorial first-hand observation, long held to be the most credible method of newsgathering, is frequently absent. If the writer happened to be present at an event, he often combined both reporting and editorializing in the same story.

Many accounts carry no writer's name or byline, yet frequently they include first-person observations or otherwise allude to the writer and his beliefs. Many stories contain as much fiction as they do reporting. Among the most egregious exemplars of this reporting style is that of former player, manager, and Baseball Hall of Famer Hughie Jennings, whose column about Louis Sockalexis in the 1920s has led to a veritable cascade of untruths and myths that have been repeated by journalists over the years, often without attribution to Jennings. I have tried to set the Sockalexis record straight, where I could, or to raise questions where the melding of fact and legend make it appropriate.

In his two volumes of profiles about prominent Maine sporting figures, Don MacWilliams further undermines the Sockalexis legacy by asserting that the Cleveland team was already nicknamed the Indians in 1897 rather than that this name was adopted because of the presence of American Indian Louis Sockalexis. Maine sportswriters, citing MacWilliams, have repeated the error. Newspapers around the state revived Williams' erroneous contention when Sockalexis was inducted into the Maine Sports Hall of Fame in 1985.

The author of the history of the Cleveland Indians franchise, Franklin Lewis, wrongly asserted that it was "a fan contest" in 1915 that led to the permanent selection of the Indians nickname and then claimed, without attribution, that it was a fan who proclaimed that the selection should be made "to honor" Sockalexis. Because Lewis is wrong about a fan contest (the team owner asked four Cleveland newspaper editors to make the decision), modern-day skeptics frequently doubt his position about the fan's alleged tribute. This is particularly true of those opposed to what they regard as the team's racially insensitive nickname and logo. Unfortunately, there is no mention of Sockalexis's name in any of the news accounts concerning the 1915 adoption of a new nickname. Yet a 1915 editorial in the *Cleveland Plain Dealer*, commenting on the nickname Indians, makes it clear that Louis Sockalexis is indeed entitled to the legacy of being the inspiration for the nickname.

In the early 1960s Baseball Hall of Fame historian Lee Allen also made a highly questionable determination regarding the legacy of Louis Sockalexis, stripping him of the title of first American Indian player. Instead, Allen anointed James Madison Toy, merely on the word of a descendant and absent any documentation whatsoever.

More recently, the legacy of Sockalexis has even been battered in fiction. Luke Salisbury, a college English teacher and Society for American Baseball Research member from Boston, published a fictional account in 1992 of the escapades of an American Indian athlete "freely modeled on real-life baseball legend Sockalexis," as the book's cover announces. Salisbury had previously written a highly useful profile describing the historical figure of Sockalexis. The newer, thinly veiled work of fiction accurately depicts several of the Penobscot's real-life experiences, but it is arguably libelous when it adds elements of criminality that are unrelated to the real Sockalexis. Entitled *The Cleveland Indian*, it carries the subtitle "The Legend of King Saturday." This novel shows a full-figure portrait of Sockalexis, one of the few remaining and best known, with a portrait of the 1899 Spiders in the background. Drenched in various indignities, the fictional hero is not only a phenomenal athlete but also an amoral criminal and murderer.

Even the academic world is not much interested in the real Louis Sockalexis or in his legacy, if the research and writings of Ellen J. Staurowsky, Ed.D., associate professor of sport sociology at Ithaca College, constitute the benchmark. Beginning in the late 1990s, Staurowsky put herself in the national fray, traveling to Cleveland and elsewhere around the country, decrying racist nicknames and logos in the sports world on behalf of American Indians. She has written and made available nationwide the position paper "An Act of Honor or Exploitation? The Cleveland Indians' Use of the Louis Francis Sockalexis Story."

Sculpting her brief but error-laden biography of the historical Sockalexis (largely taken from the mistake-riddled paper of then Maine school student Trina Wellman), Staurowsky makes this misguided assumption: "Traced to its earliest origins, the appropriation of Native imagery by the Cleveland Spiders and sports journalists was not an attempt to honor Sockalexis or Native Americans in general. In 1897, usage was simply a spontaneous occurrence rooted in the practice of the times that had expedient motives at core." That usage, Staurowsky argues, was to sell newspapers and sell tickets to baseball games. At the outset of the appearance of Sockalexis in Cleveland, this assessment rang close to the truth. Sportswriters loved to use a range of metaphors for warring, scalping savages and every available image of Sockalexis for the sheer novelty and spectacle of him as a recognizable Indian. Cleveland owner Robison, with serious attendance problems and no Sunday ball-playing options, must have been delighted with such a powerful box-office attraction.

As Sockalexis's demonstrated abilities were equal to and often superior to those of all the other star baseball players of 1897, however, the tone in the newspaper articles changed significantly, from derisive to respectful, and many of those sportswriters drawn to watch him reflected that change. The tone was still blatantly racist, but it was nevertheless wholly respectful. Only when the extent of his drinking problems became common knowledge did Sockalexis face overwhelming ridicule and abuse. Ultimately, the nickname Indians celebrates the Cleveland franchise's featured attraction for the first three months of 1897. Not only was Sockalexis the player fans most wanted to see and the player the press most often wrote about, he earned that attention and respect because of his exceptional skills.

At present, for all the furor the Cleveland professional baseball team continues to face from those angered by the use of the nickname "Indians" and the Chief Wahoo mascot and logo, these symbols neither exploit nor honor Louis Sockalexis. I agree with Staurowksy that no honor or respect is being paid Sockalexis by continuing the use of the upsetting spectacle that is the grinning caricature, Chief Wahoo. The Cleveland organization will, I hope, take the important initiative of adopting a more attractive, more respectful mascot and logo in the very near future.

Uncertainty is a plague to the imagination and there is still much about the life of Louis Sockalexis that may never be revealed. What did he think about his life in baseball and afterward? Was alcohol his great failing or only a crutch that supported him in the face of other demons? Was there a great love of his life? Was Louis really one of the arrested hoboes in Aroostook County and why was a Massachusetts newspaper the only one to link him to the incident while all the Maine newspapers that reported it made no mention of his name? And did his father really make that fantastic canoe trip down the Atlantic, from Maine to Cape Cod to Washington?

My search to authenticate the legendary canoe trip revealed no official record of it. I included a detailed description of the trip because it is a wonderful story and I cannot unequivocally dismiss it as myth.

I hope the Penobscot tribe understands my inclusion of all that I could find about Louis Sockalexis's life, even its less exemplary aspects. Despite his failings, I liked Louis... and I was upset when I found things that put him in an unflattering light. On balance, I hope I've treated Louis Sockalexis justly and accurately, and as a man still to be greatly admired and remembered.

Finally, I found the far-too-lengthy omission from the Maine Sports Hall of Fame of Louis Sockalexis and his second cousin, Andrew Sockalexis, a grievous oversight. Both athletes deserved to have been charter members. However, information from this manuscript helped to overcome one other oversight. I discovered, in the fall of 1997, that neither Louis nor Andrew Sockalexis was a member of our national American Indian Athletic Hall of Fame. Working with the Penobscot nation, I was pleased to play a role in their election and induction into the Hall of Fame.

Acknowledgments

For me, a lifetime runner, researching, writing, completing the editing, and now publishing this book has been the younger man's biggest dream come true and the older man's most satisfying marathon finish ever.

It has been both a humbling experience and an exalting one, particularly discovering that while, daily, it might have appeared to be a solitary effort, I was never really in the throes of the celebrated "loneliness of the long distance runner," thanks to some very special support.

This book might never have been completed but for the extraordinary researching efforts of a treasured friend who has been a friend since our college-boy days together at Northeastern University in Boston more than 30 years ago. Richard B. "Dixie" Tourangeau tirelessly traced baseball games of Louis Sockalexis at Boston area libraries and, literally for years, helped investigate several key loose ends concerning Sock to help me. Tourangeau, a member of the Society for American Baseball Research, is editor of the popular "Play Ball!" calendar produced by Tide-mark Press. He was one of the three spearheading forces behind the successful lobbying effort that resulted in the rightful enshrinement of Arky Vaughan into the Baseball Hall of Fame. His phone calls, with news of yet another exciting "find" in the library, seemed to perpetually keep me believing that this manuscript had far too great a value for me to do anything but see it through to the finish line. Dix "homered" time and again...and it's a special treat to know that one of my best friends in life played so vital a role, not only in finding many gems, but also by supporting me when the task I'd set for myself seemed insurmountable.

I really don't have the words to ever properly thank publisher/editor Scott Kaeser and Tide-mark Press for making the dream of this book come true.

Very special thanks go to my close friend, Dr. Peter Millard, for his support over many years and invaluable computer assistance with the manuscript. And, likewise, to office mate, Ted Perrin, for his computer help at "end game" time.

I'm particularly grateful to the late Penobscot Indian historian S. Glenn Starbird, Jr., for his wise counsel, significant leads, and support. I sadly regret Glenn did not live to see the completed manuscript. I'm also saddened that Sockalexis cousins' blood relative Ann Padovano, too, did not live to see this book published. She and her husband Steve and her brother, Angelo Quito, were all wonderfully supportive of my efforts.

I'm honored as well by the wonderful support I've received from Penobscot Nation Tribal Governor Barry Dana, an extraordinary man and an extraordinary leader. Thanks, too, for information and a photo provided by James Neptune, director and curator of the Penobscot Nation Museum as well as Carole Binette, Penobscot Nation Census Coordinator.

For information and help provided to me, I'm indebted to the late Edna Becker and the late Louis Edward Sockalexis, baseball researchers Larry Rutenbeck and Cappy Gagnon, and to Professor Bill Baker of the University of Maine History Department.

Absolutely invaluable was the researching support and informational assistance I received from the following: the staff at the University of Maine at Orono library; librarian Charlie Campo at the *Bangor Daily News*; library archivist Lois Hamel and assistant athletic director for marketing and media relations Frank Mastrandrea, College of the Holy Cross, Worcester, Mass.; Bill Burdick, manager, photo services, National Baseball Hall of Fame Library, Cooperstown, N.Y.; Bob DiBiasio, vice president, public relations, Cleveland Indians professional baseball team, Cleveland, Ohio.

A special thanks goes to running friend, Laura Zegel, who uncovered information about James Madison Toy when she researched Toy's life in his home area while she was "temporarily displaced" in Pennsylvania. And thanks as well to running pal, Judd Esty-Kendall, who corralled a piece of information about Sockalexis's last ball-playing days in the Bangor area.

On a personal level, I'm deeply thankful for the loving support I received over the many years of the project from: my dad, Al Rice, of Scottsdale, Arizona, and my daughter, Meisha Rice, of Bangor; my best friend from high school, "brother" Mike Swenson of Orono; my former father-in-law, Arnold Leavitt of Auburn; and my ex-wife, Cheryl Leavitt of Bangor.

Further, there are the extraordinary friends who never seemed far from my side when I needed them for inspiration of any kind on this extraordinary marathon "run": Dr. Millard and wife Emily Wesson, Danny and Tammy Paul, Newell Lewey, Giles Norton, Jim Falvo and Kris Pletan, Kim Moody and Dave Roberts, Marc Violette and Margaret Lanoue, Fred and Joan Merriam, Katrina Bisheimer, David and Katherine Wilson, Robin Emery, Steve Norton, Marly Swick, Eric Ling, Tim Kane, Liam Purdon and Dianne Ferguson, Paul Durbin, Steve Craig, Sam Schuman, Tom Atwell, Bill Barker and Betsy White, Marilyn Miller, Larry Rothstein, John Mello and Lynn Rognsvoog, Bob and Claudia Eaton, Linda Tikonoff, Terry Duffy, Sean Casey, Howard Trotzky, Dr. Stephen Typaldos and Dawn Zimmerman.

I also want to acknowledge some of the students who have inspired me in just the way I'd hoped to inspire them. They include: Misty Ridnour, Andy Gipe, Andy Doebele, Alan Langley, Nicki McAvoy, Glen McNally, Dustin Heath, Courtney McNally, Jedediah Blum-Evitts, Dorianna McNally, Patrick Rodgerson, Meredith Trask, Kandace Forge, Noah Hale, Crystal

Levesque, Adam Williams, Tia Achey, Will Hughey, and Matt Achey, to name just a few.

Also, I'm grateful for support I've received for years from so many, many friends from the running communities throughout Maine, including all my Sub 5 Track Club mates, and even four running heroes of mine…Billy Mills, Roberta "Bobbi" Gibb, Bill Rodgers and Bruce Bickford…and many, many more "runners of roads" I've known and been inspired by over the years.

Since I found inspiration in a myriad of places, I feel I'd be remiss if I didn't mention the following as well: Vic Hathaway and Studio B classical music on the Maine Public Broadcasting radio every afternoon; Gifford's ice cream; the carriage path trails of Acadia National Park; and the purring support of Kokiko, the "book puss," that special muse in a cat's body who gave me nuzzles and playful attention frequently when I was on marathon typing jags.

And, in my current universe, "Pre," the fabulous pet cat, and the real star in my constellation, artist par excellence, the talented and lovely Stella Ekholm.

Notes

CHAPTER 1

1. Sockalexis genealogy, provided by Glenn Starbird.
2. Mayo.
3. Rideout.
4. Mayo.
5. Salisbury.
6. Rideout.
7. Grayson.
8. John.
9. O'Donnell.
10. Ibid.

CHAPTER 2

1. Salisbury.
2. *Bangor Daily News*, December 25, 1913.
3. *Worcester Telegram*, April 11, 1895.
4. Dooley.
5. *Worcester Telegram*, April 20, 1895
6. Ibid.
7. Parpal.
8. Biographical sheets on Louis Sockalexis, Holy Cross Sports Information Department
9. *Worcester Telegram*, April 27, 1895.
10. Hatch.
11. Dineen.
12. Smith.
13. *Catholic Free Press*, January 27, 1956.
14. Ibid.
15. *Worcester Telegram*, April 9, 1951.
16. *Catholic Free Press*, January 27, 1956.
17. Biographical sheets on Louis Sockalexis, Holy Cross Sports Information Department.
18. *Rockland Courier-Gazette*, June 18, 1970.
19. *Bangor Commercial*, September 9, 1895.
20. Dineen.
21. *Bangor Daily News*, December 25, 1913.
22. Dooley.
23. Ibid.

24. Ibid.
25. Ibid.
26. Ibid.
27. *Boston Journal*, October 18, 1896.
28. *Worcester Telegram*, October 18, 1896.
29. Parpal.
30. Smith.
31. Ibid.
32. Dineen.
33. Smith.
34. Salisbury.
35. Letter from William J. Fox, dated July 20, 1949. Holy Cross Library Archives.

CHAPTER 3

1. Salisbury.
2. Ibid.
3. Gagnon.
4. Ibid.
5. *South Bend Tribune*, March 18, 1897.
6. Gagnon.
7. Salsinger.
8. Ibid.
9. Ibid.
10. Ibid.
11. Phillips.
12. Ibid.

CHAPTER 4

1. Salsinger.
2. *South Bend Tribune*, March 18, 1897.
3. *The Sporting News*, March 13, 1897.
4. *South Bend Tribune*, March 18, 1897.
5. Salsinger.
6. Hatch.
7. Jennings.
8. Allen.
9. *The Sporting Life*, April 10, 1897.
10. *Cleveland Press*, March 19, 1897.
11. *The Sporting Life*, March 27, 1897.
12. Ibid.

13. Phillips.

14. Salisbury.

15. MacWilliams.

16. Salisbury.

17. Lee Allen, letter to Mrs. Hannah Toy. James Madison Toy file, Baseball Hall of Fame Library, Cooperstown, N.Y.

18. Mrs. Jean Wigel, letter to Lee Allen. James Madison Toy file, Baseball Hall of Fame Library, Cooperstown, N.Y.

19. *The Sporting News*, June 15, 1963.

20. J.F.A. Pietsch, letter to Lee Allen. James Madison Toy file, Baseball Hall of Fame Library, Cooperstown, N.Y.

21. *The Sporting Life*, January 26, 1887, in James Madison Toy file, Baseball Hall of Fame Library, Cooperstown, N.Y.

22. Rutenbeck.

23. Toy.

24. Mack.

25. "Sockalexis — The Greatest Crusader?" *The Holy Cross Purple*, 1950.

26. *The Sporting News*, April 3, 1897.

27. *The Sporting Life*, March 27, 1897.

28. John.

29. *Bangor Daily Commercial*, April 12, 1897.

30. *Boston Daily Globe*, April 15, 1897.

31. Ibid.

32. Salisbury.

33. Ibid.

34. Hatch.

35. *The Sporting News*, April 17, 1897.

36. Phillips.

37. *The Sporting Life*, May 1, 1897.

CHAPTER 5

1. *The Sporting News*, April 24, 1897.

2. *Cleveland Plain Dealer*, March 26, 1897.

3. *Cleveland Plain Dealer*, April 7, 1897.

4. *Cleveland Press*, April 16, 1897.

5. *Cleveland Press*, April 19, 1897.

6. *Cleveland Press*, April 23, 1897.

7. Mack.

8. *Louisville Courier-Journal*, April 23, 1897.

9. *Cleveland Plain Dealer*, April 27, 1897.

10. *Cleveland Press*, April 27, 1897.

11. *Sports Illustrated*, September 17, 1973.

12. Mack.

13. *The Sporting Life*, May 1, 1897.

14. *Boston Daily Globe*, May 1, 1897.

15. *The Sporting Life*, May 1, 1897.

16. *Cleveland Plain Dealer*, May 1, 1897.

17. *The Sporting Life*, May 1, 1897.

18. *Cleveland Press*, May 3, 1897.

19. *Milwaukee Journal*, May 6, 1898.

20. *The Sporting Life*, May 6, 1898.

CHAPTER 6

1. *The Sporting Life*, May 1, 1897.

2. Ibid.

3. *Cleveland Plain Dealer*, May 4, 1897.

4. *Cleveland Press*, May 5, 1897.

5. *Boston Daily Globe*, May 6, 1897.

6. *The Sporting News*, May 8, 1897.

7. *Boston Daily Globe*, May 6, 1897.

8. *Cleveland Press*, May 7, 1897.

9. *Boston Daily Globe*, May 8, 1897.

10. *Cleveland Plain Dealer*, May 15, 1897.

11. *Cleveland Plain Dealer*, May 8, 1897.

12. *Cleveland Plain Dealer*, June 16, 1897.

13. Ibid.

14. *Cleveland Press*, May 17, 1897.

15. Phillips.

16. *Boston Daily Globe*, May 17, 1897.

17. Phillips.

18. *Boston Daily Globe*, May 17, 1897.

19. Phillips.

20. *Boston Daily Globe*, May 17, 1897.

21. Phillips.

22. Ibid.

23. *Boston Daily Globe*, May 17, 1897.

24. *Cleveland Press*, June 10, 1897.

25. Ibid.

26. *Cleveland Press*, May 18, 1897.

27. *Cleveland Press*, May 20, 1897.
28. *Cleveland Press*, May 18, 1897.
29. *Cleveland Press*, May 20, 1897.
30. Ibid.
31. *Cleveland Press*, May 28, 1897.
32. *Cleveland Press*, May 20, 1897.
33. Ibid.
34. Phillips.
35. *Cleveland Press*, May 21, 1897.
36. *Cleveland Press*, May 23, 1897.
37. *The Sporting Life*, June 12, 1897.
38. *Cleveland Press*, May 24, 1897.
39. *Cleveland Press*, May 29, 1897.
40. Phillips.
41. Ibid.
42. Ibid.

CHAPTER 7
1. *Boston Daily Globe*, June 1, 1897.
2. *Cleveland Press*, June 1, 1897.
3. Mayo.
4. Phillips.
5. John.
6. Phillips.
7. *Boston Daily Globe*, June 3, 1897.
8. Ibid.
9. *The Washington Post*, June 6, 1897.
10. Phillips.
11. Ibid.
12. Ibid.
13. *Cleveland Press*, June 8, 1897.
14. Phillips.
15. Ibid.
16. Ibid.
17. *Cleveland Press*, June 10, 1897.
18. *Cleveland Press*, June 12, 1897.
19. Salisbury.
20. Hatch.
21. Ibid.
22. Salisbury.
23. *Cleveland Press*, June 17, 1897.
24. *Bangor Daily News*, December 25, 1913.
25. *Boston Daily Globe*, June 17, 1897.

26. Salisbury.
27. *Cleveland Press*, June 17, 1897.
28. Salisbury.
29. Grayson.
30. *The Sporting Life*, June 19, 1897.
31. *The Sporting Life*, June 12, 1897.

CHAPTER 8
1. Feldman.
2. *The Sporting Life*, May 15, 1897.
3. Phillips.
4. *New York Journal*, May 7, 1897.
5. Mayo.
6. *Boston Herald*, May 10, 1897.
7. *Boston Daily Globe*, May 10, 1897.
8. *Boston Traveler*, May 12, 1897.
9. *Cleveland Plain Dealer*, May 7, 1897.
10. *Bangor Daily Commercial*, May 6, 1897.
11. *The Sporting Life*, May 15, 1897.
12. Phillips.
13. Ibid.
14. Ibid.
15. *New York Herald*, June 17, 1897.
16. *Cleveland Press*, June 22, 1897.
17. *Cleveland Press*, June 23, 1897.
18. *Cleveland Press*, June 24, 1897.
19. *Cleveland Press*, June 26, 1897.
20. *Cleveland Press*, June 30, 1897.
21. Ibid.
22. *Cleveland Press*, July 2, 1897.
23. *The Sporting News*, June 19, 1897.
24. Jennings.
25. Salisbury.
26. Ibid.
27. Ibid.
28. *Bangor Daily News*, December 25, 1913.

CHAPTER 9
1. *Cleveland Press*, July 6, 1897.
2. *Cleveland Press*, July 7, 1897.
3. Phillips.
4. Ibid.
5. *Cleveland Press*, July 9, 1897.

6. *Cleveland Press*, July 10, 1897.
7. Ibid.
8. Ibid.
9. Ibid.
10. *Cleveland Press*, July 12, 1897.
11. *Cleveland Press*, July 13, 1897.
12. *Boston Daily Globe*, July 13, 1897.
13. *Cleveland Press*, July 13, 1897.
14. *Cleveland Plain Dealer*, July 13, 1897.
15. *Boston Daily Globe*, July 13, 1897.
16. Ibid.
17. Ibid.
18. *Boston Daily Globe*, July 20, 1897.
19. *The Sporting Life*, July 19, 1897.
20. *The Washington Post*, July 23, 1897.
21. *Cleveland Press*, July 25, 1897.
22. *Cleveland Press*, July 26, 1897.
23. Phillips.
24. *The Sporting News*, July 24, 1897.
25. *Cleveland Press*, July 31, 1897.
26. *Boston Daily Globe*, July 31, 1897.
27. *The Sporting Life*, August 7, 1897.
28. *The Sporting News*, August 7, 1897.
29. Salisbury.
30. *Cleveland Plain Dealer*, July 22, 1897.
31. Ibid.
32. Phillips.
33. Smith.
34. *Cleveland Press*, August 5, 1897.
35. Phillips.
36. *Cleveland Press*, August 12, 1897.
37. *Cleveland Press*, August 14, 1897.
38. Phillips.
39. Ibid.
40. *Cleveland Press*, September 13, 1897.
41. *Cleveland Press*, September 14, 1897.
42. *Cleveland Press*, September 15, 1897.
43. *The Sporting Life*, September 11, 1897.
44. *The Sporting Life*, September 18, 1897.
45. *Cleveland Press*, September 17, 1897.
46. Phillips.
47. Ibid.
48. Jennings.

49. *Official Encyclopedia of Baseball.*
50. *The Sporting Life*, May 12, 1906.
51. Phillips.
52. *Official Encyclopedia of Baseball.*
53. Salisbury.

CHAPTER 10
1. Jennings.
2. Ibid.
3. Feldman.
4. *Cleveland Press*, May 8, 1897.
5. *Cleveland Press*, July 31, 1897.
6. Jennings.
7. Feldman.
8. Salisbury.
9. *Cleveland Press*, June 8, 1897.
10. Phillips.
11. Ibid.
12. Phillips.
13. *Cleveland Press*, September 18, 1897.
14. *Cleveland Press*, October 8, 1897.
15. *The Sporting News*, October 9, 1897.
16. *The Sporting Life*, November 3, 1897.
17. *The Sporting News*, October 2, 1897.

CHAPTER 11
1. *The Sporting Life*, November 3, 1897.
2. *Cleveland Plain Dealer*, March 14, 1898.
3. *Cleveland Plain Dealer*, April 1, 1898.
4. *Cleveland Plain Dealer*, March 22, 1898.
5. *Cleveland Plain Dealer*, March 19, 1898.
6. Phillips.
7. *Milwaukee Journal*, June 3, 1898.
8. *Milwaukee Journal*, April 2, 1898.
9. *Cleveland Press*, April 13, 1898.
10. *The Sporting News*, April 2, 1898.
11. *Cleveland Press*, April 22, 1898.
12. *Milwaukee Journal*, April 30, 1898.
13. *Worcester Telegram*, April 18, 1898.
14. *Cleveland Press*, April 19, 1898.
15. Ibid.
16. Ibid.
17. *Cleveland Press*, April 21, 1898.

18. *Cleveland Plain Dealer*, quoted in *The Sporting Life*, May 7, 1898.
19. *Milwaukee Journal*, May 6, 1898.
20. *Cleveland Press*, May 12, 1898.
21. Ibid.
22. *Cleveland Press*, May 13, 1898.
23. *Cleveland Press*, May 15, 1898.
24. *Cleveland Press*, May 31, 1898.
25. Jennings.
26. *Pittsburgh Leader*, October 6, 1898.

CHAPTER 12
1. Robinson & Salzberg.
2. Ibid.
3. *The Sporting Life*, January 28, 1899.
4. Robinson & Salzberg.
5. Ibid.
6. Ibid.
7. *The Sporting News*, March 18, 1899.
8. *The Sporting Life*, April 29, 1899.
9. *The Sporting News*, May 27, 1899.
10. *Boston Daily Globe*, May 14, 1899.
11. *Pittsburgh Post*, May 14, 1899.
12. *Pittsburgh Dispatch*, May 15, 1899.
13. *Boston Daily Globe*, May 17, 1899.
14. *Cleveland Plain Dealer*, May 17, 1899.
15. *The Sporting News*, June 24, 1899.
16. *The Sporting News*, July 1, 1899.
17. *The Sporting News*, July 29, 1899.
18. Robinson & Salzberg.
19. *The Hartford Courant*, May 21, 1899.
20. *The Hartford Courant*, May 24, 1899.
21. *The Hartford Courant*, May 31, 1899.
22. Ibid.
23. *Springfield Union News*, May 31, 1899.
24. *The Hartford Courant*, June 18, 1899.
25. *Waterbury Republican*, July 15, 1899.
26. *Waterbury Republican*, July 18, 1899.
27. *Waterbury Republican*, July 19, 1899.
28. Ibid.
29. *Waterbury Republican*, August 24, 1899.
30. *Waterbury Republican*, August 31, 1899.
31. *The Sporting Life*, September 2, 1899.
32. *Waterbury Republican*, September 13, 1899.
33. *Waterbury Republican*, September 15, 1899.
34. *Waterbury Republican*, September 16, 1899.
35. Ibid.
36. *Waterbury Republican*, September 17, 1899.
37. Ibid.

CHAPTER 13
1. *Holyoke Daily Transcript*, April 18, 1900.
2. *Holyoke Daily Transcript*, August 23, 1900.
3. Ibid.
4. *Holyoke Times*, August 24, 1900.
5. *Springfield Union*, August 26, 1900.
6. Ibid.
7. Ibid.
8. Ibid.
9. Unnamed newspaper clipping with no date, Sockalexis file, Baseball Hall of Fame Library, Cooperstown, N.Y.
10. Wellman.

CHAPTER 14
1. *Boston Daily Globe*, May 2, 1902.
2. Ibid.
3. *Washington Star*, quoted in *Lowell Sun*, May 16, 1902.
4. *Boston Daily Globe*, June 6, 1902.
5. Ibid.
6. Ibid.
7. *Lowell Sun*, June 19, 1902.
8. Ibid.
9. *Lowell Sun*, August 2, 1902.
10. *Lowell Sun*, September 2, 1902.
11. *Lowell Sun*, September 7, 1902.
12. Phillips.

CHAPTER 15
1. Hatch.
2. Ibid.
3. Ibid.
4. *Bangor Daily News*, August 31, 1965.
5. Ibid.
6. *Bangor Daily Commercial*, May 24, 1907.
7. *Bangor Daily News*, August 31, 1965.
8. Ibid.
9. Ibid.

10. *The Washington Post*, February 16, 1909.

11. *Bangor Daily News*, September 14, 1910.

12. *Bangor Daily Commercial*, September 13, 1910.

13. *Aroostook Times*, September 14, 1910.

14. *Brockton Enterprise*, September 13, 1910.

15. Ibid.

16. *Aroostook Times*, September 21, 1910.

17. *Portland Press Herald*, August 7, 1949.

18. *Bangor Daily Commercial*, April 25, 1912.

19. *Bangor Daily Commercial*, July 20, 1912.

20. *Bangor Daily Commercial*, September 13, 1912.

21. *Kennebec Journal*, August 2, 1913.

22. *Worcester Telegram*, August 9, 1913.

23. Ibid.

24. Ibid.

25. *Old Town Enterprise*, August 23, 1913.

26. Thompson.

27. Ibid.

28. *Old Town Enterprise*, February 23, 1934.

CHAPTER 16

1. John.

2. Jennings.

3. Lieb.

4. Jennings.

5. *Bangor Daily News*, December 25, 1913.

6. Jennings.

7. Feldman.

8. *Bangor Daily News*, December 25, 1913.

9. Ibid.

10. *Old Town Enterprise*, December 29, 1913.

11. Ibid.

12. Ibid.

13. Ibid.

14. *Bangor Daily Commercial*, December 28, 1913.

15. *Cleveland Leader*, December 29, 1913.

16. Jennings.

17. Ibid.

18. Hatch.

19. Mayo

20. Mack.

21. Leavitt.

22. Phillips.

23. Powers.

24. Gowdy.

25. Ibid.

26. Ibid.

27. *Boston Herald*, May 18, 1934.

28. *Old Town Enterprise*, June 30, 1934.

29. Ibid.

30. Fitzgerald.

31. *Old Town Enterprise*, January 19, 1956.

32. *Bangor Daily News*, January 21, 1956.

33. *Cleveland Press*, May 30, 1978.

34. *Bangor Daily News*, June 17, 1987.

35. Cartwright.

36. *Bangor Daily News*, January 4, 1994.

CHAPTER 17

1. MacWilliams.

2. *Cleveland Press*, March 30, 1903.

3. Ibid.

4. Ibid.

5. Ibid.

6. *Cleveland Press*, March 31, 1903.

7. *Cleveland Press*, April 1, 1903.

8. *Cleveland Press*, April 2, 1903.

9. *Cleveland Press*, April 4, 1903.

10. *Cleveland Press*, April 6, 1903.

11. Ibid.

12. *Boston Daily Globe*, September 14, 1907.

13. Lewis.

14. Ibid.

15. *Cleveland Plain Dealer*, January 17, 1915.

16. *Cleveland Leader*, January 17, 1915.

17. *Boston Daily Globe*, January 16, 1915.

18. *The Sporting Life*, January 23, 1915.

19. *The Sporting News*, January 23, 1915.

20. *Cleveland Plain Dealer*, January 18, 1915.

CHAPTER 19

1. Murnane.

Bibliography

Allen, Lee, "A Letter to Mrs. Gilligan," *The Second Fireside Book of Baseball* (New York: Simon and Schuster, 1958), p. 11.

Allen, Lee, letter to Mrs. Hannah Toy, James Madison Toy file, Baseball Hall of Fame Library, Cooperstown, New York.

Anderson, Will, *Was Baseball Really Invented in Maine? A Lively Look at the History of Professional Baseball in Maine and at Every Mainer Who's Ever Played in the Majors* (Portland, Maine: W. Anderson, 1992), pp. 28–29, 109–113.

Cartwright, Steve, "Living in the shadow of a baseball legend," *Talking Leaf*, November 1978.

Cunningham, Bill, "Sockalexis Set Pace for Purple: Blazed Trail to Majors for Crusaders — Had Great Debut — 39 H.C. Men Have Followed His Path," *Boston Post*, May 4, 1937, p. 12.

Dineen, Edward A., "Lewis [*sic*] Sockalexis," *Holy Cross Purple*, April 1919.

Dooley, Dick, "For Sockalexis, year of football," *Bangor Daily News*, June 12, 1974.

Feldman, Jay, "The Rise and Fall of Louis Sockalexis," *Baseball Research Journal 1986* (Society for American Baseball Research), pp. 39–42.

Fitzgerald, John A., ballad to honor Louis Sockalexis, *Holy Cross Purple*, 1934.

Fox, William J., letter from, written in 1949. Collection of the College of the Holy Cross Library Archives.

Gagnon, Cappy, letter to Ed Rice concerning Sockalexis's expulsion from Notre Dame in 1897, dated December 12, 1987.

Gowdy, Hank, "The Voice of Sports: Sockalexis Named Indians/A Legendary Holy Cross Star from Maine Made Such an Impact on Cleveland Baseball the City Renamed its Team for Him," *Boston Sunday Herald Traveler-Advertiser*, November 19, 1972.

Grayson, Harry, *They Played the Game, the Story of Baseball Greats* (New York: A. S. Barnes and Co., 1944).

Hatch, Francis W., "Maine's All-time Great Baseball Player," *Down East Magazine*, August 1963, pp. 37–39, 59.

Hodgdon, Keith, "Yesterday: The Cleveland Indian," *Sports Illustrated*, September 17, 1973.

Hotaling, Dan, "Louis Francis Sockalexis." In *Nineteenth Century Stars*, by Mark Rucker and Robert L. Tiemann. Kansas City, Mo.: Society for American Baseball Research, 1989.

Hurley, Jim, "A Brief History of Sock's Career," *Old Town Enterprise*, February 23, 1934.

Jennings, Hugh, "Rounding Third," newspaper syndicated column, North American Newspaper Alliance, 1926.

John, Frederick, "Sockalexis…the greatest baseball player of them all," *Bangor Daily News*, March 8, 1975.

Leavitt, Bud, "Louis Francis Sockalexis," *Bangor Daily News*, December 22–23, 1979.

Lewis, Franklin A., *The Cleveland Indians* (New York City: G.P. Putnam's Sons, 1949).

Libby, Steve, "Tragedy Halted Career of Great Maine Major League Baseball Player," *Lewiston Journal Magazine*, January 21, 1984.

Lieb, Frederick G., *The Detroit Tigers* (New York: G.P. Putnam's Sons, 1946).

"Looking Back," profile and photograph of James Madison Toy, *Beaver County* (Pennsylvania) *Times*, August 5, 1985, p. 1.

MacWilliams, Don, *Yours in Sports: A History of Baseball, Basketball, Boxing and Bowling in Maine* (Lewiston: Monmouth Press, 1969), pp. 17–19.

Mack, Connie, *My 66 Years in the Big Leagues: The Great Story of America's National Game* (Philadelphia: Winston, 1950), p. 32.

Mayo, Jr., Nick, "Maine's Greatest Athlete: Memories of Baseball Greats Bring Back Fabulous Deeds of Sockalexis," *Bangor Daily Commercial*, February 5, 1950, p. B-3.

Murnane, T.H., "The Dreamer," *The Baseball Magazine*, Vol. I, No. 1, May 1908, p. 36.

Nadel, Eric and Craig R. Wright, "Baseball's Legendary Indian Player," In *The Man Who Stole First Base: Tales From Baseball's Past* (Dallas: Taylor Pub. Co., 1989), pp. 131–32.

O'Donnell, Dick, "Louis Sockalexis: His dad was on baseball warpath," *55-PLUS*, June 3, 1987.

Official Encyclopedia of Baseball, by Hy Turkin and Sherley Clark Thompson. 2nd ed. (New York: A.S. Barnes and Co., 1959), *s.v.* "Sockalexis, Louis Francis (Chief)."

Oxendine, Joseph B., *American Indian Sports Heritage*. 2nd ed. (Lincoln: University of Nebraska Press, 1995), pp. 251–55.

Parpal, John T., "Packachoag Brave," *Holy Cross Purple*, April 1936.

Parrish, Melvin M., "James Madison Toy—A Baseball Legend," *Good Reading*, May 1988, Vol. 25, No. 5, pp. 20–21.

Phillips, John, *Chief Sockalexis and the 1897 Cleveland Indians* (Cabin John, Maryland: Capital Pub. Co., 1991).

Pietsch, J.F.A., letter to Lee Allen, James Madison Toy file, Baseball Hall of Fame Library, Cooperstown, New York.

Powers, Joseph H., poem entitled "Sockalexis," *Holy Cross Purple*, April 1919.

Rideout, Olen B., "Playing Baseball in Houlton, Maine with Louis Francis Sockalexis," *Down East Enterprise*, August 1965, p. 93.

Robinson, George and Charles Salzberg, *On a Clear Day They Could See Seventh Place: Baseball's Worst Teams* (New York: Dell Pub., 1991).

Rutenbeck, Larry, from his biographical and baseball game research article on "Louis Sockalexis," and phone conversation with author, December 1999.

Salisbury, Luke, "The Riddle of the Indian," In *The Answer is Baseball: A Book of Questions That Illuminate the Great Game* (New York: Times Books, 1989), pp. 141–160.

Salisbury, Luke, *The Cleveland Indian: The Legend of King Saturday*, (Brooklyn, New York: The Smith, 1992). [A work of fiction "freely modeled" on the life of Louis Sockalexis].

Salsinger, H.G., "He was the greatest — for a brief span: The Facts about Sockalexis," *Baseball Digest*, June 1954, pp. 54–56.

Smith, Robert, "The Wild Irishman and the Gentle Indian." In *Baseball: A Historical Narrative of the Game, the Men Who Have Played It, and its Place in American Life* (New York: Simon & Schuster, 1947), pp. 154–155.

Sockalexis family genealogy chart, courtesy of the late Glenn Starbird, historian, Penobscot Nation, Indian Island, Maine.

Sports Information Office, College of the Holy Cross, Worcester, Massachusetts, information sheets on Louis Sockalexis.

Staurowsky, Ellen J., Ed.D., "An Act of Honor or Exploitation? The Cleveland Indians' Use of the Louis Francis Sockalexis Story," *Sociology of Sport Journal*, vol. 15, 1998, pp. 299–316.

Thompson, Stephen I., "The American Indian in the Major Leagues," *Baseball Research Journal 1983*, Twelfth Annual Historical and Statistical Review of the Society for American Baseball Research.

Toy, James Madison, author's phone conversation with living relative and namesake of the man generally regarded as "the first man to play major league baseball with a Native American background," February 2000.

Walker, Harry, "Sockalexis the Great: Maine's Indian Ballplayer," *Bittersweet*, July 1983.

Wellman, Trina, "Louis Francis Sockalexis: The Life-story of a Penobscot Indian" (Augusta, Maine: Department of Indian Affairs, 1975).

Wigel, Mrs. Jean, letter to Lee Allen, James Madison Toy file, Baseball Hall of Fame Library, Cooperstown, New York.